THREE MAJOR PLAYS

Henrik Ibsen

THREE MAJOR PLAYS

PEER GYNT
ROSMERSHOLM
WHEN WE DEAD WAKEN

Translated by David Rudkin

OBERON BOOKS
LONDON

Rosmersholm and *When We Dead Waken* were first published in these translations by Oberon Books in 1990.

When We Dead Waken translated from The Collected Edition, Gyldendal Norsk Forlag, Oslo, 1952.

Rosmersholm translated from the original First Edition, Gyldendalske Boghandels Forlag, Copenhagen 1886.

First published in this collection in 2006 by Oberon Books Ltd.
521 Caledonian Road, London N7 9RH
Tel: 020 7607 3637 / Fax: 020 7607 3629
e-mail: info@oberonbooks.com
www.oberonbooks.com

A catalogue record for this book is available from the British Library.

ISBN: 1 84002 233 7

Cover design: Andrzej Klimowski

Printed in Great Britain by Antony Rowe Ltd, Chippenham.

Contents

Foreword

After 'Brand', 'Peer Gynt' followed almost of its own accord.
I wrote it in South Italy on Ischia and in Sorrento. Thus far removed
from one's readers, one loses one's inhibitions.

IBSEN CLAIMED THAT 'Peer Gynt is a real person who lived in the Gudbrandsdal' and yet he also declared, referring specifically to *Peer Gynt,* that 'everything I have written is most minutely connected with what I have lived through, if not personally experienced; every new work has had for me the object of serving as a process of spiritual liberation'.

Ibsen completed his 'dramatic poem' on 14 October 1867, when he was thirty-nine years old.

The year (1867) of composition of *Peer Gynt* saw also: the establishment of Austria-Hungary as a dual monarchy; the execution of the Emperor Maximilian in Mexico; Garibaldi's 'march on Rome'; the death of Baudelaire, and the births of Arnold Bennett, John Galsworthy and Luigi Pirandello; the birth of Marie Curie, and the death of Michael Faraday; the first manufacture of the bicycle; Livingstone's exploration of the Congo; the publication of the world's first paperback – Goethe's *Faust, Part One* – by the University Press in Leipzig; the publication of Karl Marx's *Das Kapital* Volume One; the completion of the railway through the Brenner Pass; the discovery of gold in Wyoming, and of diamonds in South Africa. *The Origin of Species* had been in circulation for seven years; Wagner was halfway through composition of *Der Ring des Nibelungen*; Sigmund Freud was a boy of eleven at the Sperl Gymnasium, Vienna.

●

My decision to use a stylised rural Ulster speech, for the language of Peer's youth, was doubly prompted. Soon into working the opening scene I was hearing voices from my own boyhood, in their native tones of mid-Tyrone and South Armagh. Also, I wanted the *Peer Gynt* company to feel beneath their feet, not a plasterboard 'poetic' Norway, but a living authentic terrain; to inhabit a tangible landscape, with its own culture, communal demons, hardships and code of laws. Many Ulster rural words in fact are standard Norwegian, though for clarity only one such has been admitted to the present text. Aase's idiom especially, peasant, Protestant, fiery and lugubrious by turns, finds no true equivalent in any mainland English. (Flat Urban Academic – the only English too many critics understand – will simply bury the play. It will bury our theatre too.) Ibsen scholars here and in Norway have endorsed my choice: which warms me, for I felt very cold and alone when I took it.

Ibsen's original is a dramatic poem for some theatre in the head. The whole, taking some five to six hours to perform, most of it in *Hiawatha* metre, would be indigestible. Ibsen's own cuts – savage, for the 1876 première; and for the 1902 revival, mutilation beyond belief – are a counsel of despair; the despair of a man who recognizes that the totality of his play can never be intelligibly realized on stage. So far as his own text goes, he is probably right. A translator, however, has choices. In England, the usual expedient is to hack out whole scenes and counterpoints. As a consequence, the play has bequeathed in this country a blurred 'unrealized' impression. Rather than cut, I decided on distillation: compressing each scene, beat, line; impacting its energy into a minimum number, not of words, but of syllables. The narrative, outer or moral, must be kept forever moving forward. I wanted also to highlight the profound integrity of the play as *organism*: its tight structural coherence; the symphonic onward development as its vital images – such as eye, glass and window; crown; ladle; clasp and hook; pig; fantasies of riding – grow, and come to bitter fruit. Apart from some early Aase material about Peer's childhood, and a non-dynamic scene of hers (with two peasant women, after Peer has left her on the roof) and the character of Huhu (see *Endnotes*), every narrative beat is present, each station in the moral argument is present and in place. Within each beat, internal excisions have been made. The luxuriant African monologues have been much reduced – in the culinary sense, their meaning condensed. Suppressed text can often be implied: by gesture, tone of voice, or somehow else telescoped into what remains. (Such material must of course be restored to the printed page, and will be found here, enclosed in square brackets.) At a late stage in rehearsal – and again, during preview, where audience must be our guide – further, last cuts were made. These, where too severe for the page, also have been restored.

Peer himself attracts more speculative comment than probably any other character since Hamlet. Obviously, at the back of him, Faust is somewhere: the play is a mid-nineteenth century definition of 'selling one's soul to the Devil'. Further back, we may discern the Parable of the Talents. We are at first surprised when (Matthew xxv. 25) the Third Servant proudly reveals the Talent he has so long kept safely buried in the earth, and the Master banishes him to outer darkness. So is Peer surprised, by the Buttonmoulder's quiet terrible insistence on recycling him, as life-material misused. The parable too has been misused, along Gyntian lines, as an injunction to capitalism – a cultural notion grotesquely alien in a Galilean context. Peer's garbles of Scripture are no authorial indulgence. Peer gets every message wrong; and, as we watch him so amusingly miss the point with Memnon, it dawns on us that here is a man with no capacity for self-regeneration. He has ever feared the death each old self must die. This anxiety in him, akin to phobia of heights or water, corrupts his dealings with other people. He dare not relate to anyone else as a human equal. He must objectify people, make functions of them, reduce them to elements in a scenario of his own – in order to conserve his 'self' intact.

In such moral, psychic disorder, Ibsen specifically locates Peer's capitalist impulse. Peer's fantasies of triumph, of economic vengeance, culminate in his hymn to Gyntiana, where he shall mould the earth anew in image of 'himself'. So many paradoxes here: the unconscious urge to let the water of life surge into his own inner desert; the exaltation of a utopian vision, that echoes Marx' own paean to capitalism, yet is in effect the schizophrenia of a man in total alienation from the earth. Thus Peer's arrival in the asylum is tragically just – with the 'added complication', as Begriffenfeldt observes, that Peer's clinical insanity is the norm of the human world to come. Ibsen's prophetic insight is horrific here. All that remains, is the Peer of Act Five: reduced, by the Strange Passenger, to a mere anatomy; thereafter, encounter by encounter, peeled to nothing; acknowledging, at last, that Protestant sense of individual solitude and insignificance that in the Reformation found its utterance, and further woe. For it was then, we are told, that public clocks began to strike the quarter. Time is Money – as Scripture most definitely does not say. That Reformation's true inheritor is modern Economic Man; and Peer's his archetype – running, running, running, against a Night that is forever coming and already here. In this dark universe Love does exist, and that Eternal Feminine by which we may transcend, and Be. But Peer's sin – he calls it that – has thwarted her to a maternal posture; and her eyes are gone. The Buttonmoulder is more real than Solveig now.

●

I sense that *Rosmersholm* has, with its one long forbidding looking name, held the play back somewhat with English language audiences. Their loss: for if there's any Ibsen play that speaks to us now, it is surely this – with its pitiless unmasking of the moral evasions whereby we shy from being free.

Ibsen might have been wiser to persist with an earlier title he had considered for this play: *White Horses*. There's an uncompleted first draft so named. It's a revelation of Ibsen's critical-creative process: at once intuitive and rigorous. The 'white horse' is an ancestral phantom appearing to the House of Rosmer when a death is near. It's active in the play in many metaphorical forms too – not least the self-appointed 'liberator' Rebecca herself, who physically brings whiteness onto the stage, in the crochet shawl that she is working to complete. But Ibsen had recently used a conceptually similar title, for the play that we in English know, to Ibsen's annoyance, as *Ghosts*. He settled on a more objective title, the name of the family estate – though outside Scandinavia even that name can be misunderstood: the *–holm* denotes an island amid flowing water, in this case the lethal millrace.

Title or not, there's no denying that the play itself is difficult. Certainly its leading characters are not likeable. Yet they are of urgent significance to us; indeed, they discomfortingly resemble us. For all their talk of liberation, they are in terror of freedom and its chaos, and – again like us – they can make only tepid and incomplete gestures of being free. In their pathological flight from freedom, Ibsen locates the death-wish that dooms our culture.

In performance, two tempting paths especially must not be taken. John Rosmer is *not* to be played as feeble and negative. Within his limitations, this pathetic man does show courage; and I recommend the actor to build his character from that. (Rather as he might build a miser from his one act of generosity when he gives a beggar a farthing.) The complementary error is to make a feminist heroine of Rebecca West. One can see why blue-stockings made an icon of her; one distinguished writer even adopted her name. But Rebecca, however bold her progressive attitudes in the provincial Norway of 1886, is yet devious, manipulative, high-handed – and above all a self-righteous murderess, who has systematically procured the death of a vulnerable loving wife. ('Poor Beäta' as they keep calling her: the one healthy person in the whole configuration.)

And it would be smug, to feel superior to Rosmer in his fear of sex. The text, and the back-story, furnish all the clues we need as to why this man is so inhibited and frigid. He genuinely does have, in his own despairing words, 'a great capacity for joy'. If that line strikes us as laughable when it comes, we're not alone; better Ibsen scholars than I am will argue that Ibsen could visit his scorn on the 'progressives' too. There's certainly some very bitter and painful comedy in this piece. But I don't hear a laugh-line in those words of John Rosmer. I hear the desolate cry of a man who can imagine indeed the great release of love, and the true freedom of spirit, that are in our human nature to experience and to achieve, but who knows they can never be his.

In this question of sex, we need to look honestly at Rebecca too: struggling as she has done to burn her own sexuality out of her, and calling that a setting free. (In her beautiful image, of her new-won peace as 'like that hush that stills a crag of seabirds at the midnight sun', we have a sample of one reason why, in discussing

Ibsen's 'prose' plays, one must put the 'prose' in quotes.) Rebecca may claim – and believe – that she unsexes herself as a sacrifice for love, because sexless love is the only love that Rosmer dare. But what then of that terrible moment in the blackly brilliant Act Three, where she is brought face to face with the appalling possibility that the step-father figure who has sexually used her was her real father? An astonishing play, rebarbative and compelling – and urgent too to our own self-deceiving culture. A remorseless journey inward, pitiless in its unmasking of evasion and denial, a dramatic mechanism tight as a trap.

●

From the beginning, the status of *When We Dead Waken* has been problematic. We have, I think, its (deceptive) simplicity to thank for this. Its scheme is so stonily bald, its execution so drastic, Ibsen's last has seemed, to some, not fully achieved as a play. Some even thought its author senile. But a great master, in his last works, will often cut aside the once devious procedures of his craft.

Yet, as with stone itself, we need only look close at this play, to see how it teems with microscopic life.

Unusually for Ibsen, the action here progresses onward and upward through three separate landscapes. Each is higher and wilder. (We must remember that Ibsen's settings, these meticulously defined landscapes of his, are worded for his *readers*; the stage-designer can only represent their essentials in some suggestive way.) In Act One we're on the ground, in tamed and scissored parkland of a spa. There's cultured vegetation; a fountain; and a back-cloth of fjord, away to painted distant islands in a painted sea. There's something rigid, orchestrated, in the figures of the guests and functionaries too; almost prophetic of Resnais' *Marienbad* (where, incidentally, a poster for *Rosmersholm* is glimpsed on an interior wall). In Act Two we are high up, near a mountain sanatorium. Here the landscape's a bleak measureless waste, to (again, painted) a vast upland lake and distant peaks beyond. But the element of water here also comes physically forward: where was fountain before, now there's a rockface with plunging waterfall; and a stream, flowing onstage. For Act Three we are higher yet; up near the very peak of the mountain. We're on the edge of a chasm, below a snowfield; and, where all was sultry and still below, here a snow-storm is gathering above. The living water frozen now, and angry.

Not only the life-giving element of water goes through a 'poetic' transforming process. In the hotel grounds (Act One) there's also an overgrown pavilion, like a neglected and weed-strangled heart. This will 'become' (in design terms, perhaps physically so) the half-fallen 'pigsty' on Act Three's chasm edge. (That'll be all that morally remains of Rubek's 'splendid lakeside villa' too.) And for all that the climate of Acts One and Two is heavy with sterility and death, both environments are in the precinct of a place of cure. The element of *healing* is already present. Again, while in Act One the other human figures glimpsed (mainly women) are sickly and enfeebled, in Act Two they are children singing and playing. Yet even this promise of new life can be turned inside out – when Rubek and Irena, unable emotionally to go forward, regress to children, and play with flowers and leaves for swans and boats. In furnishing and costume, too, there is an evolution. The wicker-chairs before the Spa hotel give way to the cold stone bench of Act Two; in Act Three there'll be no reposing at all. The Rubek himself of Act One, 'distinguished' in smoking-jacket over light summer-clothing, in Act Two will have a rug wrapped round him: he is aged in an instant. Yet in the finale, it is as though all age is past: he almost marches upward to his death. Meanwhile, Irena's white – in Act One, marmoreal, stiff, the garb of a statue walking in her sleep – softens at the last to white fur and swansdown: and, at the catastrophe, explodes outward to embrace Ibsen's entire Creation in a swirling shroud of living snow. It's worth noting here, too – in a dream, we'd know it – that on the edge of this ultimate chasm, that very element of stone by which Rubek has 'lived' now lies all about him, débris, shattered and fallen.

And looking close at Rubek himself, what do we see? Outwardly, an aging sculptor, who once created work of world stature, but who has long since sold out, and lives the life now of an indulged celebrity, nourishing himself on a secret contempt for the clientèle who have made him rich. Is this Ibsen's 'portrait of the artist as an old man'? Elements of Ibsen's own life will always be visible in the weft and warp of his art; but for all the Ibsen-biographical details that enrich this character's texture, Rubek – like his own busts – proves no mere 'portrait-figure' pure and simple. He is something on stage more vital – and terrible – than that.

It is as though Ibsen has diffracted from himself a negative aspect he espies there, and bodies that forth as the character onstage, to articulate him there, and put him to ordeal and judgment. Rubek is a flawed facet of Ibsen, writ large: much as, thirty years earlier, the contrasting twin figures of Brand and Gynt had each been. And in the aging Rubek's talk there are echoes of the soul-destructive 'satanic' bargains that those younger headlong fellows each in his own cause had struck. Inevitably, then, this character Rubek will be, in some self-endangering way, a man unwhole; and his great failure as an artist, an enlargment of a defect Ibsen guiltily sensed in his own art.

And here we come to the origins in him of the figure of Irena. (In the translation, I foreignize the spelling of her name, to be sure that we hear the *Irene* that Ibsen heard.) The character onstage is an aging demented woman, whose capacity for spontaneous feeling was long ago stunted by Rubek in the self-regarding service of his art. Ibsen himself, we know, felt some such guilt as this; and that would energize his characterization here. But in Ibsen there was an even deeper haunting, a sense that he had somewhere taken a wrong road on his artistic journey: that in turning to 'prose' (as he thought it) he had forsaken his true gift, of poetry; he had sinned against his Muse. In this respect, Irena originates in Ibsen's Creation just as Rubek did: as a diffraction of Ibsen himself. She is the living image of his creativity abused, a 'lady' white in living death and angry with him. Yet – by that wonderful healing paradox ever at work in our soul, that Ibsen's art so accurately reveals – she has come, not to punish him, but to offer him one last chance of change and redemption. Perhaps, by that same paradox, Rubek himself has even summoned her: in his confessional dialogue with his young wife Maja at the heart of the play, there's a hint of an unconscious intent of his in coming to this place. For such is the beginning of healing.

But in Irena the living character *onstage*, with biography in her own right, there's an apparent contradiction. She castigates Rubek for not touching her all those years ago; in the next breath she admits that, had he tried to, she would probably have killed him. We encounter here – as also in for instance *Rosmersholm* – a typical intractability of Ibsen's that his sullen honesty bequeaths us. In the earlier play, Rebecca also seems to be drawing the emotionally paralyzed male protagonist towards rebirth; but for all the rightness of where she's leading him, her personal motives prove dishonest and somewhat unwhole. The case with Irena is similar. Neat (and currently fashionable) though it would be, to see Irena as a vital loving woman damaged by a frigid and exploitative male, the text does not permit that. Since Rubek and she parted, she claims to have lived a life visiting vengeance on all his sex: posing in obscene revue; driving would-be lovers to insanity and suicide; defending herself against all comers, with a progression of sharp instruments – needle, stiletto, knife… But in her young days with Rubek, before the fatal word was even spoken, the first of those lethal instruments was already in place. We are compelled toward the conclusion that, for all her talk of her hot young blood, a pose of naked unattainable Madonna was, from the beginning, the only attitude she could adopt with men. Irena thus would be perfect casting for his 'Virgin of the Resurrection'. To look at her biographically, as an actress must, we see that perhaps what drew Irena to Rubek long ago was his very frigidity. She felt 'safe' with him. She would have killed him had he touched her, and the weapon was already to hand. To use a current cant term, she feels an 'anger' toward all men indiscriminately. But seen poetically, within the cosmos of the play, she is Rubek-Ibsen's 'feminine', angry specifically with *him* – a just anger – and she is here for that anger to be resolved.

Conversely, the other two figures in this ill-matched quartet – the frustrated young wife Maja, and the earthy Wolfheim – embody, in the cosmos of the play, those visceral energies that Rubek and Irena have forfeit and have transcended now. In the surface process of the play, the elder couple advance upward toward annihilation, while the younger pair descend toward life on earth: in the deeper process, the ill-sorted elements of Feminine and Masculine are repairing to their proper zones. Maja and Wolfheim are the harder to play for this. There are narrative decisions that Maja makes onstage that, alchemically correct in the scheme of the play, are for the character herself not truthfully actable: her decision, in Act One, to go and watch Wolfheim's dogs feeding, for instance; her abrupt surrender to him on the edge of the chasm in Act Three… One can motivate these only by an appeal to a Freudian 'return of the repressed' or (in Maja's case possibly the same) a desire for chaos. Likewise, the posture in which Wolfheim constantly appears, an abrasive and unlovely physicality, feels uncomfortably written, and is awkward for an actor to make truthfully his own.

Why is he unlovely? In defining Wolfheim, Ibsen plainly had certain mythic figures in mind: the satyr, the faun, the wolf himself. It's quite priapic, the landscape that this Wolfheim inhabits: with his imagery of poking bears in thickets, swallowing red-meat knuckles whole, the slopes 'below, where the forest is thick…' To say nothing of the amazing exchanges in Act Three, where Maja can see his shanks, his beard and ('very clearly') his horns. It must have been noted long ago how pre-Lawrentian a figure this huntsman is. Like Mellors for instance, Wolfheim is his author's polemic construct, but unlike Mellors he is not an erotic one. Ibsen's satyr is presented as revolting. But it would be sentimental and facile – and Ibsen is morally too rigorous – for Maja's choice to be between an unattractive old man and a desirable young one. It's no dilemma where the choice is easy; and, whatever their desires, sexuality is so often a *difficulty* for Ibsen's characters. It is accurate that Wolfheim should appear to us as the revolting face of male sexuality, the fell and hideous huntsman – for that is all that, at this present stage of her growth, poor Maja can see. She has been imprisoned with Rubek so long; and could well have begun to have her own sexuality curdled by her child-wife relationship to him. Ibsen is careful to specify that Wolfheim is in fact of *unseductive* appearance: 'matted hair and beard' and 'no longer young'. And just as Rubek is mirrored afar by two fading ghosts of himself, in Irena's two lost husbands, so conversely Wolfheim brings onstage two living doubles of his straining male vitality: the man Lars, and the hounds he's holding back on leash. (Lars, Ibsen omits even to mention in his character list – as though subconsciously acknowledging him a *doppelgänger* of Wolfheim's with no narrative status of his own.)

●

Ibsen's 'last' play I called this; we all do. He did subtitle the play a *dramatic epilogue*, but it seems he meant thereby to draw a line under only the preceding six or so plays which he felt to form a sequence, not that he intended this as his 'last'. That, he said, he would write in verse, if he could be sure which play his last would be. In fact he was looking forward to developing his dramatic method further, onward into poetry again; and, so far from being his farewell, *When We Dead Waken* stands on the threshold of that final phase of creativity.

But it was not to be. A stroke felled him; then another. He lived out the last half-dozen years of his life, a paralyzed man, unable mentally or physically to write. His last efforts were those of a child, playing with carved wooden letters of the alphabet.

There's no great case, then, for reading this play as Ibsen's *final* reckoning with himself. But reckoning of a sort it was. Ibsen had been reckoning with himself consistently, from the moment he first found dramatic voice. The glory of Ibsen is that he externalized this private rather morbid introspection, into universal images, mythically so dynamic, that his idiosyncratic inner world is now part of the texture of civilization's discourse with itself. And it's in this mythic cosmos of his Creation, charged with its own organic life, that even in – especially in – the so-called 'prose' plays, the true poetry of Ibsen's drama is. In *When We Dead Waken* is the consummation of this poetry – not in the language itself, that's for sure, but in the imagery it conjures, and the transformations there at work.

David Rudkin
Warwickshire, 2003

PEER GYNT

Characters

PEER GYNT

AASE
his mother

ASLAK
the smith

INGRID
the bride

MADS MOEN
the bridegroom

MADS MOEN'S FATHER

SOLVEIG

SOLVEIG'S FATHER

HELGA
Solveig's sister

INGRID'S FATHER

SOLVEIG'S MOTHER

FARMER at Hegstad

SHEPHERD GIRLS

SHE-IN-THE-GREEN

TROLL-KING

BÖYG

KARI
a neighbourwoman

HAG

URCHIN

ACT IV: AFRICA

TRUMPETERSTRAALE

COTTON

BALLON

EBERKOPF

ANITRA

THIEF

RECEIVER

Herr Doktor BEGRIFFENFELDT

FELLAH
madman

HUSSEIN
another madman

ACT V: NORWAY

Ship's CAPTAIN

BOATSWAIN

Strange PASSENGER

COOK

PASTOR

BUTTONMOULDER

OLD MAN

SKINNY ONE

Wedding-guests, Trolls, Apes, Arabs, Asylum-keepers
and Inmates, Sailors, Mourners

This translation of *Peer Gynt* was commissioned by the Royal Shakespeare Company and first performed on 9 June 1982 at The Other Place, Stratford-upon-Avon, with the following cast:

PEER GYNT, Derek Jacobi

AASE, Brenda Peters

ASLAK / TRUMPETERSTRAALE /
BEGRIFFENFELDT, David Troughton

INGRID / SHE-IN-THE-GREEN, Sinéad Cusack

MADS MOEN / HUSSEIN, Robert O'Mahoney

MADS MOEN'S FATHER / PASTOR / SKINNY ONE,
John Carlisle

SOLVEIG, Katy Behean

SOLVEIG'S FATHER, Derek Godfrey

HELGA, Sian Kenny

SOLVEIG'S MOTHER / KARI, Jennie Goossens

FARMER / TROLL-KING / COTTON / SHIP'S
CAPTAIN, Jeffery Dench

SHEPHERD GIRL / ANITRA, Josette Simon

SHEPHERD GIRLS, Cathy Finlay, Lesley Sharp

URCHIN, Paul Basson

BALLON, David Shaw-Parker

EBERKOPF / STRANGE PASSENGER /
BUTTONMOULDER, Derek Godfrey

FELLAH, Robert Clare

Wedding-guests, trolls, etc. were played by members of the Company.

Director, Ron Daniels

Music, Stephen Oliver

ACT ONE

Mountain farmstead. Mill; stream. Summer.

AASE: Lies.

PEER: True!

AASE: You swear to that.

PEER: Swear what for?

AASE: Ach ye daren't. All blather.

PEER: It happened as I say!

AASE: Peer son how you can look at me. Spring: when help on the farm's most needed. You off away above that snowline somewhere, chasin' reindeer. Month long, now home an' look at ye. Tatthers, gun lost, no carcase wi' ye. But hunters' tales, oh ay, the like I never heard. This reindeer buck then. Where'd ye find him.

PEER: West, on Gjendin.

AASE: That so!

PEER: The wind bore at me, bitter. A clump of alder screened him. Gouging for lichen in the crust of snow.

AASE: Was he.

PEER: Not a breath. Not a move. Ear pricked. Creak of his hoof. Glimpse of one branch of horn. Inch by inch, amid the boulder, I worm my road. Unseen of him I up one eye. Such gloss, such size, you never saw.

AASE: Nor like to.

PEER: I fire! he's dropped! I'm astride that spine; his left ear seized, knife up for the plunge at the base of his skull! Heyyy, that monster, the snort of him, wild! He's up; head reared, knife an' sheath dashed from my empty hand; thighs of me clamped till his sides in antlers' tongs; and we're away, full tilt along the Edge.

AASE: Lord –

PEER: Did ever ye see Gjendin Edge? Three miles and more of it before ye, honed as a scythe. Plunge down to left an' right of ye, glacier, scree, grey rakes of riven rock. Three thousand feet below, the still black water of a mountain sea. We rip the air. I never rode the like. Before me the

25

glister of many suns. Midway down, between us and that
water, brown backs of eagles aswim in the void. One
glimpse, they're specks behind. Icefloes, split and smash
upon those shores. No sound to me. All I hear, a dizzy
demon whirling, screech sway swirl about my head…

AASE: Och, Lord above –

PEER: A brink! Sheer scar below; impossible. At the beast's
very foot on its edge, from what cranny had hid him up
flaps a great ptarmigan all squawk and alarm. The buck
half shies; one bound skyward: we're out, above that
plummet to the water!

(*AASE clutches at a tree.*)

Black mountain wall behind us, in fathomless plunge,
shearing the cloud, a flock of gulls that scream, wheel,
scatter; down our onslaught, ever down. Below us a
glimmer. Pale, like the belly of a deer! Mother, our own
image! In that mirror of mountain lake, up from its bed
come sweeping to the water's crust, as we to meet it!

AASE: Och, son – What –

PEER: Buck from sky, buck from deep, in a moment clash,
a tempest of foam. We flail in the water. Long pull. Good
while. At last we make the northern shore. He swimming, I
hold on. Then I home.

AASE: But the buck, boy!

PEER: Still there for all I know. Find him, have him.

AASE: And your neck not broke? Your thighs, nor your
back…? Lord be thanked, Thine Arm about my son!
– What? I'll say nothing. What's britches torn, to the peril
of a lep like that? – Aa! You're the devil wi' words! Poor
Suffering Saviour, Peer Gynt the lies you tell! This story
I've heard before… I was twenty… Gudbrand Glesne was
the hero then, not Peer Gynt, not you, you –

PEER: Me too. Such things don't have to happen only once.

AASE: Would God I lay dead. At my last sleep in the black of
the earth. Plea or tears, I leave ye cold. Peer Gynt beyond
redeeming!

PEER: Dear lovely wee mother. True all ye say. Gladden your
heart –

AASE: Glad? me? pig for a son? How can it not hurt sore,
penniless widow helpless in this world, when all I meet
with is contempt? Your father's father, his were days. How
much of that grandeur has come down to us? Coin by the
bushel he left, your father gave wings; scattered on the
wind. In parish after parish, a purchase of land. A wagon
to drive in, gilded wi' gold. What that man squandered...
Great winter feast, not a guest but smashed glass an' bottle
on the wall behind him...

PEER: Where's last year's snow?

AASE: Listen to your mother! Look at this farm. Half the
windows stopped wi' rags. Hedge and fences fallen,
livestock naked to all weather, land left idle; each month
more seized against our debt.

PEER: Yak yak yak. Luck will droop. It stands again.

AASE: You're the fine one! You should be a rod and staff to
my frail old age. You've brawn enough. It's time ye showed
care to this farm, garnered the crumbs of your inheritance.
Devil the use you've been to me. Ye slunge all day at the
fire, pokin' the cinders. From any gatherin' ye go to, ye've
the girls run screamin'. You've me a ridicule wherever I turn.
You fight wi' dregs of humanity –

PEER: Leave over.

AASE: Well? Mighty shindig there at Lunde a while back:
were you or not the start of it? Pack of ye; mad dogs.
Wasn't it you broke Aslak the blacksmith his arm for him?
least knocked his finger out of joint –

PEER: Who put that in your head?

AASE: The crofter's wife could hear the howls of him.

PEER: Me.

AASE: You?!

PEER: Ay, mother, I came out worse.

AASE: What?!

PEER: He's the powerful man.

AASE: Who?

PEER: Sure, Aslak the smith.

AASE: I spit on you. That glassy-eyed squabblesome pickled
waster of a man, the better of my son?! How do I hold up
my head –

27

PEER: Oh mother, mother…

AASE: What? Another of your lies?!

PEER: This once. There. Dry these tears. I show ye. My left fist's a vice; it bows him to the ground. My right's a hammer from on high –

AASE: Will you never learn peace? You bring me to my grave –

PEER: Not at all. You're worth a nobler destiny by far. Kind ugly wee mother, I tell you. This land about shall come to honour you. Give me but time, and I've done something… big.

AASE: You?!

PEER: Who knows what future comes his road?

AASE: I'd sooner you'd what wit it needs to darn your britches.

PEER: A King I'll be! An Emperor!

AASE: Heaven help me; the last of his wits is gone.

PEER: I shall! Give me but time.

AASE: Ay. Time.

PEER: Mother, you see.

AASE: Enough o' that! You're cracked altogether. Right enough: you might have made something of yourself. If you'd woken up to what's aroun' ye. Daughter at Hegstad Farm had a notion o' you. A match there ready, had you put mind to it.

PEER: Say ye so…?

AASE: Oul' father of hers is stubborn in his way, but no backbone. It's Ingrid calls the tune. Step by dodderin' step he grumbles after. Och, son, imagine. A girl of means. All that freehold coming her way. You could have been the shining bridegroom there. Not this black an' raggit thing ye are.

PEER: We go a-courtin' then.

AASE: Like where?

PEER: Hegstad.

AASE: Fool, mahn! That road is closed.

PEER: How so?

AASE: You ridin' reindeer through the air; down here Mads Moen gets the bride.

PEER: Mads Moen? that fright to womankind?

AASE: Him she'll marry.

PEER: Wait here. I'll hitch the cart.

AASE: I'd not exert yourself. The weddin's tomorrow.

PEER: I can be there by tonight.

AASE: And heap more scorn on my poor head?

PEER: Mother. Trust me. This'll work out fine. Hey up! No time to fetch the mare, we'll do without the cart –

AASE: Put me down –

PEER: I'll carry ye there. Splash!

AASE: God in Heaven Peer! You'll have us drowned!

PEER: I'm born to a loftier end.

AASE: Ay, on a rope. Beast, you!

PEER: You sit still! It's slippy under. Treacherous here…

AASE: Asshead!

PEER: You shout. That harmed no one. Shelving now…

AASE: Don't drop me!

PEER: Heyyy! Peer and the Reindeer! I'm the reindeer, you are me! Gallopa-gallopa-gallopa-gallop…

AASE: You've me demented!

PEER: There. Quiet water. Up we come. Give buck a kiss. Pay for the ride –

AASE: This for the ride.

PEER: Ow! Mean fare!

AASE: Now put me down.

PEER: To Hegstad an' the weddin' first. You slip in a word for me wi' that oul' dotard. ['Och, Mads Moen, that man's no good. Peer Gynt now, there's a fella…']

AASE: I'll do that! I'll give him testimonial o' you! Front and after.

[PEER: That so?

AASE: He'll have his dogs set on ye for a tramp before I've done.]

PEER: I think I'll leave you here.

AASE: I'll be after!

PEER: Mother. You? All that way?

AASE: I've the mood on me now, I could clash my teeth in a jawful o' flints! Set you me down! [They'll know the man ye are!] Where's this you're taking me?

PEER: To sit you up on the roof of the mill.

AASE: Lift me down.

PEER: Then you listen.

AASE: Snatters!

PEER: Mother…

AASE: (*Shies a turf at him.*) Lift you me down! This instant, boy!

PEER: No fear. You sit still. You kick, or reach wi' your legs, or pull clods o' that roof out, you could come a mighty bump.

AASE: Beast, you!

PEER: Mind how ye lather about!

AASE: And you a changeling not my son, one breath from me you'd disappear!

PEER: Mother. Thing to say.

AASE: Yaach.

PEER: Better ye wished my errand well. Will ye do that?

AASE: I'll welt ye one. For all your size!

PEER: Cheerio then mother dear. Sit patiently. I'll not be gone long. Mind how ye lather about.

AASE: Peer! Och God he leaves me! Mighty rider! Mighty liar! PEER!… Up across the field there… Someone help me!

(*High. A fence.*)

PEER: Hegstad below. Soon there. Ingrid in, I wonder, by herself at all? No chance. Guests wi' presents. Swarmin' on the farm like midges. Best turn home…
The sneers o' them behin' your back. Whispers. It burns your guts. For a drop o' somethin' strong now. Or some power: to pass among their midst unseen. Or be a stranger… Strong stuff's best. Then the laughter has no sting.
(*A MAN and a WOMAN pass below, with wedding gifts.*)

MAN: …His father a drunk, the mother unwell…

WOMAN: Small wonder the boy turned out no guid…

PEER: Me? Let them. I am alive. Their natter can't take that from me.

...Some cloud, thon. Shape of a horse. Rider... Saddle, halter... Oul' witch on her broomstick after... Scouldin' an' shriekin'! 'Beast, you!' Hi there Peer! All a sudden she's afeared. Peer Gynt rides out ahead. Multitudes follow. His steed is crested with silver and shod in gold. He's gauntlets, sabre, scabbard. His cape sweeps long, silk-lined. Splendid are his train. But none so stalwart on his steed as he. None so dazzles in the light of the sun. The people stand clustered along the fence. They doff their hats as they gaze up in wonder. The women all curtsey. Everyone knows him. The Emperor Gynt. Shillings and sovereigns he scatters like shingle. And all his neighbourhood grow rich from his largesse. He rides on high above the waters of the deep. The princes of England line their shore to welcome him. And the daughters of England too. And England's mighty Lords, and England's King, all rise from their feast at his coming. The King lifts off his crown. He speaks –

ASLAK: Who have we here? That drunken hog Peer Gynt.

PEER: Your Majesty –

ASLAK: Arise, Sir Peer.

PEER: Hell, Aslak, what do you want?

ASLAK: Still sleepin' Lunde off?

PEER: Steer clear o' me...

ASLAK: Oh I shall. Well well fellow-me-lad. These six weeks, where've you been? Away inside the mountain, trollbound?

PEER: I've done wonders.

ASLAK: Such as.

PEER: Above your heads.

ASLAK: Yui goin' to Hegstad?

PEER: No.

ASLAK: Ingrid there was sweet on ye I hear. Time was.

PEER: You black-avised old crow...

ASLAK: Easy, easy. She passed ye over. There's others. I never. Jon Gynt's son. Come on down. Fine company. Fresh ewe-lambs, and vintage widows...

PEER: Away to Hell.

ASLAK: Must be one'll have ye. Good night then. I'll remind
 ye to the bride. (*Gone.*)

PEER: She can wed who she likes. To me no matter. – Ach.
 …Britches rent. Awful rags… If I'd a change o' clothes…
 To get my hand in their vitals the way of a butcher
 and wrench the scorn from out o' them…! Who's that
 whispered? I heard – Nobody. I'm away home to me
 mother…
 (*Dance music on a fiddle yonder below.*)
 Dance…! Girls, look! The swarm o' them! Seven, eight to
 a man! Dagh, Death on your black horse, I have to join
 the company. Mother but. Sat on that roof. Heyyy! The
 stamp an' the kick o' them, out over the grass! Lord, but
 that mahn has a way with a fiddle. [Boom an' thunder o'
 mighty water down a falls.] And all those flaxen heifers
 o' girls! Death, flog your black horse: I have to join the
 company!

 (*Before the farm. GUESTS sit in groups, some on logs;
 FIDDLER on table-edge. YOUNGER FOLK stamp,
 fling in violent peasant dance.*)

A WOMAN: (*Joins one group.*) The bride? Havin' a wee cry
 but who heeds that?

KITCHENMASTER: Come on friends. Let's see the bottom
 o' this keg.

A MAN: Thank you, Sor; you fill us up too quick.

A LAD: (*Whirling a GIRL past. To FIDDLER.*) Louder, you!
 More power to your bow!

GIRL WITH HIM: Welt the strings! the way they'll sound out
 over the fields!

OTHER GIRLS: (*Around a LAD high-kicking.*)
 – The kick of him!
 – The spring in his legs!

[LAD KICKING: The rafters are brave an' high out here! The
 walls are wide!]

MADS MOEN: (*Tugs FATHER's sleeve.*) Da? She won't; she's
 too stuck up.

MADS MOEN'S FATHER: Won't what?

MADS MOEN: She's locked herself in.

MADS MOEN'S FATHER: Find the key!

MADS MOEN: I don't know where to look!

MADS MOEN'S FATHER: Mads Moen I despair of you.

A LAD: Here comes trouble.

ASLAK: Who invited him?

KITCHENMASTER: He's not.

ASLAK: (*To GIRLS.*) Peer Gynt talks to you, ignore him.

A GIRL: Sure he's not here!

PEER: Which of yous huzzies has most life?

GIRLS: – Not me.

PEER: You then –

THIS GIRL: I've not the time.

PEER: Then you –

THIRD GIRL: I'm away home.

PEER: We've all night yet, you out o' your mind?

ASLAK: She'll dance wi' grandad there.

PEER: (*To an ELDER MAN.*) Where's the girls not spoken for?

ELDER MAN: Fin' them.

PEER: (*Skulking aside.*) Eyes of them. Smiles… What they're
thinkin'. Jabs at ye. Rasps like a file on the teeth of a saw…
(*SOLVEIG, little sister HELGA, severe PARENTS
arrive.*)

FARMER: New folk.

ANOTHER: From the West?

FARMER: Hedal.

OTHER: That right?

PEER: (*Stands before SOLVEIG'S FATHER.*) May I dance wi'
your daughter?

SOLVEIG'S FATHER: Ye might. First let us greet the people
of the house.

KITCHENMASTER: A drink now ye've come.

PEER: Thanks no, I'm here for a dance… Such light of her. I
never saw before. She glanced down from my eye. Till her
shoes, white pinafore… An' clung so to her mother's skirts,
prayerbook an' kerchief in her hand. I must take sight on
her again… (*After…*)

LADS: (*Coming out.*) Hi Peer. Away already?

PEER: No.

LAD: You should be.

PEER: Let me through.

LAD: Afeared of Aslak?

PEER: Why?

LAD: Lunde.

SOLVEIG: (*In doorway.*) Was it you asked to dance?

PEER: Sure. D'ye forget me so soon? Come on.

SOLVEIG: Not too far, Mother says.

PEER: Mother says, Mother says. When were you born?

SOLVEIG: You mock at me.

PEER: [You're not much more than a child at that.] How old
    are you?

SOLVEIG: I take my First Communion soon.

PEER: We'd talk more easy if I knew your name.

SOLVEIG: Solveig. You?

PEER: Peer Gynt.

SOLVEIG: Och God.

PEER: What now?

SOLVEIG: My garter's loose. I must tighten it up. (*Gone.*)

MADS MOEN: Da? She won't.

MADS MOEN'S FATHER: Won't what?

MADS MOEN: Won't.

MADS MOEN'S FATHER: What?!

MADS MOEN: Unlock the door.

MADS MOEN'S FATHER: You're fit only to tie in a stall.

ONE WITH HIM: Don't chide the creature. He'll find his road.

A LAD: Peer? A drop o' the stuff?

PEER: No.

LAD: Och, a wee taste.

PEER: You've some on ye?

LAD: Could be. (*Pulls.*) Ach. Boys but that's fierce.

PEER: Pass that over.

SECOND LAD: And I've some.

PEER: No.

SECOND LAD: Be a mahn. A drink, you!

PEER: Just a tipple…

GIRL: (*Sotto.*) Let's go.

PEER: You frightened o' me?

THIRD LAD: Who's not?

FOURTH LAD: We seen at Lunde. Tricks you can do.

PEER: That was nothin'.

FIRST LAD: He's off.

LADS: – Why?

– Why?

– What else can ye do?

PEER: Tomorrow.

LADS: Now!

GIRL: Can you do magic Peer?

PEER: I can summon the Devil.

MAN: My granny done that before I was born.

PEER: Liar. No one can do what I do. One time I conjured him into a nut. Through a hole in the shell a worm had bored.

SOMEONE: There'd need to be that.

PEER: He cursed, he wept, no bribe he did not offer me.

ONE: But in he went?

PEER: I bunged a pin in the hole. The rummel and the growl of him –

GIRL: Go to God.

PEER: Like a bee in there.

GIRL: You've him still trapped?

PEER: He's away this ages. How I fell foul of Aslak.

LAD: That so?

PEER: I went to the forge. Aslak, says I, will ye crack me this nut? I will, says he. He set it on his anvil there. But he's that heavy a hand: he ups wi' his sledge –

VOICE: An' flattened the Devil?

PEER: He swung a mighty blow. The Devil won't take that. He up through the rafters in a sheet of flame an' cleft the wall.

SOMEONE: What happened Aslak?

PEER: Scorched hands. Since when we're not friends.

SOMEONE: Some yarn.

ANOTHER: One of his better.

PEER: You sayin' I invented that?

MAN: I know you didn't. It minds me of a tale my granda
   used to tell.

PEER: Liar! It happened to me.

MAN: What hasn't.

PEER: Hear you me. I can ride mid-air on a charger. Much I
   can do, believe you me.

ONE: Do a wee ride through the air.

ANOTHER: Ay, darlin' Peer –

PEER: I'll need no askin' from none o' you! I'll sweep like a
   storm over all your heads! I'll have this parish on its knees
   to me!

OLD MEN: – The boy's cracked.
   – Buffoon!
   – Gab!
   – Fibmouth!

PEER: Yous'll see!

MAN HALF DRUNK: Ye'll dust your coat-tails sooner.

OTHERS: – Ye'll be mashed to a pulp!
   – Ye'll get a black eye!

MADS MOEN: Peer? That true? ye can ride through the air?

PEER: All true. I am no ordinary mahn.

MADS MOEN: Have you the cloak can make ye disappear?

PEER: Hat ye mane? A have. – Solveig...! You're here! Now
   let me show you how to dance! I'll sh–

SOLVEIG: Let me go.

PEER: Why?

SOLVEIG: So wild.

PEER: Come on you. Och, don't be crooked...

SOLVEIG: Best not.

PEER: Why?

SOLVEIG: You've drink taken.

PEER: ...For a knife... To twist through each one o' their
   hearts.

MADS MOEN: I was thinkin' would you help me? get in at
   the bride?

PEER: Bride where?

MADS MOEN: Storehouse.

PEER: Mm.

MADS MOEN: Peer? Try.

PEER: Mm? Ye must manage that yourself – Ingrid? storehouse? (*To SOLVEIG.*) Ye'll dance then? ...I've the look of a tramp an' you're ashamed of me!

SOLVEIG: No. Not that.

PEER: That! And A'm half cut! Because you'd hurt my pride! Och come on!

SOLVEIG: Perhaps I want to, but I daren't.

PEER: Who are you afraid of?

SOLVEIG: My father, most.

PEER: Father. Ay. A silent man. Sorry he's alive. Is he?

SOLVEIG: What shall I answer?

PEER: Churchgoer is he? An' you an' your mother? Answer!

SOLVEIG: Let me go in peace.

PEER: No! I've powers. To be a troll by night. At stroke of twelve I'll be at your bed. I'll hiss an' I'll spit an' I won't be the cat. I'll drain your blood out into a cup. I'll wolf your little sister alive. I'll bite you all over your thighs an' your back. Oh Solveig dance with me.

SOLVEIG: You were ugly then.

MADS MOEN: I'll give you a bullock if you help me.

PEER: Done. (*They go.*)

(*Disturbance.*)

KITCHENMASTER: Quiet there!

ASLAK: (*Offs jacket.*) Gynt or I. We'll settle this...

ONE: You show him.

ANOTHER: Nagh, let them slang it out...

ASLAK: Past words...

SOLVEIG'S FATHER: Take command of yourself.

HELGA: Mother are they going to hit that man?

LAD: Get him to fly an' the like. That's funnier.

OTHERS: – Kick him out.

   – Spit in his eye.

   – Aslak...?

ASLAK: Gynt's day's over.

SOLVEIG'S MOTHER: Your fool of a man. Not much thought of, is he?

AASE: (*Comes, brandishing a stick.*) Is my son here? Let me but lay my hands... I'll welt the daylight out of him...

ASLAK: That stick'll not touch him.

SOMEONE: Let Aslak sort him out.

OTHER: He'll clobber him.

ASLAK: I'll wring his neck.

AASE: My son? You try! We're his mother, we've teeth an'
claws! Where is he? PEER!

MADS MOEN: Sweet Lord on Calvary! Da... Ohh... Ohh...

MADS MOEN'S FATHER: What is it now?

MADS MOEN: Peer Gynt...

AASE: They've murdered him!

MADS MOEN: No! He's... Look! On the hill!

ALL: With the bride!

AASE: Beast, you!

ASLAK: Up that rock like a goat.

MADS MOEN: My bride slung over him like a pig!

AASE: God strike you d– ! – Aa! The boy near fell!

INGRID'S FATHER: (*Coming bareheaded.*) My daughter! On
her wedding day! – I'll hang him for this!

AASE: God damn me if I let you!

End of Act One.

ACT TWO

Early morning. High.

PEER: Get you away from me.

INGRID: After what we have done? Go where?

PEER: As far as you like.

INGRID: The deceit of it.

PEER: Save your breath. You go your road, I go mine.

INGRID: Our sin has bound us.

PEER: God damn memory. God damn womankind. Save the one.

INGRID: Who?

PEER: Not you.

INGRID: Who?!

PEER: Away back home you. To your father.

INGRID: Oh my sweet love –

PEER: You shut your mouth.

INGRID: You can't mean this.

PEER: I mean it.

INGRID: You seduce me, now forsake me…

PEER: What have you I should stay for?

INGRID: The farm. The –

PEER: A prayerbook in a kerchief in your hand? [A mane of gold?] A shy glance when I look at you? Have you? You take your First Communion soon? Do you?

INGRID: Peer –

PEER: When I entreat can you say no?

INGRID: The man's gone mad.

PEER: Are you a vision of pure light? Answer!

INGRID: Peer –

PEER: You've nothing.

INGRID: They can hang you for this.

PEER: Let them.

INGRID: Marry me. Think what you gain. Land; position…

PEER: At a price too high.

INGRID: You seduced me!

PEER: You were willing.

INGRID: I was desperate!

PEER: I was out o' my mind.

INGRID: You'll pay!

PEER: Small cost, if it makes me free.

INGRID: You're set on that?

PEER: Stone hard.

INGRID: Good. We'll see who wins.

PEER: God damn memory. God damn womankind.

INGRID: (*Off.*) Save the one.

PEER: Ay. Save the one.

(*Higher. Wind-seethe, water-lash. AASE against the elements, SOLVEIG clutching after.*)

AASE: Everything's against me with the might of its wrath. Sky, and water, and ugly mountain. Stormclouds roll down, to lose my son his road. Man too: out after him with death. God damn me, no! I cannot lose my son! What got into the fool of a boy at all? Och daughther, who'd ha thought? Him, all blather an' lies; strong in nowt but his talk; put never a hand to a good day's work... I could laugh and cry... [I'm the cause. His father you see... squandered all we had on drink. Took to the roads for a pedlar. Myself and the wee lad left at home. Stories I'd tell him. Anny oul' story, to keep the world out. Princes and trolls, all manner o' beasts...] Bride-reft. Who'd ha thought that notion'd fix in his head?

Peer? Peer?... No sign.

(*SOLVEIG'S FATHER, MOTHER, sister HELGA come.*)

SOLVEIG'S FATHER: Bodes black for him.

AASE: Poor wanderin' lamb.

SOLVEIG'S FATHER: Lost sheep indeed.

AASE: He's no such thing! My Peer's a rare man. None his like.

SOLVEIG'S FATHER: Pitiful woman.

AASE: So might I be. My son's the fella of a man.

SOLVEIG'S FATHER: His heart is stone, his soul is damned.

AASE: The Lord could never be so cruel!

SOLVEIG'S FATHER: You think your son so much as can sigh for the wrong he has done?

AASE: He can ride a reindeer through the air.

SOLVEIG'S MOTHER: Are you mad?

SOLVEIG'S FATHER: What's that ye say Mother?

AASE: No deed too mighty but he'll do. If he's long enough spared…

SOLVEIG'S FATHER: Better you saw him hanged.

AASE: Sweet Saviour no!

SOLVEIG'S FATHER: The hangman's hands can mould a contrite heart.

AASE: Ye's have me deeved wi' your talk! We have to find him!

SOLVEIG'S FATHER: And save his soul.

AASE: And life! If he's in quagmire, we must haul him out. If trollbound in the mountain, chime bells after, to break him from their thrall…

SOLVEIG'S FATHER: A sheeptrack.

AASE: God reward ye, ye help me find my way…

SOLVEIG'S FATHER: A Christian must.

AASE: Ay. Heathens, them ones. There's none'd come up in this wild with me.

SOLVEIG'S FATHER: They knew your son too well.

AASE: He stands above them all! Now he'll be lucky to live.

SOLVEIG'S FATHER: Footprint of a man.

AASE: He was here!

SOLVEIG'S FATHER: Up there's our summer pasture. You take that side, we this.

(*SOLVEIG left with AASE.*)

SOLVEIG: Tell me some more.

AASE: About my son?

SOLVEIG: Everything.

AASE: You'd tire hearing.

SOLVEIG: Not so soon as you would, telling.

(*High. Distant peaks. Shadows lengthening.*)

PEER: Whole parish after me. Rifles and cudgels. Ingrid's father out front, the yammer of him. Peer Gynt, a wanted man. Pound Hell out of Aslak is one thing. Here's another. This is to live. I feel in me, the coming strength and power of a bear. To sunder. To upturn. To stem the water in its fall.

To smite! To rend the pine up by its roots. This is to live; that can both harden and exalt a man. To Hell wi' watery lies!
(*Three upland SHEPHERD GIRLS, long high on mountain air and solitude, shriek, jodel and cry.*)

GIRLS: Trond in the mountain! Baard! Kaare! Come to our beds!

PEER: Who's that you're calling?

GIRLS: Trolls! Trolls! Trond come tender! Baard come wild! We've no one to our beds! Wild is tender! Tender is wild! We play with trolls for want of a man.

PEER: Where are your men?

GIRLS: – Can't come no more! (*Laugh.*)
– Mine had the sweetest names for me. He married a widow, one foot in her grave.
– Mine's away north with a gipsy's daughter. The two o' them, trampin' the roads.
– Mine put our bratling to sleep. Now his head stands grinnin' on a pole.
– Trond in the mountain! Baard! Kaare! Come to our beds!

PEER: (*Jumps amid them.*) I'm a three-headed troll! One each!

GIRLS: You?!

PEER: Try me!

GIRLS: Quick! To the hut! We've drink!

PEER: Pour it out!

GIRLS: – Tonight we'll not be lonely in our beds!
(*ONE kisses him.*)
– The touch of him! He burns! Like redhot iron!
(*ANOTHER.*)
– He snaps like a pike! From the blackest mountain lake…

PEER: (*Dances amid them.*) With a sorrowing soul and lust in my thought! A laugh in my eye, and a sob in my throat!
(*The three of them dance him away.*)

GIRLS: Trond! Baard! Kaare! Are ye's come till our bed?!

(*Strange sunset stillness. PEER alone.*)

PEER: Castles… Castles…rise… Gate there, so bright… I reach and it's gone… The weathervane lifts his wings to fly. Rainbow-shimmer shears my eyes. Bells far, but jangle in

my ear. My brow, so heavy. This throb in my skull. Redhot
band about my head…

[Ride over Gjendin Edge. All a story… Shin up the rock
wi' a bride. Drink the Sun round. Hunted. A tumble wi'
three mad girls. All a story…]

Twin brown eagles sail that sky. Wild geese fly south. I
flounder here and flail, mire to my knees. I'm coming
too! The wind's keen edge shall scour me. I'll up on high.
Above all this, away… My ride through the air shall
cleanse my heart. Daughters of England, look up indeed.
Not for you our coming, horse nor I. Though I might
swoop down…

Where the Hell are those eagles gone?

There's the peak of a gable comes thrusting up. Each
cranny, it grows. That house I know: my father's father
built. Here's no old rags, no fence about to fall. Each
window gleams. There's company in the hall tonight. The
clergyman taps with his knife on the glass. The smash of a
bottle the Captain threw. It shattered the mirror but what
does it matter. Och mother be quiet let them squander it
all. My father is rich and he's giving a feast. Sure aren't
the Gynts a mighty clan? Did ever ye hear such a din
and a howling, a carousing and roistering fit for a Lord.
The Captain cries: Jon Gynt, bring forth your son! The
clergyman raises his glass. So in, Peer Gynt, to be weighed
in the scale. On every voice the shout and the song: Peer
Gynt from greatness come, WHO GREAT SHALL BE!
(*Leaps up. A protrusion of the mountain fells him.*)

(*Tree-sough. Stars. Birdsong. SHE-IN-THE-GREEN.
PEER GYNT with lover's gestures after.*)

SHE: That true?

PEER: True as I'm Peer Gynt. True as you're a lovely lady. Do
be mine. I'll be such a good husband. You'll need neither
treadle nor spin. I'll fill you with food till you burst. I'll
never pull your hair.

SHE: Nor beat me?

PEER: The thought! We princes don't ill-treat our womenfolk.

SHE: You a prince?
PEER: That's right.
SHE: My father's King of Dovreland.
PEER: Then we are well met.
SHE: His palace is inside this mountain.
PEER: I'll bet my mother's is bigger.
SHE: You heard of my father: King Brose?
PEER: You heard of my mother: Queen Aase?
SHE: When my father is angry the mountain cracks.
PEER: When my mother starts scolding, the rocks roll down.
SHE: My father when he dances kicks ever so high.
PEER: My mother can ride the wildest water.
SHE: That's all you have to wear, those rags?
PEER: You should see my Sunday suit.
SHE: This silk and gold are my weekday wardrobe.
PEER: Those weeds and straw?
SHE: That's the whole point! You have to see with Dovre
    eyes. What looks a dismal scree to you's my father's
    kingdom really.
PEER: It's just like that at home! What looks like rubbish is
    really gold. A stuffing of cloths is glittering glass!
SHE: Black seems white and nasty seems nice.
PEER: Great is little and filthy clean.
SHE: Aren't we the appropriate pair.
PEER: Fits find each other as they say.
SHE: Then let us be married! My bridal steed. Come hither,
    ho!
    (*Enter a monstrous pig, rope for a bridle, saddle a*
    sack. PEER mounts with SHE-IN-THE-GREEN, in
    posture of the knight and damsel.)
PEER: Forward ho! We'll charge the gates of your father's
    kingdom! Gee up my mighty steed! Gallopa-gallopa-
    gallopa-gallop…
SHE: I was so lonely till you came, and wanly loitering. Life's
    full of surprise.
PEER: By their mount shall ye know them!

(*Within the mountain. TROLL-KING on throne; crown, sceptre. COURT disorderly and seething. PEER seems arraigned.*)

TROLL-COURT: – Kill him! Kill him!

– The Christian's son has wronged our Royal Master's fairest maid!

TROLL-YOUTH: – Chop his fingers!

– Pull his hair!

TROLL-WENCH: Bite his bottom!

HAG WITH LADLE: Make broth of him!

HAG WITH CLEAVER: Shall I spit him and roast him or brown him and stew him?

KING: Simmer down! (*To COUNCILLORS.*) Let's not pretend. We're not the force we've been. We could be finished for all we know. Human assistance is not to be despised. The boy's well made. No blemish; seems hefty enough.

So. You crave our daughter's hand.

PEER: And the Kingdom as dowry.

KING: Half now, the rest when I pass on.

PEER: Done.

KING: Not so fast. Now your commitments. Breach any, the contract's void, you don't leave alive. One. Utterly to forgo all world outside. Day; action; light of the sun…

PEER: Small loss, if that make me a King.

KING: Two. Tell me…

SENIOR COURTIER: You'll need a wisdom tooth to crack this nut.

KING: What is the difference between troll and a man?

PEER: None I see. Big troll would roast me, little would claw me. So would man, if he dared.

KING: True. And we've more in common. Yet morning is not fall of night. How's this for a difference? Beneath the shining vault, Man's motto is: Be yourself. Troll's motto here: Yourself be enough.

SENIOR COURTIER: Deep.

PEER: Murky.

KING: 'Enough': that mighty sundering oath be your watchword from now – !

PEER: But –

KING: – if you are to be master here.

PEER: What the Hell. It could be worse.

KING: Next. To appreciate our humble and homely regime.
(*Food, drink.*)
Cake from cow. Mead from bullock. Pleasant or foul, is not
the issue. This is all good Dovre fare.

PEER: You can keep it. I'll never acquire the taste o' that.

KING: The bowl comes with the diet. Gold. And with the
bowl, my daughter's fancy.

PEER: Mm. It is written: Curb your nature. The drink will
taste less foul with time. Pour away.

KING: Wisely said. You spit it out?

PEER: I shan't when I'm used to it.

KING: Next. All Christian clothing off. Know, that to our
greater Dovre glory, everything here's good mountain
wear. Nothing from the valley. But that silk bow on the end
of your tail.

PEER: I've no tail!

KING: We can soon put that right. Chamberlain! Bring this
man my Sunday tail.

PEER: No! You make me look ridiculous.

KING: None courts my daughter with his afters bare.

PEER: You make a beast of me!

KING: The contrary, dear boy. A fitting suitor. Yours shall be
an orange bow. Our highest order.

PEER: All man in me, brushed off so easy. How one adapts.
Tie on!

KING: Troth, an amenable knave.

SENIOR COURTIER: Let's see you twitch it.

PEER: Leave me some dignity. You'll be wanting my religion
next.

KING: Oh no. No interest in that. [No matter what loathsome
values you subscribe to in that heart!] By outward and
visible Troll we['ll] know each other.

PEER: I must say, I expected much worse.

KING: We deserve our reputation no more than men do.
Good. That's the serious business done. Let us now
gladden ear and eye, with Dovre harp, and Dovre dance.

[Music!]

(*So.*)

SENIOR COURTIER: How's it looking?

PEER: Mm...

SENIOR COURTIER: Feel free to speak.

PEER: Hideous. A bellcow clats at a gut with her hoof. In knee-socks a prancing sow...

TROLL-COURT: Eat him!

KING: Remember he sees as a man!

TROLL-WENCHES: Tear out his eyes!

SHE: Aoww! Boo hoo! How can I dance with all this going on?

PEER: Oh it's you. A joke at the feast: not meant to be unkind.

SHE: You swear to that!

PEER: The dance and the music are gorgeous. Cross my heart.

KING: Remarkable. His nature will cling to a man. My son-in-law, so flexible in all that we required of him: I felt for sure all man in him was quite expelled. Man will reassert himself. Alas my son. Still too much damnable Man: and that must be put right.

PEER: What do you mean?

KING: A little chink in this left eye... Then out with this right windowpane... You have to see the beauty of the bride.

PEER: Non-sense...

SENIOR COURTIER: Dovre sense.

KING: (*Spreads glazier's tools.*) Think of the pain, this shall ultimately spare you. What's an eye: but wellspring of the bitter wash of tears.

PEER: Truth in that... And Scripture says: If thine eye offend thee... I do get my sight back?

KING: Friend, nevermore. Stay where you are! Way down here is easy. My gates don't open out.

PEER: You'd keep me here?

KING: Prince Peer. You've makings of a troll. If troll you'd be –

PEER: For wife and a well-run estate there's much I'd forgo. But there are limits. All I've agreed so far can be reversed.

Tail untied, Christian clothes back on... But to shed all my
humanity for ever. A troll, the rest of my days. No going
back. That's a commitment I cannot make.

KING: You anger me! You abuse my daughter –

PEER: That's not true!

KING: You lusted for her in your heart.

PEER: That counts wi' nobody.

KING: Man never changes. Moral from the teeth out. Lust not
count eh? It's work'll soon be evident enough.

PEER: An old trick, that, an' I'm not fallin' for it.

KING: You're a father within the year my boy.

PEER: Let me out o' this place – !

KING: That little son'll haunt you! In a goatskin!

PEER: I dream this.

KING: Amazing how these crossbreeds grow.

PEER: Sir. Lady. Surely we can meet half way. I'm not a
prince. In fact I've nothing. From any angle, I'd be no
great acquisition.

(*SHE-IN-THE-GREEN is taken ill and carried off.*)

KING: Splinter him against the wall!

TROLL-YOUNG: – Oh Dad, can't we play with him first?

– Eagle and owl!

– The wolf game!

– Cat and mouse!

KING: All right! But not for too long. I'm upset, and I want
my sleep. Goodnight. (*Goes.*)

(*TROLL-YOUNG descend on PEER with joyous cries.*)

PEER: Let go of me, you little fiends!

TROLL-YOUNG: Come on everybody! Bite his bottom!

PEER: Ow! Cellar door...

TROLL-YOUNG: Block it!

SENIOR COURTIER: Playtime.

PEER: (*One biting his ear.*) Aoww! Stop that! Little monster!

SENIOR COURTIER: Watch who you're talking to! That's a
real prince!

PEER: ...A rat-hole...

TROLL-YOUNG: Block it!

PEER: I'd rather the father than these.

TROLL-YOUNG: Slash him!

PEER: So much of me! To be only a mouse!

TROLL-YOUNG: Ring him round! Ring him round!

PEER: To be only a flea!

TROLL-YOUNG: Get his eyes!

PEER: Help! Mother! I'm dying!

(*Bells sound as from outside the mountain. TROLLS scatter screaming.*)

TROLL-YOUNG: Bells! Him in the Black, with his flock...!

(*Pitch darkness. PEER flails about him with a branch.*)

PEER: Who are you? Speak!

VOICE: (*In the dark.*) My self.

PEER: Out o' my road.

VOICE: Go round, Peer. The hill has space enough.

PEER: (*Elsewhere. Blocked.*) Who are *you*?

VOICE: My self. Can you say that?

PEER: Can and do. Beware my sword! Ha ha! King Saul slew hundreds, Peer Gynt slew thousands! – Who are you?

VOICE: My self.

PEER: Idiot answer. Keep it for you tell me nothing. What are you?

VOICE: The Mighty Böyg. In your way, unseen, and endless in the dark.

PEER: Böyg, out o' me road.

VOICE: Peer Gynt, go round.

PEER: Through ye! Got you! (*Forward. Blocked.*) How many of yous are there here?

VOICE: One. The only. Böyg you hurt, and Böyg not hurt. Böyg lifeless, Böyg alive.

PEER: Trolls have smeared my sword useless. (*Throws branch away.*) I've still my fists!

VOICE: Ay ay. Head down and elbows out. The way to the top.

PEER: (*Comes at him again.*) Back or on, the way's as far. Out or in, the way's as tight. There he is! And there! He's all about me. Leap clear, I'm in his coil again! [Tell me your name!] Let me see you: what sort of thing ye are!

VOICE: Böyg.

PEER: (*Gropes.*) Living. Yet not alive. Slime to the touch. Yet nothing to be seen. Nor any form to him. Defend yourself!

VOICE: Böyg has more sense.

PEER: Lash out at me!

VOICE: What need?

PEER: Fight me! [I'll make you!]

VOICE: Böyg never fights. Yet always wins.

[PEER: For something I could take on! Not this Nothing. He's snoring! You! Böyg!

VOICE: What?]

PEER: Savage me!

VOICE: Böyg wins everything by doing nothing.

PEER: Teeth, nails, tear at my own flesh! To taste the warmth of my own living blood!

(*A beat of mighty wings.*)

BIRD CRY: Böyg, is he near?

VOICE: Step before step he comes.

BIRD CRY: Sisters afar! Fly to the encounter here!

PEER: Och girl: if you would save me, do it now! Not just look down, but pitch your silver prayerbook in his eye!

BIRD CRY: He's falling!

VOICE: We have him.

BIRD CRY: Sisters! Hurry!

PEER: A wearying hour of this, to buy my life? Too much…

BIRD CRY: He's down! Böyg take him now. Take him now.

(*Bells sound afar. A Lutheran hymn.*)

BÖYG: (*Shrivels in a gasp.*) He was too strong for me. He has women behind him…

(*Sunrise. Mountain pasture wall. PEER wakes. Looks about him with bleary eye. Spits.*)

PEER: I'd give my eye teeth for a pickled herring.

(*Spits again. HELGA with a basket.*)

You is it? What do you want?

HELGA: Solveig –

PEER: Where?!

HELGA: Yonder that wall.

SOLVEIG: (*Hidden there.*) Don't you come any nearer[; I'll run away] –

PEER: Afraid I'll grab at you?

SOLVEIG: Should be ashamed.

PEER: This night gone, you know where I was? I had the King of Dovre's daughter after me. She clung like a clegg.

SOLVEIG: As well we rang the bells.

PEER: I'm not one to stray. What's that?

HELGA: She's took off home. Solveig! Wait!

PEER: You. I've something in my pocket. A silver button look. It's yours. If only you put in a word for me.

HELGA: Let me go, let me –

PEER: Take it.

HELGA: Let me go. There's food for ye in the basket there.

PEER: For God have mercy on ye if ye don't!

HELGA: You frighten me!

PEER: Please. All I mean. Ask her. Not to forget me.

(*Lets her go. She runs.*)

End of Act Two.

ACT THREE

Forest. Autumn; snow falling. PEER felling an obdurate tree.

PEER: Ay, oul' fella. Tough ye might be, down ye come.
I'll hag ye through, for all your armour vest. Shake yuir
gnarled fist at me. You've the right. But to your knees, old
mahn! Not true! Not true! A tree only. Fir tree. Timber's
toil enough, without this dreaming! You're an outlaw, Peer.
Hounded to these woods. No mother here, set supper
before ye. Fetch your own food, raw, from forest and
stream; chop pine for your own fire, smash boulders if ye'd
have four walls, for roof hump your own lumber to your
door... Fine house shall this be... Steeple and weathervane
proud on its ridge. Mermaid carved for gable-end, all fish
below. Glass I must lay hand on; that folk on their way
down there look up this height and wonder: what glitter's
yon? Not true! Not true! You're an outlaw Peer. A hovel
roofed in bark's the most ye'll have against drizzle and
frost... Who's there? Who's that? Oul' mahn of Hegstad?
How could he be here... Someone is here... (*Hides.*) Boy
only. He seems afeared.
(*BOY glances about him.*)
What's that he has beneath his jacket? Sickle?
(*BOY stands. Looks round. Lays out his hand just so on
fence.*)
Aa!
(*BOY leans and sways.*)
Ugh... He's chopped a finger off... Bleeds like a pig...
(*BOY wraps fist in cloth and runs.*)
Hell of a lad. He chopped a finger off. One whole finger.
One un-replaceable finger, clean away. Of his free will! Of
course. Now the Army can't conscript him for their wars.
Sure he'd rather stay home. But a finger off for ever. To
think of that; wish that: one thing; to want that... But to do
it...! Beyond me...

(*A room in recent disorder. AASE at a loss. KARI, neighbourwoman, trying to help her.*)

AASE: Whole house stripped. Ingrid's oul' father. All belongs to him now. Farm and inheritance. Not even ma clothes to call me own. A shame on them, punished us so hard.

KARI: Ye've the house till ye die.

AASE: Ay. Cat and meself, on charity.

KARI: How that son's cost ye.

AASE: Him? Spake sense. Ingrid's back home and ended up all right. Might ha' known they'd gang together. Peer was the only offender there, oh ay! Fool of a boy.

KARI: Should I send for the Pastor? Might be you'll need him sooner nor ye think.

AASE: Pastor…? Could well be… Ye will not! I'm the boy's mother! He's a right to what help I can! While them ones pluck him… Here's a coat A saved him. Needs patchin' up. Would God A could ha sneaked him the fur blanket as well. Where's the leggin's?

KARI: Somewhere in that.

AASE: Will ye look at this. Oul' castin' ladle. He played with this as a child… Buttonmoulder. Melt, shape, stamp… I mind the day. We'd company. Wee boy comes in and asks his father for a lump o' tin. 'Tin?' says himself. 'Take coin of the realm. Silver… Make a button o' that, and stamp yerself Gynt son of Jon!' God forgive the mahn. The drink. He knew neither tin nor gold. Och look at these, all holes. They'll need to be darned.

KARI: They will that.

AASE: I'll darn these so, then away to me bed… I feel that failed… Here's two wool shirts! These tha missed!

KARI: So tha hahve.

AASE: These'll come in. You put one asi– No. We'll take both. That he has on him is worn that thin.

KARI: Them's not yuirs to take now Mother Gynt, that's sin!

AASE: Ay. Well. Your sins be forgiven ye, the Pastor says.

*(Before new hut. Reindeer-horn over door. Snow fallen.
Dusk. PEER hammering.)*

PEER: I must have bolts to me door. Against all trolldom,
man and womankind. Bolts. To keep all angry gremlin
out. They come with dusk. Rat tat. Peer Gynt let us in. You
think us, we are here. They pither and clouster beneath
the bed. Whisk the ashes. Ach! Nail and boord won't keep
those from yuir duir. They're in your head.

*(SOLVEIG has come far through snow, in shawl;
bundle in hand.)*

SOLVEIG: God bless the work. No. Don't turn me away.
Word came; I am here. You have to welcome me.

PEER: Solveig...? [It – Solveig...?!] No dread now, to come so
close?

SOLVEIG: You sent word with my sister. Word came after: on
the wind; then word in stillness. Word came in all of you
your mother told me. Word was in my dreams. Bleak night
and barren day were word, here should I be. Down there,
the life in me was almost gone. Heart dead to laughter,
dried of tears. I had no knowing what your feelings were.
Mine I knew.

PEER: But your father?

SOLVEIG: In God's wide earth I've none to call my father
nor my mother now. I've cut adrift from that all.

PEER: Solveig my love. To come to me?

SOLVEIG: To you, none other. You must be my friend and
comfort now. Worst was to leave my little sister. Worse yet,
to sever from my father. Worst above all, from her had
held me till her breast. Worst but, of all that, God have
mercy, the pain of parting from them all. From them all.

PEER: You understand the sentence I am under? Farm and
inheritance lost? Outside this forest, any can lay hold on
me?

SOLVEIG: I hurried to be here. I needed to ask each turn of
my road. What can be up there for you? they said. I told
them. Home.

PEER: Let me look at you. No: where you are. Look at you...
Pure light... [Lift you... No weight at all...] I could carry

you Solveig and not weary ever. But I'll not sully you. I'll hold you, pure at the length of my arm. So precious to me, so warm… This I've built, so poor and ugly. I pull it down…

SOLVEIG: Poor or grand, it is after my heart. In this wind's shock I breathe so free. Down there was stifling me to death. As much for fear of that I left. The wind in these trees: it's both a silence and a song. Here's home.

PEER: For the rest of your days?

SOLVEIG: No going back now.

PEER: You are mine! Oh let me see you in the house! Go in! I'll fetch wood for a fire. You shall sit easy and never be cold.

(*SOLVEIG in.*)

My king's daughter! Found and won! This has to be a palace now!

(*Axe up –*

A HAG in green rags, face marred with the neb of a troll. An ugly URCHIN after, limping; bottle in hand.)

HAG: Good night to ye. Peer-be-Nimble.

PEER: Who the –

HAG: Old friends. Neighbours.

PEER: News to me.

HAG: As you built yuir hut, up went mine.

PEER: I'm in a great hurry.

HAG: Ye always were. I trudge after: but I catch up.

PEER: Mother, have you the wrong mahn!

HAG: And had before. When ye promised so big.

PEER: Promise? Me? Non-sense.

HAG: Night ye drank at our house: d'ye not remember?

PEER: Remember what I never knew?

HAG: Offer yuir father a dhrink. A think he nades wun.

PEER: Me? Father o' that?

HAG: Tell a pig by his hide. You've eyes. He limps, look. As you in yuir soul.

PEER: You lay that get at ma duir…? Legs on him that length?

HAG: He shot up quick.

PEER: An' you!? Neb on ye like a witch?!

HAG: There speaks a feeling mahn. What fault mine my looks are gone? Looks I had when ye took me astray to the hills. Autumn after, this was born. And a bad time with him, the Devil had ma back that seized. I'm ugly from that day. If you would see the looks I had, show that one the door.

PEER: Get you away from me.

HAG: Never!

PEER: I'll cleft your head.

HAG: Try that. I'll visit ye every day. Spy in at your door. On the two of ye. Sat side by side on that bench in there. And wax you tender, Peer, I'll in and ask my share. That one and I, it shall be turn and turn about wi' you. Farewell dear mahn. You wed tomorrow!

PEER: I dream this.

HAG: One thing more. Take charge of your son. He'll keep ye tethered. Gyntlet, to your father.

URCHIN: (*Spits at PEER.*) I'll chop you down! You wait! You wait!

HAG: (*Kisses boy.*) Hasn't he the right idea? And won't he be the image of his father when he's grown? A pity on ye, Peer. All for the one wild urge…

PEER: Worse on another.

HAG: Ay. So. The blameless get scorched, the Devil said. When his mother cuffed him for his Da bein' drunk.
(*Gone; BOY after, pitching bottle behind him.*)

PEER: There crashed my palace to the ground. She, so near: all this sudden, walled from me. Here's ugly now[; my joy grows old]. Go round, said the Böyg. Go round, mahn! No straight road to Solveig now. [Yet some road there must be…] What's that that Bible says… Repent…? I disremember. [Shatter a bell: mend her fragments how ye like, the note is never true again.] That hag was never here. She was here. The thought of her will dog me through that door. Ingrid… Those three on the hill… Will they up too; and nudge her from my knee? Go round… Were these arms fir-stem long, already have I held her to me much too close; my harm and smirch of her are done…

SOLVEIG: (*In doorway.*) Peer?

PEER: Go round.

SOLVEIG: What?

PEER: Don't come out! It's nearly dark. I've something I'm
carrying here.

SOLVEIG: I'll help you. Let me share…

PEER: Wait there! I must manage this alone.

SOLVEIG: Well don't you take too long.

PEER: Have patience, girl. However long… You wait.

SOLVEIG: Ay. Wait.

(*Room of before. AASE on deathbed. Night.*)

AASE: Will the boy never come? So much to say till him. So
little time. My end, so sudden on me… A treated him too
hard…

PEER: Mother?

AASE: Son! Och son… You took a chance. Down here you're
good as dead.

PEER: What matter? I had to come.

AASE: Now I may go in peace.

PEER: Mother? Go? Go where?

AASE: Peer, son, ma last road. And that near done.

PEER: My luck. Trouble left behind, now trouble here. Are
yuir feet an' hahn's coul'?

AASE: They are. Near spent, so A am… When my eyes cloud
over, you shut them son. See to a coffin. Daycent, mind…
One thing more… ·

PEER: Mother. Time for that.

AASE: Ay. See what little them ones left.

PEER: Not that either. Sure I know I'm the cause. Don't cast it
up to me now; what guid?

AASE: Not you. The damn dhrink. Our ill came all from that.
A man's no knowin' what he does. An' yui'd been ridin'
that reindeer, yuir head was turned…

PEER: Ach let that story lie. All that. What's sad can keep.
Till ye – Till another day. We'll just sit talkin' Mother you
an' I. On anny oul' matther. What's a'k'ard or thorny or
hurtsome or sore put out of our minds. – Oul' cat still alive.

AASE: She maks that mournful a noise through the night. Ye
know that sign.

PEER: What's news down here?

AASE: There's tell of some girl, has her heart on the high lahnd…

PEER: Mads Moen settle down?

AASE: Her parents weep; she takes no heed. You shuid drop by. Might be yui cuid help.

PEER: Aslak the smith –

AASE: Agh. That filthy oul' smiter. I tell ye the wee girl's name. She –

PEER: Mother. I said. What's a'k'ard or thorny or hurtsome or sore, put out of our minds. D'ye want a dhrop o' watther? Can't ye straighten yuir legs? Short bed… Isn't it this A lay in as a child? Mahn dear… Yui'd sit where I sit now. Draw up the cover to me chin. Sing some oul' song. Or lullaby…

AASE: Ay. The sled ride. Ye remember that game? Times yuir father was away. Quilt for a rug. Thon fluir a fjord all ice…

PEER: Best of all, our fine horse Mother, d'ye mind that?

AASE: A do surely. Kari's cat there, we tuik the loan of. It sat on that log chair…

PEER: To the castle west of the Moon. To the castle east of the Sun. To Soria Maria Castle in Araby land, we'd take the road both high and low. A stick from the cupboard you'd use for a whip –

AASE: Ay, me the driver…

PEER: Ye'd give the horses their head. Ye'd turn as we travelled along. To ask was A cold… God bless your dear ould ugly loving soul… What is it ails ye?

AASE: Ma back's the Devil… This hard oul' boord…

PEER: Lie straight. I hold ye. There. You lie easy.

AASE: No. A have to be away…

PEER: Away where?

AASE: Away. That's all A want…

PEER: Non-sense. You draw up the cover. I'll sit here. We'll sing as you done before. The night's soon over.

AASE: I'd as lief you brought the prayerbook. I'm that uneasy in my heart…

PEER: In Soria Maria Castle the King and Prince have
company. Lie back in the sleigh on the cushions. I'll drive
ye there over the moorland.

AASE: Mahn dear, they've not invited me?

PEER: We both are. Tsk tsk. Trit trit trot... Are ye coul' there
Mother? We're on the move. Gallopa-gallopa-gallopa-
gallopa –

AASE: That jangle I hear...

PEER: The harness bells!

AASE: They sound so ampty.

PEER: We're crossing a fjord!

AASE: I'm afeared! That roar A hear... Great wild sigh of a
sound above...

PEER: The wind in the pines! We're over moorland now. Just
you sit still.

AASE: That glitter an' twinkle o' lights ahead...

PEER: From the windows and gates of the Castle! They've a
dance on! Hear them!

AASE: Ay.

PEER: I spy the Dean's wife: puttin' out the coffee an' dessert.

AASE: Lord. I meet her?

PEER: Often as ye'll like.

AASE: Here's some grand do, ye bring me till, daft son...

PEER: Gallopa-gallopa-gallopa-gallop...

AASE: Peer watch the road.

PEER: It's wide enough.

AASE: This ride... I feel so unwell... So tired...

PEER: Up there's the Castle now! Our journey's near over!

AASE: I'll lie an' close me eyes. I leave it to you, son...

PEER: Gallopa-gallopa-gallopa-gallop... There's the world
and his wife in the Castle tonight. Who's this Peer Gynt
and who's his mother? What's that ye say, Saint Peter Sir?
Not let her in?! Ye'll look a while before ye find again a bag
of bones so true. We'll not talk about me. I can turn from
your castle door. To me all one. But her, you'll honour and
respect; and treat her right. Aha. Here's God the Father.
'What's this, Hall-Porther Peether! Mother Aase gets in
free!' – See mother? What's that A toul' ye? Laugh the

other side their faces now. Mother? What's this [strange]
milk about yuir eyes? Are ye in your mind at all? Don't
gaze at me! Mother speak! It's me your son!
Horses, you rest. The ride is done.
Thank you for all your days. The welts ye gave me; songs
ye sang… Now you thank me.
(*His cheek to her dead lips.*)
For the ride.

KARI: Peer? Lord but does she sleep sound. Or –

PEER: She is dead. See her buried with respect. I must set out.

KARI: Far?

PEER: For the sea.

KARI: Far as that!

PEER: And way beyond.

End of Act Three.

Interval.

ACT FOUR

A shore. Palms, hammocks. (Yacht anchored afar: Norwegian and US colours.) Sundown; a dinner party ending. Host: PEER GYNT – late forties, impeccable turnout. Four rebarbative guests, each a ludicrously true specimen of his own worst national kind.

PEER: Gentlemen. Pray: imbibe. If Man was made for pleasure, pleasure be it. Lost is lost, the Scripture says: and gone is gone. [What can I offer you?]

TRUMPETERSTRAALE: Brother Gynt. Such hospitality!

PEER: Thank me but thank my money too. My cook, my steward…

COTTON: Here's to all four I say. (*Clink.*)

OTHERS: – Prosit.
    – Skaal.
    – Santé.

BALLON: Msieu. You ev eh…gout, un…ton, un…je ne sais quoi…

EBERKOPF: Ein Desh, you mean? ein Sheen. Of Inner Speculation. Of Verltcitizenhoot. His Vision shears ze Clouts. He bears ze Shtemp of Refelation. Ein UrNatur, yet mit Experience of Leif. All in one Men. How to explain this?

PEER: No marital commitment. A man must be himself alone. Not a beast of burden for others and their needs.

EBERKOPF: Such Freedom surely has its Preis. In Shtruggle…

PEER: Struggle I have always honourably won. I once came near to being trapped. A lady dear to my heart. Of royal blood –

BALLON: *Royale?!*

PEER: Hopelessly above me.

BALLON: What eppened? Ze familee were opposed?

PEER: Quite the reverse. Circumstances made our marrying a matter of some urgency. Then the girl's father started hinting at terms. I should change my name; my attitudes;

61

submit to ennoblement... Conditions quite distasteful to
me. Unacceptable. I bowed out; with grace: flatly refusing
all his ultimata; renouncing my bride... It cost me blood:
with seven of the younger brothers in a duel. But that same
blood I shed taught me my value as a living man; and
pointed to a greater Destiny [that shaped my course].

EBERKOPF: The mere empiricist sees only each scene as it
heppens. His life's a fumbling in ze dark... You grasp ze
Pettern that ordains it all. And vizzout formal education!

PEER: I have thought. Pondered. Read: widely if not deep.
I came to learning late; had not the leisure. A fragment of
history from here and there. The odd dose of religion – for
reassurance in bad times; one could never swallow that
wholesale. A man should learn only what can be put to
work for him.

COTTON: Pragmatic.

PEER: Dear friends. Consider my career. A penniless
immigrant in America. The cruel struggle for my daily
bread. But Life, my friends: I cherished that. For Death,
they say, is bitter. And Luck did smile on me. Good old
Fate cleared every obstacle away. And I learned Versatility.
Within ten years, among the shipping fraternity my name
was Gold. I trafficked in Prosperity herself.

COTTON: What trade was that?

PEER: Negroes mainly, for South Carolina. Heathen idols for
the Chinese.

BALLON: Fi donc!

TRUMPETERSTRAALE: For tusen!

PEER: I came to feel misgivings too. A moral revulsion
indeed. But believe me: an enterprise on such a scale,
once in motion – deploying thousands – is the devil to
stop. And I could have cause to regret that. Age however
was creeping up on me. Late forties, that sprinkle of grey
hairs. For all my health, a painful awareness: who knows
when that dread hour may strike, and judgement fall upon
a man, and he go numbered with the saved, or damned?
Conscience on the one hand, self-preservation on the
other: there had to be some compromise. Each spring, I

sent to China heathen idols. Autumn after, men of God.
With socks, Bibles, rum, rice –

COTTON: But at a profit?

PEER: Naturally. For every idol sold, a coolie baptized:
the two trades fought and fed each other inexhaustibly.
Proceeds to me.

COTTON: And the African merchandise?

PEER: There too morality prevailed. [And the trade had its
hazards. Abolitionists, piracy, storms at sea. I said: Peter,
lay off.] My last consigment – excellent specimens – I
settled on some land I'd bought in the South. Fattened
them up: a model community – happy; schools; moral
standards – I saw to that. I was a father to them all. I sold
the whole plantation, hair and hide. They say who does
no harm does good. I trust that when I'm brought to book,
any errors of my past will prove balanced by my good
work since.

EBERKOPF: To a Leif-Prinzipal: in one Men, ected to ze full!
(*Clink.*)

PEER: Well. We Norsemen know at least this. Keep one foot
always safe on solid ground, poised for retreat: and the line
of the retreat well open. A national characteristic, and my
one inheritance.

BALLON: You are from Norway msieu?

PEER: Originally. But of the world by temper. From
America I learned to use my chances. From Germany,
my scholarship... From France my comme il faut, mes
mots justes; from England, that redoubtable marriage of
Industry with Self-Interest; from the Jews, how to wait;
from Italy, a touch of dolce far niente; I once, in dire need,
had recourse even to Swedish steel.

TRUMPETERSTRAALE: Aja! Svensk staal! Skaal! Skaal!
(*Clink.*)

COTTON: All very well, Sir. But now you've made your
money what are you going to do with it?

PEER: Do?

ALL: Yes...?

PEER: Travel... Why I shipped you four aboard at Gibraltar.
To worship at my Golden Calf.

(*All laugh*.)

COTTON: No one goes sailing simply to sail. You must have some scheme in mind.

PEER: Oh yes. To be Emperor.

ALL: – Ha ha.

– Emperor?

– Kaiser?

– Empereur?

COTTON: Emperor where?

PEER: Of all the world.

BALLON: Mais…mais comment…

PEER: Through the power of Gold. That's been my governing design from the beginning. As a boy I dreamed I rode out over oceans on a cloud. And came a cropper. But my intent never wavered. Some writer I think once said: Win the whole world, yet lose your Self, you win but a crown on a cloven skull.

EBERKOPF: What is Gynt's 'self'?

PEER: This world in my head. All its fantasies; desires. All its notions. Needs. All by which I live and feel and breathe and am. I'll mould the earth anew, through Gold, in image of that. We sail tonight.

ALL: Hein?! Tonight…? We?!

PEER: I have received information. Greece is in revolt.

ALL: – Die Griecher?

– Les Hellènes?

PEER: Turkey has a rising on her hands.

ALL: Hurrah! Hurrah! (*All toast Greece afar.*)

BALLON: Vive la Grèce! En avant par les portes de la Gloire! Je vous aide avec mon épée de la France!

EBERKOPF: Courage, brothers! Courage there!

COTTON: I agree! Greece, independent! Contracts for all!

TRUMPETERSTRAALE: To it, Hellas! Cast off your Turkish joke! Drive your oppressorsh out!

BALLON: (*Arms around PEER's neck.*) Mon cher ami –

EBERKOPF: (*Seizes PEER's arm.*) Freiheitsbruder!

TRUMPETERSTRAALE: (*Kisses PEER.*) Mine Wiking cousin!

EBERKOPF: Now we see: in one illuminating shtroke, the
Self of Gynt, its yearninks, espirations ent deseirs, made
real, in the real verldt!

BALLON: Voilà que ça veut dire, être Pierre Gynt soi-même!
To put his ships and moneys to the help of Hellas in her
fight!

PEER: Oh no. Not the Greeks. The Turks. I invest in the
strong.

BALLON: Hein?! C'est pas possible!

EBERKOPF: Ha ha. Ha ha. Funny yoke.

PEER: Gentlemen. I see we reach the parting of our ways.
You go to Hellas. I'll arm you, land you: free of charge.
Inflame the rebellion all you can. It's grist to my mill. You
fight the Greek fight for Freedom and Justice; and end
impaled on janissaries' lances. Forgive me for not joining
you. My cause is money alone. I am my Self. Sir Peter
Gynt. Goodnight. (*Retires to a hammock.*)

TRUMPETERSTRAALE: Svinish bashtard.

BALLON: No sense of honneur.

COTTON: Who cares about honour? Think of those
opportunities lost. The Greek market wide open, enormous
profits –

BALLON: I saw myself en conquéreur: all about me les
Grecian damsels les plus exquises.

EBERKOPF: I saw ze Kultur of ze Fazzerlandt spread Souse
to ze Sun!

COTTON: I could weep. All that capital of his. On Mount
Olympus all those copperveins, waiting only to be opened
up…

TRUMPETERSTRAALE: I go anyway. Mine Swedish svort
is versh more than Jankee golt.

COTTON: All very well. Us, packed in those rebel hordes? 'd
sink without trace. Very profitable.

BALLON: Nom du Diable! So near the pinnacle de la
Fortune! Now to stand by her grave.

COTTON: Damn coffinship of his out there. With all that
golden nigger-sweat…

EBERKOPF: Of course! Ze kepital notion! Eil machen!
  Schnell, schnell. Ve hev his Empire by its sroat. HA!
BALLON: Msieu?
EBERKOPF: I seize his power. I expropriate ze yat!
COTTON: What's that?
EBERKOPF: I greb the whole verks! (*Gone.*)
COTTON: Mm. I'd do well to be in on this… (*Goes.*)
TRUMPETERSTRAALE: After such hospitality?!
BALLON: Pas du tout comme il faut. Main enfin… (*Goes.*)
TRUMPETERSTRAALE: Ja vel. (*Follows.*) But I protest!

  (*Night. PEER comes running.*)
PEER: This isn't happening. My yacht, full pelt for the open
  sea…? I refuse to believe this! Could be the death of me…
  I DREAM THIS! Monsters of friends. Oh Judge above!
  It's me! Peter Gynt! Father don't let me die! Bring them
  back! Stop them! DO SOMETHING! The world can look
  after itself a moment; concentrate on me! Deaf as ever…
  What use is a God like that? Hey. I sold the plantation.
  Those missionaries I sent to China: surely one good turn –
  (*Yacht explodes. PEER cries; falls. Soon last glug.
  Silence.*)
  The Sword of Wrath… All souls to the bottom: plop. Could
  have been me on that… Luck? I have been spared… Thine
  Arm was about me, for all my wrong! Ah… Extraordinary
  security one feels. Especial protection. In this desert? No
  food, no water? HE'll see to that. I'm not in that much
  danger really. HE won't let His little sparrow starve.
  Humility. The Lord shall provide. Just give Him a minute
  or two. Forward, head high! What's that? in those reeds,
  that growling, a lion – Lion? Yaach. Beast has more sense.
  Keeps well away. He knows his master. All the same…
  [Those nodding palms…] Up a tree I'd be safer. More so
  if I knew a hymn or two… Morning is not fall of night
  indeed: a text often pondered. Mm. Lofty thoughts. Feel
  good. Better than being rich. Build but on Him! A personal
  Father above…! But no sense of economics. (*Gone.*)

(*Night still. ARAB SLAVES come rending their garments and their hair; an OFFICER after.*)

SLAVES: – Aa! The Sultan's white horses are missing!
– Aa! The Sultan's sacred robes have been stolen!

OFFICER: Find them! A hundred strokes on his soles for every man who fails! (*Gone.*)

(*Grey daybreak. PEER in Darwinian estate: up a palm tree, flailing vainly about him with a frond.*)

PEER: I wish Hell had these monkeys. Not my idea of a good night's sleep at all. You again? Fiend! Pelting me with fruit now. Mm. Not fruit. Revolting creature, your ape. I must put paid to these bastards somehow. Grab one. Throttle him, flay him; wriggle into its coat some way or other: that'd fool 'em. [All Man in me, brush off so easy?] Adaptation… Here's more of them. Whole swarm[; the tree's alive] …Monsters! Shoo! If I had something like a tail I could put on… I'd look a little less different… [Padding about up there, who's that?] Old fella. Fists of him, full with filth. Bus Bus. He looks a creature of some reason. No no. Bus not throw. Of course not. It's me. Pip pip! Me friend. Ai! Ai! See? I speak your breogue. We are cousins. Of a sort. Bus get sugar in the morning. Aa! Animal! Whole lot in my face. Revolting. Might this be food? Taste: indeterminate… Taste's not the issue. Which philosopher *is* that? 'Spit out now, you shan't when you're used to it…' Oy oy. Here come the young. (*Flails about him.*) This really is too bad. Man: Lord of Creation: reduced to – Aa! Aa!

(*Early morning. ARABS creep in: from one side, one with stolen robes, riches etc. (Restless horse heard off. – Sh!) From other side an ARAB to receive.*)

THIEF: Allah is good.

RECEIVER: Great is Allah.

THIEF: Cavalry! Lances! (*Panic.*)

RECEIVER: Ai-ai! I see my nopper rolling in the sand!

THIEF: My father was a thief. What else can I be?

RECEIVER: My father was a receiver: we are who we are.
(*Fleeing…*)

THIEF: The horse! The robes!

RECEIVER: Were never to be ours! Great is Allah! (*Both gone.*)
(*Silence. PEER comes, whittling a pipe from a reed.*)

PEER: Bliss of the morning. The scarab trundles his little
ball. From shell creeps forth the snail. Morning! Gold in
its mouth. Remarkable, the power of new light of day: so
sure I feel, so increasingly strong. I could tackle a bull. All
about, so still… Nature. Too little have I heeded this. This
is Living! Not walled up in those great towns. Pestered
by one's fellow men. That lizard: snapping its jaws: not a
thought in his head. So innocent, the animal estate. Each
goes his Maker's way. Each is what he is: in shape and
stamp that nothing can efface. Himself: in play or fight, the
Self he ever was. (*Lorgnettes to his nose.*) That toad. Encased
in sandstone there. Head only protruding: his eye, like a
glass through which he considers the world. Himself, is
enough. What great classic *is* that? Wisdom of Solomon?
Damn' memory. Not what it was… (*Sits.*) [A moment in
the shade. Ferns… Edible roots… Not human diet really.
Still. 'Curb your nature. Whoso abaseth himself shall be
exalted.' Exalted I shall be. No question. This is a mere
test.] (*Cigar.*) Endless emptiness. Ostrich strutting there.
This void: so sterile; scorched. Profitless. What did God
mean? Earth lying here so idle. A carcase, that since its
Creation has not rendered its Maker so much as a thanks.
What Nature squanders. That the sea over there? that
twinkling? Mirage. Sea's behind me, West. Dammed out by
those dunes.

That's a thought. That ridge is not so wide… Cut a canal.
Bring pouring in to this desert's throat the water of life!
Whole redhot graveyard, transform to a salt sea bay! This
stifling heat, dispel; cloud, dew, verdure; towns. White sails
shearing like dizzied gulls the old caravan routes; south
of Sahara a coastline waiting only to be civilized! Steam
shall power the factories of Timbuktu! Explorers pass to
the Upper Nile in sleeping-cars! On an opulent oasis in
the midst of my sea I'll breed Norwegians! Valley blood
and Arab mixed, what a race! Around the shelving strand

I'll found Peeropolis! This world is old. Gyntiana inherit!
Brave new earth! Men yearn for freedom everywhere.
Come to my shores! Be born again! Born free! [Needs only
the capital. With a key of gold, unlock the deep…] Let's get
started. Capital. From east or west… Oh for a horse… My
Kingdom, half my k –
(*A neigh off. And soon he's seeing:*)
Robes? Jewels? A sword? Real…?
(*Neigh there again.*)
I've read of will moving mountains; but a horse…
(*Horse.*)
Horse it is. Think him, he is here. (*Robes himself.*) Sir
Peter… Turk. Life's full of surprise. By their mount shall ye
know them!

(*ARAB GIRLS. ANITRA. PEER GYNT in Muslim
luxury.*)
ARAB GIRLS: (*Sing.*)
> Behold it is He!
> Our Prophet, our Lord,
> our Master all-knowing
> to us has come riding the desert sea.
> Before us He stands!
> Our Prophet, our Lord,
> His way ever sure,
> like a ship has come gliding the sea of the sands.
> Touch flute and drum:
> our Prophet is come.

ANITRA: (*Sings.*)
> His steed: was milk of Paradise so white?
> His gentle eyes: were stars above so bright?
> [Kneel; bow our heads: what child of dust can bear
> the burning of such eyes as dazzle there?]
>
> Across the sands He came.
> Bright at His breast like flame
> leapt pearls and gold.
> Banishing thirst, simoom and night,
> His Coming touches all to Light.

The signs foretold
Himself proclaim:
Our Lovely One
in vesture of an earthborn son.

ARAB GIRLS: (*Sing.*)
Touch flute and drum:
Our Prophet is come.

PEER: I have read somewhere – print doesn't lie – no man's a prophet at home. This suits me much better than shipping. Never quite rang true, that. Not the real me. Identity based on what you own? A house built on sand. [Ha! My tiepin they were doffing their hats to in America, not me.] A prophet now… Nothing external about that. This is me being worshipped. Me. Fancy. And just blundering into it like that. Here I came, here these daughters of Nature were. No deceitful intent on my part. If my every word is a Prophetic Utterance to these, that's how these want it. I'm their Prophet. Simple. I can always back out. If need be, vanish as I came. My horse stands ready. I am, in short, Master of the Situation.

ANITRA: Prophet? Lord?

PEER: Well slave?

ANITRA: Sons of the desert are gathered before Thy tent. They crave a Sight of Thee.

PEER: No! They must worship from afar. I can listen from here. Men my child are a feeble collection. [Oh Anitra you cannot imagine the barefaced robb– wrong, my child, that men have done me.] We'll not talk of that. Women, dance for me. The Prophet would forget the memories that pain him so.

[ARAB GIRLS: (*Sing.*)
The Prophet is good.
The Prophet is sad:
such wrong to Him the sons of dust have done.
The Prophet is kind.
Oh sinners be glad:
He opens Paradise to everyone.]

PEER: Very tempting she is too. Somewhat exotic in design.
But where's the norm? Each realm has its own currency.
Her feet could do with a wash. Arms too; especially that
one. [I'd say, though, that counted rather for her...] Anitra.

ANITRA: Lord and Master.

PEER: You quite allure me child. The Prophet is moved. So
much so, I'll make you a Houri in Paradise.

ANITRA: My Lord, that cannot be.

PEER: It shall be! True as I live!

ANITRA: I have no soul.

PEER: We can put that right.

ANITRA: Lord? How?

PEER: I shall provide. Stupid you might be. [As to my grief
I have observed.] But there's always room for a soul. Let
me measure. Of course there's room. Not for a great soul;
nothing penetrating or profound. But soul enough, for you
to know some self-respect.

ANITRA: The Prophet is kind.

PEER: But...?

ANITRA: I would much rather...

PEER: Ask! Feel free!

ANITRA: I do not care about a soul so much...

PEER: As...?

ANITRA: That lovely opal. (*In his turban.*)

PEER: Anitra! Daughter of Eve! What hope has a mere man
when as our great poet puts it 'The Eternal Feminine is
leading us on?'

(*Night. Moon. A palm tree. PEER much rejuvenated,
singing to a small guitar.*)

    I shut and locked my Paradise,
    and brought away the key.
    The North Wind bore me out to sea;
    my keel sheared south for warmer lands
    whiles all forlorn on colder strands
    fair woman wept for me.

    [Where Ocean gently curves the shore
    and proud palms sway and sigh

I set my ship afire; then high
on desert stallion hoist my sail.
He foamed beneath my flashing flail:
and now I've wings to fly.]

Oh who can trap the songbird now?
He chirrups in his tree.
No wine so fresh, no joy so free,
nor milk beneath cold northern sky
of taste so sweet nor true, as my
Anitra is to me. (*Stillness.*)

ANITRA: My Lord is calling in the night?

PEER: Yes. Yes he is. The cat woke me. He was chasing a
mouse: a terrible noise.

ANITRA: The cat I heard wasn't after a mouse my Lord.

PEER: What then?

ANITRA: The Prophet makes me blush to speak it.

PEER: Ah. The cat perhaps was moved? As I was? deeply:
when I gave you my opal?

ANITRA: The Treasure of the Earth, liken himself to a nasty
old cat?

PEER: There is one longing cat and Prophet have in common.

ANITRA: My Master's teasing streams like honey from His lips.

PEER: Sweet child. Like all girls, you will judge great men
by our appearance. True: my status; prophetic duties;
responsibility for the world and so on, constrain me in a
mask of gravity. By day. But here…with just the two of
us…you see my truer, playful self.
Come Anitra. Let us lie easy. I shall whisper, you shall
smile. Then you do the whispering, I shall smile.

ANITRA: Tell me Lord. Can Thy daughter, by listening, catch
a soul?

PEER: Ah. Soul. [The inner light and knowing.] You'll come
to that. When rosy-fingered dawn, in letters of gold, prints:
Here is day. I'll start your lessons then. Not waste this night.
Besides: soul's not the issue. What matters, is the heart.

ANITRA: Master. Thy words gleam as opals. Speak more.

PEER: I tell you, child. Some people on this earth are stuffed
so full with soul, they'll never learn a thing. I knew one

such. Heard all the sound, and none of the sense. Do you know what it means: to live?

ANITRA: Oh teach me.

PEER: To drift down the river of time, and not get one's shoes wet. To be myself through and through. Only in my manhood's potent prime can I be that. Consider the eagle; the bull; man, womankind: the loathsomeness of their decay. And their souls wither. Youth! Youth! I will be Sultan, hot and whole: not on the shores of Gyntiana but in the garden of a woman's young awakening. You are my chosen: in whose enraptured heart my throne shall stand. In that deep kingdom of your longings, am I Kalif absolute. Each fibre and each inch of you I'll know charged full with me! And in our parting all your garden dies. Nota bene. So much the better then your skull's so empty. Once burdened with a soul, you have a notion of your self. Wiser a ring round your ankle; I'll be what soul you need. (*ANITRA snores.*)
Ahh. Anitra sleeps. Passed her all by. Stamp of my power, that on the words of love, she drifts away in dreams. (*Gently pours jewels into her lap.*) [Here's jewels from your Lord. Here's more.] Sleep. Anitra, sleep. Your dreams, make man in me true Emperor.

(*Blazing day. Desert. PEER on white charger, ANITRA side-saddle before him (cf. with She-in-the-Green in Act Two).*)

PEER: Gallopa-gallopa-gallopa-gallop…

ANITRA: Put me down! I'll bite you!

PEER: You little fiend!

ANITRA: What are you playing at?!

PEER: Falcon and dove! I'm carrying you off!

ANITRA: You should know better. Old prophet like you.

PEER: Old?! Call this old?!

ANITRA: Put me down! I want to go home!

PEER: Home is it? To your old father?! After what we two have done?! Besides. I stay too long. [One forfeits respect.] A Prophet should be glimpsed, and gone.

ANITRA: You are a prophet?

PEER: I am an Emperor! (*Would kiss her.*) Oh ho! My
woodpecker bristles!

ANITRA: Give me that ring.

PEER: Oh sweet Anitra take them all.

ANITRA: Thy very word is music to my ear.

PEER: The bliss. To know oneself on such a pedestal. I'll
down: you ride, I'll lead. (*So.*) I am your slave! I flounder
and flail in the sand: till a sunstroke kill me. Anitra: I am
young. The day I cannot play the fool, oh then I'm old.

ANITRA: You're young all right. Are those all the rings you
have?

PEER: Of course I'm young. Take them! I can leap like a buck
through the air! AM I YOUNG?! (*Dances, sings.*)

> A lucky cockerel I!
> Take a peck at me my pretty little hen!
> Hey up, I dance,
> I preen and prance:
> a lucky cockerel I!

ANITRA: The Prophet perspires. I fear he may melt. His
pouch there hangs so heavy. Hand it to me.

PEER: Solicitude! There! What need has heart in love, of
gold? (*Sings.*)

> A merry fool is he!
> Young Gynt can't tell his right from his left.
> Says Peer: So what?
> Goodbye to the lot!
> A merry fool is he!

ANITRA: I flood with joy, to see my Prophet dance.

PEER: Prophet my arse. Let's change clothes. Heyyy up!
Come on: all this off –

ANITRA: The kaftan was a little long…

PEER: Eh bien alors! (*Kneels.*) Do me a sorrow. Hurt me deep.
To heart in love, such anguish is so sweet! Listen. When we
come to my castle –

ANITRA: Is Paradise a long ride away?

PEER: A thousand leagues!

ANITRA: Too far.

PEER: Listen. You'll have that soul I promised –

ANITRA: Thanks all the same, but I can do without the soul.
You craved of me a sorrow.

PEER: Ay, by God. A savage sorrow! – Not to last more than
two or three days!

ANITRA: I hear my Prophet, and obey. Goodbye. (*Slashes his
hand with crop and gallops off.*)

PEER: Of all the –

(*Alone, PEER pensively sheds all Arab garb. From
Western attire intact beneath, takes out, dons: a little
travelling cap.*)

There lies Turk. Here stand I. Came damn' near looking
a proper clown. Preening like a peacock. Not the real me.
Trollop. Had all but besotted me. How could it happen?
Am I troll or a man? To think to stop time with prancing
and dancing? Ah well. In my fine prophetic frenzy: got
well and truly plucked. Still some money in America... I'll
survive. In fact I'm free. A traveller without luggage. In a
word: Master of the Situation. Which way then.
Forward. ['Back or on, the way's as far. Out or in, the way's
as tight...' Which philosopher *is* that?...] Some new goal.
That justifies the trouble and expense. Autobiography...
Tell all... A book to teach men how to live... I know. I'll
be a scholar in antiquity. That's more like me. Follow
man's path from his beginnings. Visit the scenes! Drift
like a feather down the stream of history. Relive it as a
dream. See heroes of old in their struggle for Justice – as
a spectator of course – Great thinkers put to death, the
blood of martyrs; the rise and fall of mighty empires; age
dawn, age pass away. I'll skim the cream of Time. Must lay
hands on a book or two. My grounding was never secure.
[The exaltation I feel! to set before me such a goal! To
sever myself from friend and native soil! Blow sky-high the
wealth that I've amassed! Put Love behind me! All in quest
of the Secret of Truth! (*Wipes a tear.*) That's the mark of the
pioneer!] Oh boundless bliss! the riddle of my Destiny is
solved! [Only the persevering to be done.] I've found out
who I am! Emperor: of Human History! I'll tread the ways

of the living no more. Devoid of spirit, faith or truth, are the
doings of men. As for women: they're a feeble collection.

(*Far northern summer. SOLVEIG in middle age sits
spinning before the hut with reindeer horn above its door.
She sings.*)
SOLVEIG:

> The winter and spring could both come and pass on
> and summer after, a whole year be gone:
> I know you'll home one day, oh friend of my heart.
> I wait as I promised, when last we did part.
>
> God's good strength go with you, oh dear man my son:
> I know you'll home to me, when your journey is done.
> If you're gone on before me, and kneel at His feet,
> then in the hereafter we surely shall meet.

(*Egypt. Toward dawn. A statue in the sand. PEER
GYNT surveys.*)
PEER: Here I begin. Banks of the Nile. Statue of Memnon.
I'm all Egyptian now – on Gynt foundations. (*Sits on a
stone.*) Every sunrise, this statue sings. I'm waiting patiently.
After breakfast I'll climb the pyramid. If time allows,
I'll investigate inside. Then, Araby land… I'll be Asiatic
by then. Babylon. Her famous hanging gardens; temple
whores… Main stream of culture, all the way. One leap to
the walls of Troy. Sea-route to Athens. [The prison where
Socrates died for truth –] They've a war on. Hellas'll have
to wait. [This sun. So slow.] Where was I? Troy. Whatever
is that extraordinary noise?
(*Sun comes up. The statue sings.*)
STATUE: Half God was I.

> Singing from my ashes rise
> birds of Renewal, yet whose cries
> conflict: Great Zeus all wise
> shaped them so.
> Owl of wisdom, say: where lie
> my birds sleeping? Man below,
> learn my meaning; else you die.

PEER: It did! That statue really seemed to sing! A stone tune!
Archaic. I must note this. For scholars to ponder. 'Statue
sang. Sound distinctly audible. Text...obscure. Manifest
illusion. Nothing else of weight observed today.'

(*The great Sphinx of Gizeh (minarets of Cairo afar
beyond). PEER comes; now through lorgnettes, now
through funnel of his hollowed hand, subjects the Sphinx
to an intense scrutiny.*)

PEER: Monstrosity. Reminds me of someone. Norway
somewhere? A man? Something. Extraordinary halfbreed.
Lion and woman in one. Of course. Old fellow Böyg. I
cleft his head for him. Dreamed I did. Delirious at the
time. Well well Böyg. So. [You look like a lion from behind,
by light of day.] Still speak in riddles do you? Tell me. Hey!
Böyg! WHO ARE YOU?

VOICE: (*From behind the Sphinx.*) Ach. Sphinx. Wer bist du?

PEER: What's that? Echo in German? Remarkable.

VOICE: (*Again.*) Wer bist du?

PEER: Oh. Actually speaks the language. No one else has
noticed that. 'Echo German. Accent Berlin.'
(*From behind the Sphinx emerges HERR DOKTOR
BEGRIFFENFELDT. All manner of gestures of
repressed anxiety.*)
Oh. 'Proved later otherwise.'

BEGRIFFENFELDT: My friend. Excuse please. A question
of life. Why today are you coming here?

PEER: I'm visiting. A friend of my youth.

BEGRIFFENFELDT: How? The Sphinx?

PEER: Old acquaintance.

BEGRIFFENFELDT: Famos! All this night gone, such
hammering in my skull. I thought my head must split. You
know him, man? Quick! Tell me! Can you say what he is?

PEER: What he is? That's easy answered. He is himself.

BEGRIFFENFELDT: (*Leaps.*) The riddle of Life! in one
illuminating flash! He is himself: of that you are sure?

PEER: So he says...

BEGRIFFENFELDT: Himself. Why then: the hour is near, when the world turns upside down. (*Doffs hat.*) And your name, Sir?

PEER: Baptized Peer Gynt.

BEGRIFFENFELDT: Peer Gynt... A parable... To be expected... Peer Gynt...? Why, that must mean: He, the Unknown; He, who is coming; of whose appearing I have been foretold...

PEER: Really? And you are here to welcome me?

BEGRIFFENFELDT: Peer Gynt... The depth of that. The mystery. The cutting edge. Each word, a teaching, fathomless. What are you?

PEER: I have always done my best to be myself. My passport: tells you the rest.

BEGRIFFENFELDT: Again that word: mysterious at depth... (*Seizes him by hand.*) To Cairo! The Emperor of Revelation is found!

PEER: Emperor?

BEGRIFFENFELDT: Come!

PEER: I really am known of – ?

BEGRIFFENFELDT: The Emperor of Revelation! on the basis of Self!

(*A yard. High walls. Barred windows. Cages. KEEPERS, one coming.*)

KEEPER: Schafmann? Where's Herr Direktor?

SCHAFMANN: He went out very early.

FIRST: I think something's upset him. Last night he –

ANOTHER: Sh.

(*BEGRIFFENFELDT brings PEER GYNT in. Locks door; key into pocket.*)

PEER: Really gifted, this man. I understand hardly a word he says. – So. This is the Learned Society.

BEGRIFFENFELDT: Here they all are. Lock, stock unt berrel. Scholars the lot! Mikkel, Schlingenberg, Schafmann, Fuchs – Into the cages.

KEEPERS: Us?

BEGRIFFENFELDT: Move, move! The earth turns over. So
must we. (*Crowds them into one cage.*) Great Gynt is come.
Need I say more? (*Locks cage; drops key for ever down a drain.*)

PEER: Herr Direktor, Herr Doctor –

BEGRIFFENFELDT: I'm neither now. Because, you see…
– Herr Gynt. In strictest confidence…

PEER: Yes?

BEGRIFFENFELDT: Last night, at eleven p.m., Pure Reason
passed away.

PEER: Go to God.

BEGRIFFENFELDT: Is that not desolating? And for me in
my capacity, the added complication. This place, till now,
a home for the insane…

PEER: The insane…?

BEGRIFFENFELDT: …cannot be that any more!

PEER: Now I see where I am …

BEGRIFFENFELDT: (*Holding him back.*) But what that
means! Pure Reason: dead. Not dead. He, and self, have
parted company. Like the fox –

PEER: I really must leave –

BEGRIFFENFELDT: No, eel. Eel. A nail though his eye. He
wriggled up the wall.

PEER: Let me out of here…

BEGRIFFENFELDT: Slit his own throat all round, and flip!
out of his skin!

PEER: The man's mad –

BEGRIFFENFELDT: Since when, of course, the categories
Sane, Insane, are changed about. Land and sea are quite
upturned! What was mental disorder before, became last
night the norm of the New Age!

PEER: My time is short –

BEGRIFFENFELDT: (*Calls.*) Everybody hear me! Reason is
dead. Long live Peer Gynt!

[PEER: My dear man –]

BEGRIFFENFELDT: Come forth and greet the dawn of your
deliverance! Behold! Your Emperor!
(*The demented emerge.*)

PEER: Emperor?

BEGRIFFENFELDT: Of course.

PEER: The honour is too great… What have I done…

BEGRIFFENFELDT: False modesty, in such an hour?

[PEER: Allow me a little time… No really I… I'm
    overcome…!]

BEGRIFFENFELDT: A man who has grasped the meaning
    of the Sphinx? Who is himself?

PEER: Precisely. I am myself. More than one can say of these.

BEGRIFFENFELDT: You are so wrong. What is each here,
    but his own damnable self? Entirely and exclusively
    himself alone? No tears for any other's sorrow. No
    understanding of any other's thought. Self, through every
    fibre of the being. Self, to the outmost spring of all activity.
    Wherefore. If here be need of Emperor, you are he.

PEER: Like hell I am.

BEGRIFFENFELDT: Of course you feel depressed. You've
    not adapted. Whom shall I choose… For an example… ha!
    King Apis. How fares Our Royal Majesty?

FELLAH: (*Has a mummy on his back. Demands of PEER.*) Am I
    King Apis?

PEER: I'm sorry, I'm new to the situation, I – But to judge by
    your tone –

FELLAH: You lie too.

BEGRIFFENFELDT: Your Royal Highness must explain to
    him.

FELLAH: Yes.

See this I carry. King Apis was his name. They call him a
mummy now. And he's dead. He built the pyramids. He
carved the Great Sphinx. He scattered our enemies. For
which all Egypt hailed him as a god. They set him up in
temples, in image of a bull. I am King Apis. I see that, clear
as the sun. That perplexes you. Listen. King Apis went
hunting, you see. He stepped from his horse. He needed
privacy a moment. The ground he chose to crouch on is
my ancestral land; and from his manuring, the corn that's
grown has nourished me. For proof, if more is needed, I've
invisible horns. But no one, damn them, will acknowledge
me. Born Apis of Egypt, a peasant is all these see! What
must I do, to be visibly the King I am?

PEER: Your Highness could hang His Royal Self. Then lie in Earth's embrace: in your natural kingdom now, the tomb: in posture of the Royal Dead.

FELLAH: I'll do that. It'll feel a little strange at first. But time smooths unfamiliarity away. (*Goes aside.*)

BEGRIFFENFELDT: Now there Sir goes a personality. A man of method.

PEER: Quite so. Quite so. I can see – He's really doing it! Oh God take care of us! I feel unwell… My thoughts seem no longer my own…

BEGRIFFENFELDT: A transitional state. Soon be over.

PEER: Transitional? To where? I really must be going –

BEGRIFFENFELDT: Are you mad – ?

(*Disturbance. MINISTER HUSSEIN forces his way through the crowd.*)

HUSSEIN: I'm told an Emperor is here today. – You are He?

PEER: It seems I've not much choice.

HUSSEIN: Good. Your Excellency will have official notes for me to answer.

PEER: Aa. I… Oh what does it matter…

HUSSEIN: Excellency. Do me the honour. Dip me. (*Bows.*) I am a pen.

PEER: (*Bows deeper.*) Then I: a poor scrap of imperial vellum.

HUSSEIN: I'll be brief Sir. I'm a pen but these will use me for a blotter!

PEER: I'll be brief Sir Pen. I'm a blank sheet on which nothing is written.

HUSSEIN: They will not see! I am the pen itself!

PEER: I was once a woman's prayerbook: with a silver clasp.

HUSSEIN: Imagine: the misery. A quill: and never tasted the edge of a knife.

PEER: Imagine you: the misery. To be a reindeer buck! One leap for the sky: since, for ever plunging…

HUSSEIN: Oh sharpen me. I have to be slashed. If I've no tip, it's the end of the world!

PEER: Pity the earth, the Good Lord thought He'd made so well!

BEGRIFFENFELDT: Here's a knife.

HUSSEIN: Ahh. I'll lap the ink now! Ohh...! (*Sharpens himself.*) The joy!

BEGRIFFENFELDT: Don't spurt like that!

PEER: Stop him! Hold him someone!

HUSSEIN: Hold! That's the word! Hold me! Hold the pen! There's paper on the desk! (*Falls.*) I run dry... P.S. He lived and he died, a pen well guided.

PEER: What shall I do? What am I? Oh Mighty – Hold me! I'm all you say! Turk, sinner, troll. But help me! Something burst in my head... (*Screams.*) [You – ! I can't put a name to you just now but] HELP ME! Oh Thou above, Who watchest over all the mad...! (*Sinks.*)

BEGRIFFENFELDT: (*Leaps astride him, brandishing a crown of straw.*) Haa! The mighty in his mire! Great Gynt, your coronation's here! All hail! The Emperor of Self!

KEEPERS: (*From cage.*) Es lebe hoch der grosse Peer!

End of Act Four.

Interval.

ACT FIVE

Sea-shock. Elemental trouble coming. Rolling afterdeck. PEER GYNT, greyheaded, powerful in age; part sea-clad – jacket, boots – clothes worse for wear; self weatherbitten, harder of face. HELMSMAN – wheel heavy, CAPTAIN near.

PEER: Old man HallingsSkarv. Ridge of him, in his winter coat. Preening in the evening sun. Jökel his brother, crooked after. Still has on his green mantle of ice. FolgeFonn now, here's a girl. In her linen of snow. You not kick your legs there, fellow-me-lads. Stand where you stand. You are stone.

CAPTAIN: Double the helm here! Lanthern aloft.

(A SECOND MAN comes to the helm.)

PEER: Stiff wind blowing.

CAPTAIN: A wild night on its way.

[PEER: Can we see Dovre?

CAPTAIN: Too far inlahnd.

PEER: Where's Haarteig from here?

CAPTAIN: About there. Ye seem to know where ye are.

PEER: The last of our land we see when we leave: that lingers in the memory.] Are we in before light?

CAPTAIN: With anny luck.

PEER: Thickening in the West there.

CAPTAIN: It is.

PEER: Captain. Remind me. When we settle. I'd like to show the crew my appreciation.

CAPTAIN: Thank you.

PEER: It can't be much. My gold I've dug and lost. All I've left I've with me. But there's no one waiting for this old miser. At least I'm spared scenes on the jetty…

CAPTAIN: Here comes the storm.

PEER: You remember. Any of your crew who's in real need.

CAPTAIN: Ye're very kind. They've none of them much, ye can see. And families at home…

PEER: Families?

CAPTAIN: They all have. The Cook now; I'd say it was tightest for him. Black famine ever at his door.

PEER: Families? Waiting? Glad when these come home, ha?

CAPTAIN: Glad as the poor can afford.

PEER: But should they come to the door by fall of night…

CAPTAIN: The wife'll find some treat for the occasion.

PEER: And a lamp lit?

CAPTAIN: Two maybe. And a drop of drink forbye.

PEER: Then they sit? Warm at their fire? Children around them? Jabber, jabber, none hearing the other out? Such joy on them all…

CAPTAIN: Something like that. So yuir offer will go a long way…

PEER: You think I'm out of my mind? Fork out for another man's children? That below, I've earned with labour, hard and sore. No one's waiting for old Peer Gynt.

CAPTAIN: It's your money.

PEER: Too right it's mine. My money. Moment we're in, we settle. One cabin fare from Panama, a drink round the crew and that's that.

CAPTAIN: Excuse me Sor. Storm's almost here. (*Goes for'ard.*)

PEER: To be awaited with joy… In someone's thought, along one's road… Lamp lit? I'll see it out. I'll send these home that drunk, that foul-mouthed and brutish… those women waited with such love'll scurry screaming from the house, weans under their wing, their joy in cinders!
(*Ship lurches. PEER hard put to it to stand.*)
[Some sea, that. You'd think it was paid. Still its old self, the sea off Norway.]

CRIES: (*Off.*) Help! Ahoy!

PEER: What's that?

WATCH: Shipwreck alee!

CAPTAIN: Hard a-starboard! Close to the wind!

HELMSMAN: Survivors?

WATCH: Looks like three…

PEER: Lower the stern-boat…!

CAPTAIN: She'll swamp sooner.

PEER: What's a wet skin?! Quick, rescue them!

BOATSWAIN: Impossible in this!

PEER: They'll need help! There's a lull! Cook, you try!
Hurry! I'll pay you –

COOK: Not for twenty English pounds.

PEER: How can you be so craven? Those could have women
and children waiting at home!

BOATSWAIN: Let 'em wait. Good for the soul.
(*A massive swell heard rolling in…*)

CAPTAIN: Bear off from that sea!

HELMSMAN: She's capsized.
(*…and passing.*)

PEER: Suddenly so quiet there.

BOATSWAIN: If those were married as you say, that makes a
batch of three fresh widows in the world.
(*Sea-thrust more purposeful. PEER moves aft.*)

PEER: No faith now, binding man to man. No Christianity.
No respect for the Powers Above. I know my Master.
Night like this, I'll keep the right side of Him. I've no guilt.
Sacrifice was called for: I stood forward with my money.
Yet what good's a clear conscience to a decent man like
me, in peril on the deep? If Cook or Bos'n's hour be come,
and ship go down, Peer Gynt too gets washed away. The
sea is no respecter of the Self. I've lived too pious a life. If
I'd my time over, I'd not make that mistake again. I'd grab
the whip hand. Regardless. I have time! –
(*An uncanny OTHER PASSENGER materializes from
the dark, deathly pale at PEER GYNT's side.*)

PASSENGER: Good evening. Your fellow-passenger at your
service Sir.

PEER: I thought I travelled alone.

PASSENGER: You thought wrong.

PEER: How have we not met till now, and it dark?

PASSENGER: I don't come up by day.

PEER: Are you ill?

PASSENGER: I feel uncommonly well.

PEER: In this wild weather?

PASSENGER: Exactly. Praise be!

PEER: Praise be?

PASSENGER: Seas high as houses. My teeth water! Think what wrecks'll smash tonight! Such corpses flung ashore!

PEER: Heaven forbid.

PASSENGER: Did ever you see a strangled man? Or one's been hanged or drowned?

PEER: Really…

PASSENGER: He has a laughing look. Usually he's tried to bite through his tongue.

PEER: Go away…

PASSENGER: Just one request. If we should founder, and sink in the dark –

PEER: You think that likely?

PASSENGER: What can I say? But should I float and you drown…

PEER: Rubbish…!

PASSENGER: Suppose. A man at death's door: he softens somewhat; inclines to little charities…

PEER: Ah. Money…

PASSENGER: Not at all. But if you might be so kind. The gift of your corpse?

PEER: This is too much!

PASSENGER: The carcase only. For my scientific use.

PEER: Leave me alone.

PASSENGER: Friend. Think. Your privilege. You: laid open to the light. You: anatomised. Chiefly I seek the source of dreams…

PEER: Get away from me – !

PASSENGER: Friend, what's a body…?

PEER: Blasphemous man! You make the storm worse! We're in peril enough from the wind and water: you'll have us all drowned!

PASSENGER: Not in a mood to discuss I see. Well. Let's hope your temper improves as you go under.
(*Gone below, where a SEAMAN emerging.*)

PEER: Scientists. Freethinkers. Give a fellow the creeps. Bos'n! That other passenger. Ought to be put away.

BOATSWAIN: You are our passenger Sir.

PEER: I like this less and less. (*To SEAMAN.*) You. Who's that
went below?

SEAMAN: Ship's dog Sir.

WATCH: Land hard ahead!

PEER: My strongbox! My trunk! All luggage on deck!

BOATSWAIN: We've more to think of!

PEER: Captain. What I said. It was nonsense: lies, a joke. Of
course I'll help the Cook –

CAPTAIN: The jib's run!

HELMSMAN: Fores'l's gone!

BOATSWAIN: Groundswell ho!

CAPTAIN: She's going to break!

(*Ship founders. Confusion and elemental havoc in the
dark.*)

(*Breakers amid skerries (throughout). PEER GYNT
struggling to clamber up upturned dinghy.*)

PEER: Help! A boat from shore! I'm drowning! – Eternal
Father strong to save, and so on...! (*Clings to keel.*)

COOK: (*Surfaces the other side.*) Dear God have mercy... For
my childer's sake... Bring me to lahnd...! (*Clings to keel.*)

PEER: Off, you.

COOK: Yui off.

PEER: I'll hit you.

COOK: I'll hit yui too.

PEER: She won't carry us both!

COOK: I know!

(*They fight. COOK, one hand soon maimed, clings
desperately with the other.*)

PEER: Let go!

COOK: Och Sor... I've kids at home...

PEER: I've none, so need my life the more...

COOK: Yui've had yuir life!

PEER: Get on with it! Drown! You grow too heavy.

COOK: For Jesu's sake! Yui'll not be mourned or missed...!
Hold me!

PEER: (*So, by the hair.*) Your Lord's prayer. Quick!

COOK: I can't remember the words... I can't see!

PEER: The part that matters: hurry!

COOK: Give us this day –

PEER: Skip that! It's way past daily bread with you.

COOK: Give us this day our – (*Gone.*)

PEER: Amen boy. Cook to the last. (*Swings up over keel.*) I'm not dead yet.

> (*Uncanny OTHER PASSENGER materializes, floating easily, his left leg working. A merest grip between the dinghy's timbers with his fingernails. Fractured sea-thrash throughout.*)

PASSENGER: Good morning. We meet again. What did I tell you?

PEER: Let go! Let go! This can carry only one!

PASSENGER: The merest purchase with my finger-ends, that's all I need. About this corpse…

PEER: NO!

PASSENGER: What else of you remains to talk of now? I'm waiting.

PEER: What are you?

PASSENGER: Don't I remind you of someone?

PEER: I'd say Old Nick himself.

PASSENGER: Come come. Is He one to light you your last road of guilt and terror?

PEER: Light is it?

PASSENGER: Have you ever in your life looked deep in the well of your own terror?

PEER: I've known danger. [You mean more…]

PASSENGER: Have you but once won that salvation that terror can yield?

PEER: If you come to convert me, you choose your moment.

PASSENGER: A man's more easy saved then, at the quiet of his own fire?

PEER: How do you say a man is saved?

PASSENGER: When all's reckoned, a smile will count for as much as any grand gestures. Death has undone so many. They strut upon no stage.

PEER: Scarecrow! Leave me be! I'm not going to die! I will make land!

PASSENGER: Oh you shall. Peer Gynt can't die in the
  middle of Act Five. (*Glides from sight.*)
PEER: Hm. Only some dreary moralizer after all.

(*Silence. Inland. A mountain churchyard. Funeral.
PEER GYNT passing beyond; pausing.*)
PEER: A countryman on his last road. There but for the
  Grace of God…
PASTOR: (*Manse Ulster speech.*) The soul goes on his way
  to Judgement even now. Here lies the pod of his dust.
  Friends. Let us recall a moment our brother's journey on
  this earth.
  Not a rich man. Not intelligent. Quiet. Submissive. He
  spoke his mind, when at all, with hesitance. Hardly master
  in his own house; and would steal into church as though
  beseeching leave to join our worship.
  He came from the valley near Dovre. The mark of him we
  most remember was that right hand forever hidden in his
  pocket; and his shifting unease in company. We know the
  shame that right hand was to him: one finger missing.
  I mind well – years long gone now: war; our land in peril
  – one morning in the town of Lunde. A crowded room.
  At a table, between bailiff and serjeants, a Captain sitting;
  enlisting soldiers. The laughter of the young men thronged
  outside. A name called. One standing forward. Pale as the
  snow on a glacier's edge. Faltering. Called nearer. His right
  hand swaddled in a cloth. His gasp, gulp, his struggle to
  speak. Suddenly, his face aflame, some blurted tale about a
  mishap with a sickle, had shorn him his finger to the skin.
  The silence. The scorn those faces hailed on him, more
  loud than any words. He knew. Out! the Captain said; and
  spat and pointed to the door. They let the boy stumble his
  way between the ranks of them. He reached the door; and
  was gone.
  Six months after, he came here. With his mother, his
  woman and a baby son. He took the lease of some land
  high up where the wild begins; wed soon as he could;
  built a house; broke at the hard earth: and prevailed. As

many a brave golden patch of swaying wheat and rye bore
testament. Surely those nine fingers wrought as hard and
well as many another's ten. One spring, the flood swept all
his work away.

Ruined and bare, he began again. On a site more
sheltered, he cleared and built anew. Two winters, and that
second farm an avalanche destroyed. Unbowed, he dug; he
cleared, he carted. Before next winter's blizzards came, his
third house stood.

[And his three lively sons. School was far. A scramble
down a tight and treacherous cleft to where the parish road
began. One, the eldest, struggling best he could alone,
roped to his father should he fall; another in his father's
arms, the third on his back. Three men of substance in
the New World now, forget their father in Norway; that
wearying path he toiled, year in, year out, to see them
schooled.]

Short-sighted man. No eyes for any beyond his own. Those
mighty ringing words that stir most other hearts – nation;
land – were but a jangle of bells to him. Offender against
our law? So might he be. And State, or Church, have won
from his existence nothing. Yet one Light shines above all
Law, sure as the highest glittering peak has pinnacles of
gleaming cloud above. There, on the dome of that high
land, within the narrow round of his own kin, he saw his
calling. He was of stature there, because he was himself.
His life was as a muted string: but to its note he lived ever
true, his own man all his days.

So, peace be with you, silent warrior, who fought and fell
in your own modest struggle with the earth. We that are
dust shall not inquire into his heart. Dust's Maker shall
do that. Yet this I hope, and this I say. Our brother stands
before his Judge: scarce cripple there.

(*All go their ways.*)

PEER: That, I call Christianity. Nothing disturbing. Indeed:
Be Your Own Man: most edifying. I saw a fellow once,
hack off his own finger… Could be this is him… [First-rate
Pastor too. Could have been talking about me…] Ah well.

I've time. Home. However steep or tight the path: my own self, poor but true.

(*Mountain farmstead of play's beginning.* (*Mill in ruin, streambed dry.*) *Decay and waste. Last effects being auctioned off. Drink, noise. PEER GYNT sits aside, on a heap of junk.*)

MAN IN MOURNING: Now there's only rubbish left. Do I see strangers? Evening Sor. (*The local accents as of old.*)

PEER: (*Loss of his accent pronounced.*) Same to you Sir. All very jolly. Christening? Wedding?

MAN IN MOURNING: Homecoming I'd say. The bride, to bed, among the worms.

PEER: Worms wrangling over the rags I see.

MAN IN MOURNING: How the story ends.

PEER: Don't they all?

LAD: Look what I just bought. Peer Gynt's ladle, where he melted silver down for buttons!

ANOTHER: How about me then? The sack where his da kept his money!

THIRD: That all? I've the pack his father wore.

PEER: Peer Gynt? Who was he?

MAN IN MOURNING: In-law to Death. That I know. In-law to Aslak the smith…

MAN IN GREY: Ye forget I'm here!

MAN IN MOURNING: Yui know well as I do, Hegstad storehouse had a door stood never locked.

MAN IN GREY: Mads Moen, yui torned the blind eye…

MAN IN MOURNING: Ach… She's a husband'll keep her now. (*They stagger away.*)

PEER: Old acquaintance.

URCHIN: (*Hollers after.*) Aslak! You stay sober! Else Ma'll haunt yui!

LAD: (*With reindeer horn.*) Here's the buck Peer Gynt rode on Gjendin Edge!

ANOTHER: (*With sledgehammer.*) Hi Aslak! Was it this yui used when the Devil cleft yuir wall?

THIRD: (*With nothing.*) I've the invisible cloak Mads Moen,
   helped Peer Gynt fly off wi' yuir bride!
PEER: You there. Give me a drink. I feel my age. I've odds
   and ends I'd auction too.
LAD: Why, what have yui?
PEER: A palace. In the Dovre there. Good solid walls.
LAD: One button!
PEER: A dram, no less.
ANOTHER: Here's the quare oul' eejit!
PEER: My royal steed.
ONE: Where can he go?
PEER: Far west, to the set of the sun.
OTHERS: Have y'annything more?
PEER: A dream of a prayerbook with a silver clasp. Going,
   for a hook-an'-eye!
LAD: Dhrames be damned.
PEER: An Empire! Scramble for it!
LAD: Throw in the crown!
PEER: I do that. Beauteous straw. It fits the first man puts it
   on. I've more yet! An addled egg! A fool's grey hair. A
   prophet's beard. Going…going… To the first man shows
   me a signpost on the hill that reads: This Way.
BAILIFF: This way'll get ye locked up.
PEER: Very like. Bailiff Sir: tell me. Who was Peer Gynt?
BAILIFF: Dagh…
PEER: No. I beg. Kind Sir…
BAILIFF: A most atrocious liar, so I'm told. No deed so
   mighty but he'd done it. If you'll excuse me, I've a job to
   do… (*Goes.*)
PEER: (*To ANOTHER.*) Whatever came of this extraordinary
   man?
OTHER: (*Elderly.*) He ammigrated. It worked out bahd. Ye
   might ha knowed. He's hanged this many years.
PEER: Hanged? Is that a fact? Himself to the last. Well…
   (*Takes courteous leave.*) Thank you for your company.
   (*Pauses.*) Brave lasses and lads. Shall I pay for the drink
   with a story? Why not.
   (*A strange transfiguration coming over him.*) Out in San

Francisco, I was grubbing for gold. The town was full of
jugglers and contortionists. One sawed at a fiddle he held
with his toes. One danced a Spanish class of a fling on his
knees. I'm told of one, spouted poetry while a hole was
drilled through his skull. The Devil came, to try His luck
as an entertainer. In disguise, you understand. Magnetic
personality. And for his act, a portrayal, in grunts, squeals
and the like, of the Life of a Pig: from birth, to the shriek
of its slaughter. He took care of course to have a real pig
stowed beneath his cloak. This he prodded and pinched,
the living pig squealed forth; while he himself pulled
the appropriate faces. The act was over. He courteously
retired. The critics began. Some thought the performance
had atmosphere. Not so others. Voice too squeaky. Death-
cry too studied. All agreed: quâ grunt, overplayed. Dumb
Devil. Should have known his public better.
(*Courteously leaves them in a baffled silence.*)

(*Deep forest. PEER GYNT grubbing for wild onions.*)
PEER: Or picture me thus: I start out, Caesar of Rome; end,
Nebuchadnezzar, beast of the field. When my hour tolls, as
it must one day, I'll creep beneath a fallen tree, and heap
up over me a mound of leaves; and scrat in capital letters
on the bark HERE LIES PEER GYNT, EMPEROR OF ANIMALS.
Emperor? Onion more like. How now, Peer Gynt? I peel
ye bare. For all ye howl or beg… Outmost skin all torn.
Who's he? Shipwrecked mahn, on a capsized dinghy. Now
that scrawny passenger. Touch o' meself in the tang of him.
Next in's the man I was, grubbed for gold. Husk all dried;
if juice he ever had. Next has the look of a crown. Thanks
for that: throw you away and say no more. He's short and
stout: scholar in antiquity. Now the prophet: fresh and
sappy. And this, that peels away so easy, is one all flab, a
life of luxury made soft. Next in looks sick. Black stripes.
Black for missionary. Or for negro. Layer within layer
within layer; where is the core? Nature is witty. (*Slings onion
away.*)

The Hell with thought! I'll keep my four feet on the
ground. Life's more of a riddle nor I can master. Grab at
her, she's something else; or nothing… Where've I seen
that hut before? [Reindeer horn? Mermaid! No. Nails but…
Boards… To keep all angry gremlin out…]

VOICE OF SOLVEIG: (*Dimly heard as from within hut obscurely
seen. Sings to same air as in Act Four.*)

>My Whitsuntide candle tomorrow I light.
>The dark is near over, of winter's long night.
>[Oh, far though you wander, oh dear man my son,
>it cannot be long now till your journey is done.]
>That burden ye carry, though it drag ye so slow,
>in stillness I wait here, as I vowed long ago.

PEER: Oh! Grief of my heart! To waste what never never
comes again. Deep sin I've done. Here was my kingdom
all along.

(*He runs away.*)

(*Tumult of the wasted and denied. PEER running.*)

PEER: Run… Run… Mile upon mile, the stumps of fir are
smoke and char… Run…! Run…! [Ash, scud, dust driven
on the wind…] All I unheeded, all I shirked, flares like
the Trumpet of Doom: Petrus Gyntus Caesar fecit! I hear
the sound of children weeping… Half tears, half song…
Threadballs trundle at my feet…

THREADBALLS: We are thoughts: you should have thought
us…! We should have soared and sung! [We roll on the
ground…!]

PEER: Out of my road! Ye's snag me in!

WITHERED LEAVES: We leaves on the wind are the words
you should have lived by! For Peer's neglect we wither and
fall…!

SOUGHING BRANCHES ABOVE: We sighing trees are
songs you choked in the pit of your heart. [In your throat
we're venom now…]

PEER: Out from this… What time had I for trash like poetry?

DEWDROPS: We drops of dew are tears you never shed…!

BROKEN STRAWS: We broken straws are deeds undone…! [For Peer Gynt's doubting we are maimed…!] We flock to judgement and accuse! Pity ye then!

PEER: Mean trick ye's play on me! Indict a man for what he never did?!

VOICE OF AASE: Aase your mother! You mired me, boy! Some road. Some ride! No castle here…

PEER: Run… Run… A sexton! A sexton! Dig me my grave! I bear so many dead, and I must after…!

(*PEER running. A BUTTONMOULDER with kit and ladle suddenly crosses his path.*)

BUTTONMOULDER: Hello old Sir!

PEER: Good night to you, friend.

BUTTONMOULDER: Where's the great hurry?

PEER: To a gravewarming.

BUTTONMOULDER: Really? Excuse me Sir. My eyes are bahd. Would your name be Peer?

PEER: Peer Gynt so I'm told.

BUTTONMOULDER: Isn't chance a fine thing! You're the man I've been sent for tonight.

PEER: Me?!

BUTTONMOULDER: Can't you see? I'm a buttonmoulder. I've to put you in my ladle.

PEER: Me? What for?!

BUTTONMOULDER: To melt you down.

PEER: M–

BUTTONMOULDER: Look. Scoured and ready. Your grave's dug, your coffin's ordered. Your carcase'll be some feast for the worms. It's your soul my Master wants, and now.

PEER: [This can't be. I've had no notice!

BUTTONMOULDER: Wake or birth, the guest of honour's last to be informed.

PEER: True…] I'm rather confused… You must be –

BUTTONMOULDER: You heard. A buttonmoulder.

PEER: I see. So, Peer. There ye finish up. The Hell I will! I don't deserve an end that harsh. I've done my share of good in the world. I never sinned as such. The worst ye could say, I muddled through.

BUTTONMOULDER: Precisely. Like so many. Hence the ladle. As you observe. No epic sinner. Hardly éven average.

PEER: There you are! –

BUTTONMOULDER: Which falls far short of goodness in a man.

PEER: I'd never claim to that.

BUTTONMOULDER: Somewhere between then. Mediocre. Sin calls for vigour and commitment. You merely dabbled.

PEER: That's right. Sin no more than spattered my coat.

BUTTONMOULDER: You'll understand then. No fire and brimstone for a man like you.

PEER: Good. Then I may go.

BUTTONMOULDER: Good. Then I must melt you down.

[PEER: This you hatch behind my back; all these years I've been abroad?]

BUTTONMOULDER: That's the way. You'll know. You've moulded buttons in your time. When a casting scummed, or a button came out faulty: what did you do?

PEER: I scrapped it.

BUTTONMOULDER: My Master doesn't you see. Waste not, want not. There's where He thrives. You He made for a shining button on the waistcoat of the world. Your loop broke. So you're for the reject box to be rendered down and used again.

PEER: Me? To be cast with all and sundry into something new?

BUTTONMOULDER: Exactly that.

PEER: [Your Master's one father and mother of a miser! One mingy button?] No. I refuse. I'd liefer a stretch in good old-fashioned Hell. A hundred years if need be. At least they'd pass. One day reprieve must come. But to lose my identity in that… Come out, a fleck on someone altogether different? My Self extinct? The very soul rebels!

BUTTONMOULDER: Friend! Why all this commotion about a self you never were? Where's the death when nothing dies?

PEER: Me not my self?! Haa! Your sight is bad,
buttonmoulder. If you could see into my heart you'd find it
Peer Gynt through and through!

BUTTONMOULDER: I'm sorry. I've my warrant. Look.
'Peer Gynt. For a life misused. Faulty. Melt down.'

PEER: You're sure that says Peer? Not another Gynt: Rasmus
or Jon…?

BUTTONMOULDER: Please come quietly and not waste my
time.

PEER: No. I refuse. Mahn dear. Suppose you found out in the
morning you'd melted me down by mistake. Yours is an
awesome responsibility; you can't risk error like that.

BUTTONMOULDER: It's here in writing.

PEER: Just give me time!

BUTTONMOULDER: To do what?

PEER: To prove that I've been my self! Since that seems the
issue.

BUTTONMOULDER: Prove how?

PEER: Witnesses, statements…

BUTTONMOULDER: I'm sad to say my Master has no
truck with those.

PEER: This isn't happening. I'll take what's coming to me
when it comes. But my self… Lend me my self again one
little while. This'll not take long. A man's born only once.
He clings to the self he was made with. We agree?

BUTTONMOULDER: I'll be waiting. At the next cross
roads.

(*PEER running.*)

PEER: Run… Run… [Time is money, the Scripture says. If I
but knew where the crossroad comes…] The earth begins
to scorch my feet… Oh where is witness to be found in this
wild wood? The world's a bungle, when man must prove
what's his by right.
(*He catches up with an OLD MAN trudging bent upon
a stick, beggar's pack on his back.*)

OLD MAN: Good Sir. Spare a copper for an old man, no roof
to his head.

PEER: I'm sorry, I've no change on me…

OLD MAN: Prince Peer! Ai-ai. To meet so.

PEER: Do I know you?

OLD MAN: Surely you remember. The old man in the mountain…

PEER: Not the –

OLD MAN: TrollKing, old boy!

PEER: TrollKing? You?!

OLD MAN: Fallen so low.

PEER: Bankrupt?

OLD MAN: Cleaned out. Tramping the roads, stomach sticking to my back bone.

PEER: Hurrah! The very man! Oh here's a witness and a half.

OLD MAN: Your highness is grown so grey.

PEER: Dear father-in-law, the ravages of time. Look. We've had our disagreements; I offended your family I know. Can we set that aside? I was immature –

OLD MAN: Ay, young and foolish. Refusing my daughter. You made a shrewd move there. Saved yourself much heartache and humiliation. That girl's gone so to the bad.

PEER: Has she now?

OLD MAN: Wee boy she had though. Grown to the figure of a man. Littering the land with his young.

PEER: This is all very interesting. Look. Fact is, I'm in a bit of a jam. That night I presented myself as a suitor. Remember?

OLD MAN: Do I remember?! why –

PEER: Please. You wanted to make a troll of me. You were going to slit my eye and warp my sight. And I refused. Remember? I'm up before a kind of court and I need you to testify. How I renounced love, power, position, to be my own man.

OLD MAN: I can't swear that. That's perjury. You did become a troll. You pulled the britches on, you drank the –

PEER: Yes, but the crucial test! That I refused!

OLD MAN: You turned your back on us, that's true; but ours was the commandment you took into the world.

PEER: Commandment?

OLD MAN: That mighty sundering vow by which the troll is recognised. YOURSELF BE ENOUGH.

PEER: ENOUGH?!

OLD MAN: That's how you've lived.

PEER: I've been Peer Gynt!

OLD MAN: The thanklessness of him. I could weep. To live as a troll and never once admit to it. That's what swung you to the top of the tree! You learned it all, you owe that all to me. Now you despise me.

PEER: Me? A troll? Rubbish you talk.

OLD MAN: (*Takes out a sheaf of newspapers.*) We take the papers! It's all here, in black and red. Your doings in the world. [Bloksberg Herald. Four Fells Journal. You're famous!] An editorial, look! You don't have to stay in Norway to be a troll.

PEER: I see I'm wasting my time. Buy yourself a smoke.

OLD MAN: Dear Prince –

PEER: Let go of me! You're senile. You need a hospital.

OLD MAN: If the Prince could see his way –

PEER: Sorry. I'm down and out. Not even my self to call my own. Damn' trollery.

OLD MAN: Ah well. I'll limp my way to a town, I suppose…

PEER: What good'll that do you?

OLD MAN: I think I'll go on the stage. Says here. They're looking for national types.

PEER: Best of luck. Give the theatre my love. If I wriggle out of this I might follow you. I'll write a farce, absurd and profound. And call it: Thus Earthly Splendour Passes On. (*Runs on. OLD MAN hollering unheard after.*)

(*PEER running.*)

PEER: Run… Run… Time so short… [Me to the scrapheap? Anything rather!]

BUTTONMOULDER: (*Appears from nowhere.*) Well Peer Gynt? Where is your witness?

PEER: Crossroad? Here? So soon?

BUTTONMOULDER: Perhaps that old man –

PEER: No! He's drunk.

BUTTONMOULDER: He might be able –

PEER: No I say! Leave him.

BUTTONMOULDER: Then let's get started.

PEER: Just answer me this. What does it really mean? To be one's Self?

BUTTONMOULDER: You? ask that?

PEER: Tell me!

BUTTONMOULDER: To be oneself, the Self must die. I see that's lost on you. Let's rather say, a man should stand forth everywhere, his Maker's purpose in him shining bright.

PEER: What if he never discovers what that purpose is?

BUTTONMOULDER: He must listen to the voice within. I tell you. Stifle that: the Prince of Darkness gets his hook in.

PEER: It's all so complicated suddenly. I can see my plea of selfhood won't stand up. Look. Just now as I wandered so alone, I felt a twinge of conscience. I said: Peer Gynt, you're a sinner –

BUTTONMOULDER: We've been through all that.

PEER: No listen! A colossal sinner. I've lechered, I've lied. My life abroad, you'd be appalled –

BUTTONMOULDER: I'd have to see that itemized.

PEER: Just give me time. I'll find a clergyman. I'll get it down in writing.

BUTTONMOULDER: Sin Positive? That'd spare you the scene in the ladle. But what about this warrant?

PEER: Out of date. Facts overtook that long ago. At least let me try…

BUTTONMOULDER: Well…

PEER: Dear wee kind buttonmoulder. You're not that busy. Enjoy the air. So healthy here. Rejuvenates a man.

BUTTONMOULDER: The next cross road. And that's it.

PEER: A clergyman. If I've to clamp him with tongs. Run… Run…

(*PEER running.*)

PEER: Run… Run… This might come in handy! yer mahn said: pickin' up a magpie's wing. Who'd have thought the market-value of my sin would prove my reprieve at the eleventh hour?

(*A SKINNY CHARACTER, cassock hooked up to his knee, darts along, wielding a birdnet.*)

A clergyman! Heyyy up, amn't I the lucky mahn? Evening Pastor. Tricky bit of path here.

SKINNY ONE: Quite. But I'll go anywhere after a soul.

PEER: Oh yes? One's on his way above?

SKINNY ONE: Below, I trust.

PEER: Pastor. May I join you a step or two?

SKINNY ONE: Do. I like company.

PEER: There's something I –

SKINNY ONE: Out with it! Yes…?

PEER: I'm a decent sort. Never been in trouble with the law. Sometimes however one puts a foot wrong…

SKINNY ONE: Happens to the best of us.

PEER: A peccadillo really.

SKINNY ONE: That all?

PEER: Yes, I –

SKINNY ONE: Then don't distract me. You see who I am? Observe my fingers!

PEER: Extraordinary nails.

SKINNY ONE: Glance down.

PEER: Is that hoof genuine?

SKINNY ONE: I pride myself so.

PEER: (*Doffs his hat.*) Well well. HIMSELF. Who better qualified?

SKINNY ONE: You seem openminded. Shake hands. What did you want of me? Not money or power I hope. Trade's very bad. So few souls. The quality of Man has so depreciated. Most end up in a casting-ladle.

PEER: It's that that brings me here.

SKINNY ONE: Yes?…

PEER: I wouldn't wish to ask too much…

SKINNY ONE: A place of retreat?

PEER: Well… You yourself say. Business is slack, so you can't pick and choose…

SKINNY ONE: A room with heating?

PEER: Not too much heating. And preferably the freedom
    to come and go. And a way back out: should things
    improve…
SKINNY ONE: I'm very sorry. I really am. You've no idea
    how many such petitions I receive…
PEER: But surely my career entitles me –
SKINNY ONE: You said a peccadillo only.
PEER: Well… Now I think of it, I trafficked in slaves.
SKINNY ONE: Others have exploited human will and
    feeling.
PEER: I sold heathen idols to China!
SKINNY ONE: There are images far more foul purveyed in
    sermons, art and books…
PEER: Yes but I – I set myself up as a prophet!
SKINNY ONE: Others do that. Empty they prove, and end
    up in the ladle too. I'm really sorry, you don't qualify.
PEER: Listen. In a shipwreck – it was him or me – I half-
    deprived a cook of his life.
SKINNY ONE: I don't give a damn if you'd half-deprived
    a kitchenmaid of something else! Half this half that. With
    all respect. Fuel the price it is I can't go wasting on non-
    committal refuse like you. You'll have to adapt my friend
    to the notion of the ladle. Reconcile yourself. After all,
    what would you gain by boarding with me? True, you'd
    keep your identity. Is that so amusing? when you have
    not one memory worth either smile or screaming for?
    Nothing: to make you either hot or cold? Only a niggling
    dissatisfaction. (*Silence.*) I can't stand here hobnobbing. I've
    hopes of a luscious roast hereabout, and I don't want to
    miss him…
PEER: This roast. May one inquire what diet of sin so fattened
    him?
SKINNY ONE: I was told he was exclusively Himself. That
    after all is the issue.
PEER: Been himself?! Such people come under *your* parish?!
SKINNY ONE: That depends. There are two ways of being
    oneself. You've heard of this new invention in Paris?
    Producing pictures by light of the sun? You can achieve a

positive image; also what is called a negative. Light and
darkness reversed. Ugly in the conventional sense, but the
likeness is there: needs only bringing out. Now. Suppose
a soul throughout has pictured itself in the negative. Is
that negative scrapped? Oh no. It comes to me. I steam, I
steep, I burn, I cleanse, with sulphur and the like: until at
last it yields its positive. But if, like you, a man has virtually
rubbed himself blank from the start, alas, no end of sulphur
and potassium is needed, to produce picture at all.

PEER: This negative you're after now. Has it a name?

SKINNY ONE: Peter Gynt.

PEER: Peter Gynt?! Is this Herr Gynt himself?

SKINNY ONE: He swears so. You know him?

PEER: In a way. One knows so many.

SKINNY ONE: Time is short. Where did you last see this
man?

PEER: Down at the Cape.

SKINNY ONE: Of Good Hope? I hate that place.

PEER: I understood he'd soon be sailing on.

SKINNY ONE: I couldn't bear to miss him. I must fly South!
(*Exit so.*)

PEER: Fool. [Playing hard to get.] Bungler. No wonder he's so
thin. He'll come a crash soon enough, and his whole damn
racket. Not that I'm that secure. Expelled, one might say,
from my freehold of self.
(*A shooting star.*)
Hi brother Shooting Star! Give everyone my love! ...All in
one gulp: flare, gutter, and be gone.
(*Mist clots around him.*)
Is there no one? No one in all the whirl of space? No one
in the abyss, or heaven above...?
(*Emerging lower. Despair. He pitches his hat on the
ground. Over him now a stillness stealing.*)
Poor beyond words, the soul returns, to the grey of mist
and nothingness. Oh lovely earth, do not be angry I
trampled your grass to no good end. Oh lovely sun, the
touch of your light was wasted on an empty wooden room:
no one within to warm nor give it heart. The owner, they

say, was never home. Fool Sun, fool Earth, to give my
mother sustenance and light. The soul's so mean, where
nature gives so free. We pay heavy, for being born. I'll
up, way, high, to the giddiest peak above. I'll watch there,
one last time, the rise of the Sun; and gaze, till sight grow
weary, out across the promised land. Then toil and heap
up over me a mound of snow. Who wants can write there:
HERE LIES NO ONE. Then come what can.
(*A processional hymn is heard afar below: Lutheran
chorale, raw, foursquare, joyful:*

> 'Blest morn! when once in swords of flame
> Earthward Thy Holy Spirit came
> And touched men's tongues to Heavenly voice abounding.
> Grant us, Thy Kingdom's heirs below,
> Our earthly voice like grace to know,
> Before Thy gates in Heavenly tongue resounding.')

PEER: Oh Peer Gynt turn your eyes away. There's desert and
waste. I was dead already, long before I die! (*Would slink
away.*)
BUTTONMOULDER: (*There.*) Good morning Peer Gynt.
Your list of sins.
(*PEER shakes his head.*)
Could you find no one?
PEER: Only some travelling photographer.
BUTTONMOULDER: Time's up.
PEER: It's all up. D'ye hear that owl? Tu-whit, tu-whoo! He
smells his prey.
BUTTONMOULDER: That's the matin bell.
PEER: What's that shine there?
BUTTONMOULDER: A candle only. In a hut.
PEER: Strange sound I hear…
BUTTONMOULDER: A woman only. Singing some song…
PEER: Ah…! There! Oh there…! Seek there my list of sins…!
BUTTONMOULDER: Set your house in order.
(*In slow cold grey of dawn, the hut again becomes
visible; a candle lit within.*)
PEER: Leave me! Away from me! Were your ladle the size of
a coffin, my sin runs over…

BUTTONMOULDER: Till the third cross road then Peer. But there… (*Moves aside.*)

PEER: Back or on, the way's as far. Out or in, the way's as tight. No… Go in…? Go back…? Go home…? NO-O-O…!
(*Stricken echo seems unending.*)
Go round, said the Böyg. Peer Gynt go round no more. This time, however tight the track, go straight, to the heart.
(*He steps toward hut. SOLVEIG emerges, churchclad, with prayerbook in white kerchief in her hand. She has need of a stick to feel her way. She stands upright, yet unforbidding.*)

PEER: (*Hurls himself down before her.*) If you have sentence for a sinner, speak it now!

SOLVEIG: (*Feeling through the air to find him, her fingers all the sight she has.*) He is here! He is here! Glory to God!

PEER: Cry out the sin I've done!

SOLVEIG: Sin, boy? What sin?

BUTTONMOULDER: (*Waiting where the dark begins.*) Peer Gynt. The list.

PEER: Howl my wrong!

SOLVEIG: (*Sits beside him.*) You have made my life a song of wonder. God bless you, you are here. You are here, you are here.

PEER: And damned.

SOLVEIG: Our Maker must judge that.

PEER: I am damned! But ye answer this riddle.

SOLVEIG: Ask it me.

PEER: Ask. Ay. Since Peer Gynt left you, say where has he been? The man I had in me to be? Oh say where has he been!

SOLVEIG: That riddle is easy.

PEER: Answer then. Say where I was.

SOLVEIG: In my faith. In my hope. In my love.

PEER: Ye toy wi' words. Ye make yourself a mother to me there.

SOLVEIG: Why so I do. But who's his father? He that forgives, when the mother pleads for the child.

PEER: (*Transfigured.*) Mother. Wife. Innocent woman. Oh hide
    me. Hide me. Hide me in your love!
    (*Stillness. Sunrise. SOLVEIG sings, to the tune of*
    before.)
SOLVEIG:
      In my arms I shall rock you, oh dear man my son.
      I'll watch over your sleep now your journey is done.
      Yet all our life long, never once he left me.
      Like a child with his mother, who plays on her knee,
      Lay he deep in my heart and close to my breast.
      Now his head grows a-weary, and he would rest.
BUTTONMOULDER: Peer Gynt. The last cross road. Till
    then. Then we'll see.
SOLVEIG:
    …I'll cradle and watch you. God bless you my joy.
    You sleep now and dream there, my dear man my boy.

The End.

ROSMERSHOLM

Characters

JOHN ROSMER
Master of Rosmersholm, formerly parish incumbent

REBECCA WEST
with Rosmer in his house

SCHOOL PRINCIPAL KROLL
Rosmer's brother-in-law

ULRIK BRENDEL

PETER MORTENSGÅRD

MRS HELSETH
Housekeeper at Rosmersholm

The action takes place at Rosmersholm, an old estate in the
vicinity of a small fjord-town in Western Norway.

This translation of *Rosmersholm* was first performed on BBC Radio 3 in May 1990, with the following cast:

ROSMER, Edward Petherbridge

REBECCA WEST, Lindsay Duncan

KROLL, Charles Kay

BRENDEL, Michael Gough

MORTENSGÅRD, Nigel Anthony

MRS HELSETH, Mary Wimbush

Director, John Tydeman

ACT ONE

The living-room of the Parsonage at Rosmersholm: spacious, old fashioned and comfortable. Down front before the wall to our right, a tall Scandinavian tiled stove, dressed with fresh birch-greenery and wild flowers. Further back, a door. In the back wall, a folding door leads to the 'forstue', an enclosed veranda-like front porch. In the wall to our left, a window, and before this a stand set with flowers and plants. By the stove, a table with sofa and easy chairs. Round about on the walls there hang portraits, older and more recent also, of clergy, military officers and government officials in their uniform. The window is open, as are the door to the veranda-porch, and the veranda's outer door beyond. Outside can be seen large old trees leading in an avenue toward the parsonage. A summer evening. The sun is down.

REBECCA WEST sits in an easy chair at the window, crocheting a large white woollen shawl that is nearly complete. Now and then she peers out between the flowers, watching for someone. Soon MRS HELSETH comes in at the door to our right.

MRS HELSETH: Oughtn't I to be setting the table, Miss, for supper?

REBECCA: Yes, if you would. His Reverence won't be long now, coming home.

MRS HELSETH: Isn't that very draughty where Madam's sitting?

REBECCA: It is a little. Perhaps you'd close up in here.
(*MRS HELSETH goes over and closes the door into the porch; then makes her way to the window.*)

MRS HELSETH: (*About to shut it; seeing out.*) But isn't that His Reverence, coming over yonder?

REBECCA: (*Quickly.*) Where? (*Standing.*) Yes, that's him. (*Behind the curtain.*) Stand to one side. Don't let him see us.

MRS HELSETH: (*Back in the room.*) I say though, Miss. He's starting to walk the mill path again.

REBECCA: He walked the mill path the day before yesterday too. (*Peers out between the curtains and the window-frame.*) But is he going to –

111

MRS HELSETH: He's coming onto the footbridge?

REBECCA: That's what I'm waiting to see. (*Soon.*) No. He turns aside. Today as well, the top road round for him. Long way about.

MRS HELSETH: Lord, so he does. His Reverence must find it more than he can do, to walk over that bridge. There where such a thing has happened, where –

REBECCA: (*Gathering together her crochetwork.*) At Rosmersholm here, they cling long to their dead.

MRS HELSETH: I'd say Miss myself, it's the dead that cling so long to Rosmersholm.

REBECCA: (*A look at her.*) The dead?

MRS HELSETH: Yes, you could almost say they can't quite leave go of those that remain.

REBECCA: Whatever gives you that idea?

MRS HELSETH: It's true, or else I reckon that white horse wouldn't come.

REBECCA: Yes, Mrs Helseth, what actually is this about the white horse?

MRS HELSETH: Oh, it's pointless to talk about it. Something, anyway, the like you'd not believe.

REBECCA: And you do?

MRS HELSETH: (*Moving away, and looking out at the window.*) Oh, Madam would only laugh at me. (*Sees out yonder.*) No! That can't be His Reverence out yonder on the mill path again?

REBECCA: (*Sees out yonder.*) That man there? (*Goes to the window.*) But that's our School Principal!

MRS HELSETH: Doctor Kroll, why so it is!

REBECCA: But what a lovely surprise. He's on his way to visit us, you'll see.

MRS HELSETH: Straight out across the bridge for him, look. And her the sister of his flesh and blood. Ah well; I'll away on in then, Miss, and set that table for supper.
(*She goes out right.*
REBECCA stands a moment at the window; then waves a greeting, smiles and nods to one out there. It begins to turn dark.)

REBECCA: (*Moves away, and speaks through the door right.*) Oh Mrs Helseth, if you'd be good enough, could you manage something a little extra special for supper? You'll know what Doctor Kroll likes best.

MRS HELSETH: (*Off.*) Of course, Miss. Leave it to me.

REBECCA: (*Opens the door into the porch.*) Well, well, after all this time… Dear Doctor Kroll, how lovely to see you!

KROLL: (*In the porch, standing his stick away.*) Thank you. Then my calling does not inconvenience you at all?

REBECCA: You, Sir? You should know better than think that…

KROLL: (*Coming in.*) Gracious as ever. (*Looks about him.*) Is Rosmer up in his study perhaps?

REBECCA: No, he's out on his walk. He is a little later home than usual. But any moment he'll be back. (*Indicates the sofa.*) Please: take a seat till he comes.

KROLL: (*Laying down his hat.*) Thank you very much. (*Sits, and looks about him.*) Well, Miss West, you have brightened up the old room, I have to say. Flowers high and low.

REBECCA: Mr Rosmer likes to have about him fresh, living flowers.

KROLL: And so do you, I think.

REBECCA: Yes. I find them so lovely and soothing. That pleasure we had to deny ourselves before.

KROLL: (*Gravely nodding.*) Poor Beäta could never abide the scent.

REBECCA: Nor the colours. They would so disturb her…

KROLL: I don't forget. (*In lighter tone.*) So: how's it all going then, out here?

REBECCA: Oh, everything goes its quiet uneventful way. Each day much like the next… And with you, Sir? Your wife…

KROLL: Oh my dear Miss West, let us not talk of me and mine. In any family there'll be something or other untoward. Especially in such days as these, we live in now.

REBECCA: (*After a moment, sitting in an armchair by the sofa.*) In all these weeks of your school holiday, why have you not been to see us once?

KROLL: Well, one mustn't be forever at other people's doors…

REBECCA: If only you knew how much we have missed you…

KROLL: And then of course I've been away…

REBECCA: Yes, for the fortnight or so. You were going to all the political meetings, were you?

KROLL: (*Nodding.*) And what do you say to that? Did you ever imagine, I'd turn political agitator in my old age? Hm?

REBECCA: (*With a smile.*) You were always something of an agitator, Doctor Kroll.

KROLL: Oh yes, but that was only my little game. I tell you though, it's a deadly serious matter now. Do you read these left-wing papers at all?

REBECCA: Yes, dear Principal, I'll not deny it, I –

KROLL: My dear Miss West, it is no matter for reproof. Not as concerns yourself.

REBECCA: My feeling too. I need to stay in touch with the world. Keep myself informed.

KROLL: Not that I would in any circumstance require you, as a woman, to side with either party to the factional strife – civil strife, one could well call it – we have raging hereabouts. But you'll have read the sort of abuse these so-called tribunes of the people have chosen to heap upon my head. The unspeakable filth they have presumed to hurl at me.

REBECCA: Yes, but I'd say you've been quite trenchant with them in your turn.

KROLL: That I have. Though I say it myself. I have in my teeth now the taste of their blood. They'll live to learn I'm not a man to let my enemy walk over me. (*Breaks off.*) No, but listen… All that's too painful and distressing a subject, let's not go into it tonight.

REBECCA: No, dear Principal, let us not.

KROLL: Tell me rather: how are you managing, really, here at Rosmersholm? On your own now as you are. Ever since our poor Beäta –

REBECCA: All right, thank you; I'm managing very well here. In many ways, of course, there is a great emptiness now she is gone. Loss too, and sadness…as you'd expect. Apart from that…

KROLL: You are minded to stay on here? Permanently, I mean?

REBECCA: My dear Principal, I never give it a thought, one way or other. I am become so used now to being here, I feel I almost belong to this house myself.

KROLL: That you do. I should say you do.

REBECCA: And so long as the Master finds me of some comfort and usefulness to him, so long I reckon it would seem I'll stay.

KROLL: (*Looking at her, with some emotion.*) I must say…it is magnificent of you: a woman, laying down the years of her youth like this, in sacrifice for others.

REBECCA: Oh, what cause other would I have had?

KROLL: First, there was your crippled and unreasonable foster-father forever to contend with…

REBECCA: You mustn't think that Dr West had been so unreasonable before, up home in the Far North… What broke him were those terrible journeys by sea up there. Though true enough, once we'd moved down south here, there did follow a gruelling two years till his struggle was done.

KROLL: Were they not even more gruelling for you, those years that came after?

REBECCA: No, how can you say that? Beäta meant so very much to me… And so pitiful, poor thing, in her need of nursing and gentle caring all the time.

KROLL: It does you great credit, that you remember her with such forbearance.

REBECCA: (*Moves a little nearer him.*) Dear Principal, you say that so kindly and with such heart, I can be sure you're masking no ill-feeling there.

KROLL: Ill-feeling? What can you mean by that?

REBECCA: Well, would it be so surprising, that it caused you some pain? To see me, a stranger to this house, in charge of it now?

KROLL: But how could you concei –

REBECCA: Yet it causes you no pain. (*Reaches her hand to him.*) Thank you, dear Principal. Thank you, thank you for that.

KROLL: How could you conceive such a notion?

REBECCA: I was becoming a little anxious, you were visiting us so seldom here.

KROLL: Miss West, you could not be further from the truth. Besides which…nothing here is essentially changed. Yourself it was – yourself, no other – already at the helm in this house, as poor Beäta's lifetime drew to its unhappy close.

REBECCA: She was mistress; I the regent rather, in her name.

KROLL: Be that as it might… Let me say, Miss West… I for one would feel no objection, I assure you, should you… But such, I suppose, is not for me to say.

REBECCA: What is not?

KROLL: If things did so develop, that you were to assume the empty place…

REBECCA: I have the place I wish for, Principal Sir.

KROLL: In practice, yes. But not in –

REBECCA: (*In earnest, interrupting him.*) Doctor Kroll, you should know better. How can you be frivolous on a matter like that?

KROLL: Oh well, our good John Rosmer must feel he's had wedlock to last him and more. Nevertheless…

REBECCA: You know, I could almost smile at you?

KROLL: Nevertheless… Tell me only, Miss West…if one might be permitted the question… What age in fact are you?

REBECCA: Shame to say, I was twenty-nine last birthday. I am into my thirtieth year.

KROLL: Sure, sure. And Rosmer…what age is he? Let me see. He's five years younger than myself. Which would make him a good forty-three. That would seem quite fitting to me.

REBECCA: Oh yes, oh yes. Eminently fitting… Will you be joining us for supper?

KROLL: If I may, thank you. I had intended to stop by with you a little. There is a matter I need to discuss with our good friend… So, Miss West…to spare you further foolish thoughts, from now I'll visit here as often as possible…as in earlier days.

REBECCA Oh yes, you really must. (*Seizing and shaking his two hands.*) Oh thank you, thank you. You're really so good and kind a man, in spite of all.

KROLL: (*A little gruffly.*) Indeed? That's more than I hear said of me at home.

(*JOHN ROSMER comes in at the door right.*)

REBECCA: Mr Rosmer…do you see who's sitting here?

ROSMER: Mrs Helseth told me.

(*KROLL has risen.*)

ROSMER: (*Gentle and muted, clasping his hands.*) Dear Kroll, welcome to my house again. (*Rests hands upon his shoulders, and looks into his eyes.*) Oh, my dear old friend! I knew it: the day had to come, when all between us would again be as before.

KROLL: But my dear fellow…were you, too, labouring under that idiot delusion, all between us was not right?

REBECCA: (*To ROSMER.*) Just think…how lovely, it was a delusion only.

ROSMER: Really, Kroll, that's all it was? Why though did you withdraw yourself from us so absolutely?

KROLL: (*Grave and low.*) Because I did not wish to come here, a living reminder of your unhappy years…and of herself, who perished in the millstream there.

ROSMER: That was really thoughtful of you. You always are so understanding. But there was absolutely no need for you to stay away on that account… Come on, man, you sit down beside me here… (*They sit.*) No, honestly: the thought of Beäta causes me no pain at all. We talk of her every day. To us, she's one of the household still as ever she was.

KROLL: You actually feel that?

REBECCA: (*Putting light to the lamp.*) Yes, we do indeed.

ROSMER: It's only natural. To the two of us she meant so much. And both Rebe – both Miss West and myself know as only we can: all that was in us to do, we did, for that poor soul in her affliction. We have no cause to reproach ourselves... And so, when I think of Beäta now, it's with a gentleness and tenderness.

KROLL: Oh, you precious, magnificent pair! From now I'll come and see you every day.

REBECCA: (*Sits in an armchair.*) Well, let's but see if you're as good as your word.

ROSMER: (*Somewhat hesitantly.*) Kroll, dear friend... I've had great cause to wish our old mutuality had never been broken. It's you I've always naturally turned to for advice, all the time we've known each other. Ever since my student days.

KROLL: Indeed yes, and I set great store by that. Why, you have some particular question now...?

ROSMER: I have so many, and so much, I long so to let pour out and talk about with you. From deep in the heart.

REBECCA: Yes, Mr Rosmer, haven't you? I think it must be so good, between those who have long been friends.

KROLL: Believe you me, I've even more to talk about with you. Now that I'm active on the political front, as you are no doubt aware.

ROSMER: Why, yes, so you are. How actually did that come about?

KROLL: I had no choice, man. No choice, however I might wish it otherwise. It's not possible to stand by a moment longer, look on and do nothing. With this deplorable majority the Left have won...it's high time we... And that's why I've prevailed on our little circle of friends there in town to close ranks. And high time too, I say!

REBECCA: (*With a faint smile.*) Indeed, perhaps in fact a little late?

KROLL: No question but we should have acted earlier, to stem this torrent. But who could have foreseen what was coming? Not I for one. (*Stands, paces the floor.*) Well, my eyes are well and truly opened now. When the spirit of subversion has intruded into the school, no less.

ROSMER: Into the school? Not your school, surely?

KROLL: Oh, very much so. Into my own school. Imagine! It has come to my attention that my sixth-years – well, a number of them – have formed a secret brotherhood and, for the past term and more, been taking that paper of Mortensgård's.

REBECCA: Ah: *The Signalling Flame.*

KROLL: I ask you, what diet is that, for the public servants of tomorrow? But what saddens me most about it is, they're all the best-talented boys of their year, ganging together to conspire against me so. It's only the clodpolls and backward ones who'll have nothing to do with it.

REBECCA: And Principal, that hurts you so deep?

KROLL: Of course it does. To see myself thwarted and countered so in my life's work? (*In a lower voice.*) Though I'd almost be tempted to say, so what, let it happen. Only you've not heard the worst. (*Looks about him.*) I take it there's nobody listening at your doors?

REBECCA: Oh of course not.

KROLL: Then let me tell you: the undertow and subversion have penetrated my very house. Into my own quiet home. And utterly disrupted the peaceful family life I had.

ROSMER: (*Stands.*) What are you saying? That beneath your roof –

REBECCA: (*Goes to KROLL.*) My dear friend, what can have happened there?

KROLL: Think of it, my own children... In a word...the chief conspirator at school's my son. And my daughter has embroidered a red folder for hiding their copies of *The Signalling Flame.*

ROSMER: I'd never have dreamed it...beneath your roof...in your own house...

KROLL: No, who could have dreamed of it? In my own house, where obedience and good order have ever been the way...where, ever till now, had prevailed the simple concord of one common purpose...

REBECCA: What is your wife's reaction to this?

KROLL: Well now, that is what beggars belief most of all. That woman, who all her days, in matters great and small alike, has been of a mind with me, endorsing all my views: she is actually tending now on many issues to side with the youngsters! And says for what's happened I've myself to thank. She says I impose my will upon the children. As if that weren't exactly what we need to do!... So, that's the turmoil I have going on at home. I talk of it of course as little as possible. Such matters are best kept dark. (*He paces the floor.*) Ah well, ah well... (*Pauses, hands behind his back, gazing out at the window.*)

REBECCA: (*Has come close to ROSMER, and speaks softly, quickly, unobserved by KROLL.*) Tell him.

ROSMER: (*Likewise.*) Tonight, no.

REBECCA: (*As before.*) When better? (*She moves away and attends to the lamp.*)

KROLL: (*Comes forward into the room.*) So, my dear Rosmer, now you know: how, into my family life and over my professional calling, the spirit of our time has cast its shadow. And this baneful, corrupting and degenerative ethos am I not to contest with what weapons I can? Oh friend, be sure I shall. With written word, and spoken.

ROSMER: You've hope then of achieving results by those means?

KROLL: I do at least my duty as a citizen. As any man must, who loves his native land, and cares for what is good and true. In fact...it's for this reason, more than any, I have come to you tonight.

ROSMER: But my dear man, what do you...? How can I – ?

KROLL: You can help your old friends. Do as we are doing. Involve yourself, to your utmost.

REBECCA: But Doctor Kroll, you well know of Mr Rosmer's disinclination in such matters.

KROLL: Then he must master his disinclination. Rosmer, you're losing touch with the world. Here you sit, walled up with your antiquities. Heaven knows, all due respect to family trees and the rest. But this alas is not a time for such pursuits. You've no conceiving the predicament of that country out there all around you. I tell you, every single principle's been stood on its head. Oh, it'll be an epic task, purging the land of all that aberration.

ROSMER: I'm sure it shall. But such a task is not at all for me.

REBECCA: I reckon, also, Mr Rosmer is clearer sighted than he was.

KROLL: Clearer?

REBECCA: Well, more liberated, shall we say? More open-minded.

KROLL: What is all this? Rosmer...don't tell me you could ever be so feeble: it's not gone to your head, this passing freak majority the leaders of the rabble have?

ROSMER: Dear man, well you know how poor a grasp I have of politics. Yet I can't help feeling, in recent years the individual has come to form his own opinions more.

KROLL: Oh...and that you consider of itself a good? Anyway, my friend, you are gravely mistaken. Only examine what the Radicals are actually saying, out here and in the town. It's not a whit different from the gospel propounded by *The Signalling Flame*.

REBECCA: Yes, Mortensgård exerts some considerable influence in these parts.

KROLL: And look at him! A man with so besmirched a past. Someone who had to be dismissed his teaching post for immoral conduct...! A creature like that, sets himself up as Leader of the People! And it works for him! It really works for him! He's hoping now to enlarge his paper, so I'm told. I have it on authority, he's looking for a capable assistant.

REBECCA: I marvel that yourself and your friends don't put something up in opposition to him.

KROLL: It's exactly that we are about to do. This very day we have bought the *County Newsletter*. The matter of money presented no problem. What *did*... (*Turns to ROSMER.*) Yes, now I come to my true mission here, my friend. It's the management...the editorial management, where we're stuck, you see... Rosmer, you don't think...for the sake of all that's good and true, you might feel called upon to take it on?

ROSMER: (*Quite horrified.*) Me?!

REBECCA: No, how can you, it's unthinkable.

KROLL: You have a terror of public assemblies, I know, and the charming treatment they dish out to one there: which is only understandable. But an editor's is a more sequestered activity; or rather…

ROSMER: No no, dear friend, this you must not ask of me.

KROLL: I would dearly have loved to try my hand in that direction myself. But it's altogether more than I could take on. Already before we've begun I'm overburdened with innumerable claims on my attention. Whereas you, no longer professionally occupied… We others, of course, will be of whatever help to you we can.

ROSMER: Kroll, I cannot. I've not the gift for that.

KROLL: Not the gift? So you said, when your father procured you the living here.

ROSMER: And right I was. For which reason I went my way.

KROLL: Prove only so able an editor as you were Parson here, and we shall be well content.

ROSMER: Dear Kroll. Once and for all, my friend, I am not doing it.

KROLL: Well…but you'll lend us at least the use of your name.

ROSMER: My name?

KROLL: Indeed: the name John Rosmer will advance the paper of itself. We others are men too much identified with party. Myself I'm told stand even to be smeared as a rabid fanatic. So what hope have we, of reaching the misguided masses most of all, if we publish under our own name? Whereas you…you've always held aloof from party conflict. Your quiet upright character…sensibility of mind…your unassailable integrity, are known and prized by everybody hereabout. To say nothing of the regard and esteem you still enjoy, as one-time Parson here. And last above all, the authority of the name you bear.

ROSMER: Oh, name…

KROLL: (*Indicating the portraits.*) The Rosmers of Rosmersholm: men of church and battlefield. Of positions of high trust in public service. Men of distinction and propriety, every one: a dynasty, for nigh on two centuries residing here as the foremost in the countryside about. (*Laying his hand upon ROSMER's shoulder.*) Rosmer, it is your duty to yourself and your inheritance, to join with us in the defence of all that ever till now has been held sacrosanct in our society. (*Turns.*) How do you say, Miss West?

REBECCA: (*With a light, quiet laughter.*) Dear Principal...it all sounds unutterably comical to me.

KROLL: What's that? Comical?!

REBECCA: Yes; and I'll tell you why –

ROSMER: (*Quickly.*) No, no...leave be. Not now.

KROLL: (*Looking from one to the other.*) But my dear friends, whatever... (*Breaks off.*) Hm.
(*MRS HELSETH comes in at the door right.*)

MRS HELSETH: There's a man out there in the kitchen passage. He says he wishes to pay respects to His Reverence.

ROSMER: (*Relieved.*) Is that so? Well, bid him be so good as to come in.

MRS HELSETH: Come in here?

ROSMER: Of course.

MRS HELSETH: He's not the sort to look at you'd let come in here.

REBECCA: What is he, Mrs Helseth then, to look at?

MRS HELSETH: Not much, Miss, if you ask me.

ROSMER: Did he give no name?

MRS HELSETH: Yes, I think he said Hedgeman or some such name.

ROSMER: I don't know anyone called that.

MRS HELSETH: And he said he had another name, Uldrik too.

ROSMER: (*With a start.*) Ulrik Hetman, was that it?

MRS HELSETH: Yes, Hetman, that was it.

KROLL: That name I'm sure I've heard...

REBECCA: But that was the name *he* used to write under, that extraordinary man –

ROSMER: (*To KROLL.*) It's the pen-name of Ulrik Brendel,
   you remember...

KROLL: That worthless Ulrik Brendel. So it was.

REBECCA: And living still.

ROSMER: I understood he'd joined a troupe of travelling
   actors.

KROLL: Last I heard of him, he was in the workhouse.

ROSMER: Ask him to come in, Mrs Helseth.

MRS HELSETH: As you say. (*She goes.*)

KROLL: You'll really tolerate that character in here?

ROSMER: Come on, you know he was my tutor once.

KROLL: Yes, I know he crammed your head so with seditious
   notions, your father had to take a horsewhip and flog him
   from the door.

ROSMER: (*A touch bitter.*) Father was Commanding Officer to
   his family too.

KROLL: Dear Rosmer, for that you thank him in his grave.
   So!
   (*MRS HELSETH opens the door right for ULRIK
   BRENDEL, goes again and shuts it behind him. He is a
   prepossessing though somewhat emaciated strong and vigorous
   figure of a man, with grey hair and beard, but in the garb
   of a common vagabond, coat worn almost to nothing, shoes
   breaking apart, no shirt on him to be seen. A pair of old
   battered gloves, a dirty soft hat pressed to his body beneath his
   arm, and a walking-stick in his hand.*)

BRENDEL: (*Uncertain at first, then making straight for KROLL,
   and reaching a hand.*) Good evening, John!

KROLL: I'm sorry –

BRENDEL: Did ever you expect to set eyes on me again?
   And that, within these detested walls?

KROLL: I'm sorry. (*Points.*) That is –

BRENDEL: (*Turns.*) Of course. There we have him. John...my
   boy...you whom I most have loved...

ROSMER: (*Reaching a hand to him.*) My old teacher.

BRENDEL: Certain memories notwithstanding, how could I
   pass Rosmersholm and not look briefly in on you?

ROSMER: And right welcome, Sir, you are. Be sure of that.

BRENDEL: Ah! and this alluring lady… (*Bows.*) Herself, the Parson's Wife, who else?

ROSMER: Miss West.

BRENDEL: Then a close relation, I presume. And over there, unknown to me… A brother in the clergy, that is plain.

ROSMER: Doctor Kroll, School Principal.

BRENDEL: Kroll? Kroll? Wait a minute. Was one reading Philology in one's student days?

KROLL: It goes without saying.

BRENDEL: But *Donnerwetter* old man, I was sure I knew you!

KROLL: I'm sorry –

BRENDEL: Was it not you –

KROLL: I'm sorry –

BRENDEL: – along with other of Virtue's Vigilantes, who had me banned from the Debating Union?

KROLL: It could well be. But that's as close as our acquaintance goes.

BRENDEL: Sure, sure. *Nach Belieben,* Doctor Kroll, Sir. To me, all one. Ulrik Brendel remains the man he was, for all that.

REBECCA: You're on your way into town, Mr Brendel?

BRENDEL: The Parson's Wife hits the nail on the head! Times are, I needs must lift a finger for survival. Not as I would prefer it. But…*enfin*…necessity compels…

ROSMER: My dear Mr Brendel, is there some help to you that I can be? In one way or other, you understand…

BRENDEL: The very suggestion! How could you wish to sully the bond that unites us? Never, John…never!

ROSMER: But how are you intending to manage in town? Believe me, you'll not find it so easy…

BRENDEL: Leave that to me, dear boy. The die is cast. I stand before you, poised for departure upon an all-embracing mission. Embracing more by far than all my former forays put together. (*To KROLL.*) If one may presume to inquire of our Professor: *unter uns,* is there to be found, Sir, a tolerably respectable, reputable and spacious venue in your estimable town?

KROLL: The largest is the Working Men's Association Hall.

BRENDEL: And has our Senior Fellow some *ex officio* influence within this doubtless worthy brotherhood?

KROLL: I have no dealing with it in the least.

REBECCA: (*To BRENDEL.*) You'll need to make yourself known to Peter Mortensgård.

BRENDEL: *Pardon Madame,* what kind of imbecile is he?

ROSMER: What makes you think he's an imbecile exactly?

BRENDEL: Don't I hear it in his name, the man's low-born?

KROLL: That answer I didn't expect.

BRENDEL: But I shall master myself. I can no other. When one…such as I…stands at a turning-point in his life… Done. I establish contact with the character in question… initiate direct negotiation…

ROSMER: Truly and seriously, you stand at a turning-point?

BRENDEL: My dear boy, don't you know: where Ulrik Brendel stands, there he always truly and seriously stands? Ay, laddie, now shall I put a new self on me. Break free from that retiring self-restraint, that ever was the way with me till now.

ROSMER: How will you –

BRENDEL: I will seize hold on living, with an active hand! Step onward. Step upward. This age we breathe in is the storm-lashed turning of a year. Now shall I lay my widow's farthing on Liberation's altar.

KROLL: You too?

BRENDEL: (*To them all.*) Are present company acquainted at all with my sporadic writings?

KROLL: No, I regret to confess, I…

REBECCA: I've read a good number. They were among my adoptive father's books.

BRENDEL: Fair mistress of the house…there you have wasted your time. They are but trumpery, I tell you.

REBECCA: What?!

BRENDEL: Yes, such as you have read. My works that matter, no man nor woman knows. No one…but myself alone.

REBECCA: How can that be?

BRENDEL: Because they are not written.

ROSMER: But my dear Mr Brendel –

BRENDEL: John boy, you know me, how I am something
of a sybarite. A *Feinschmecker*. Always was. I like to take
my pleasure in solitude. There's twice the pleasure so.
Ten times. You see, boy…when golden dreams descended
upon me…swathed me about…when novel, dizzying,
unbounded concepts came to birth in me…wafted me aloft
on soaring wings…I gave them form: in poetry, visions,
images. In rough outline as it were, you understand…

ROSMER: Of course, of course.

BRENDEL: Oh, my son, the pleasure and the ecstasy that I
have known. The mysterious bliss of the creative act…in
rough, as it were, as I say…the applause, the gratitude,
the acclamation, the victor's crown: I've raked it all in,
to overflowing, in these gleeful trembling hands. Fulfilled
myself in my secret performances with an exaltation…oh
so giddyingly vast…

KROLL: Hm.

ROSMER: But never wrote it down?

BRENDEL: Not one word. That slavish toil of writing out
by hand ever did arouse a nauseous aversion in me.
Why, come to that, should I profane my own ideal
conceptions, when I could enjoy them in their purity and
for myself? But now shall they be offered up. Truly…it
is with me as with a mother, who lays her daughters in
their bridegrooms' arms. None the less, though, I make an
offering of them…offer them on Liberation's altar. A series
of papers, fully argued…the length of the land…

REBECCA: (*Quickened.*) Mr Brendel, that is magnificent of
you. You're giving the most precious possession you have.

ROSMER: Your only.

REBECCA: (*Casting at ROSMER a meaningful look.*) How
many are there, I wonder, who do so much? Who dare
that?

ROSMER: (*Returning the glance.*) Who can say?

BRENDEL: The assembly are moved. That stills my troubled
heart…and nerves the will. I put it into action then! One
matter, though… (*To KROLL.*) I wonder could our Senior
Reader inform me: does your town boast a Temperance
Society? A Total Abstinence Society? As though one need ask.

KROLL: Yes, at your service. I am its President myself.

BRENDEL: Couldn't I see it in your face, Sir? Well then, it's not beyond the bounds of possibility you'll be finding me at your door, Sir, booking in for the week.

KROLL: I'm sorry…we don't take members by the week.

BRENDEL: *A la bonne heure,* schoolmaster, Sir. Ulrik Brendel has never pestered such societies as that. But I must not protract my sojourn in this house, so rich in memories. I must to town and select myself some suitable accommodation. I'm right in assuming there's a decent hotel?

REBECCA: Won't you take a drink of something warm before you go?

BRENDEL: Warm, good lady, in what sense?

REBECCA: Some tea, or…

BRENDEL: I thank Mine Hostess for her bounty. But I would make no demands on private hospitality. (*Saluting.*) Good company, farewell! (*Goes to the door; but turns.*) Ah, which reminds me… John…Parson Rosmer…will you do your old teacher a service, for the sake of our friendship of so many years?

ROSMER: I'd be more than happy.

BRENDEL: Good. Give me the loan then…for a day or so…of a dress-shirt with cuffs.

ROSMER: Is that all?

BRENDEL: Because I go on foot, you realize…this once. I'm having my box sent on.

ROSMER: Of course. You're sure there's nothing else?

BRENDEL: Well, I tell you what… There isn't an old cast-off summercoat that you could spare?

ROSMER: Yes, yes, of course there is.

BRENDEL: And a pair of decent boots perhaps, to go with the coat.

ROSMER: I'm sure we can manage that. As soon as we know your address, we'll send the articles on.

BRENDEL: Not at all. No inconveniencing yourselves on my account! I'll take the odds and ends along with me.

ROSMER: Good, good. Then come with me upstairs.

REBECCA: No, let me do this. Mrs Helseth and I shall see to it.

BRENDEL: How could I permit so distinguished a lady –

REBECCA: Oh nonsense. Mr Brendel, come along.

ROSMER: (*Holding him back.*) You're sure…there's no other help that I can be?

BRENDEL: I really can't imagine what. Unless, dammit… now I think…! John, lad…you wouldn't happen to have eight kroner on you?

ROSMER: Let's have a look. (*Opens his wallet.*) I've two ten-kroner notes.

BRENDEL: Well, well, same difference. They'll do. Can always get them changed in town. Thank you meanwhile. Remember, two tenners you lent me. Goodnight to you, lad, my own dear boy. Goodnight, most honoured Sir. (*He goes out right, where ROSMER takes farewell of him and closes the door after.*)

KROLL: All-pitying God above…so that was the Ulrik Brendel, people once thought had in him to be something great in the world.

ROSMER: At least he's had the courage to live in his own way. I'd not call that so little to have done.

KROLL: What? A life like his? I could almost believe that man might turn your head a second time.

ROSMER: Oh no, my friend. I think quite clearly for myself on every matter now.

KROLL: I'd not be so sure, dear John. You've always far too readily let others impress themselves upon you.

ROSMER: Let's sit. I have to talk with you.

KROLL: Yes, we should.

(*They sit on the sofa.*)

ROSMER: (*After a while.*) Ours is a good and comfortable life here, wouldn't you say?

KROLL: Yes. It's good and comfortable in this house now… and peaceful too. Ay, John, you've found yourself a home now. Mine I've lost.

ROSMER: Dear friend, do not say that. What's broken now will be made whole again.

KROLL: Never. Never. The barb in the wound will abide. It can never again be as it was before.

ROSMER: Kroll, listen. You and I have been close to one another now so many, many years. Does it seem thinkable to you, our friendship could ever come to grief?

KROLL: Nothing I know of in the world could set myself and you at odds. What can have put such a thought in your head?

ROSMER: The critical importance you attach, to our being at one in views and values.

KROLL: Well, yes: but we two are as one, as near as makes no odds. At length on the great essential questions.

ROSMER: (*Softly.*) No. No longer so.

KROLL: (*Would jump to his feet.*) What's this?!

ROSMER: (*Restraining him.*) No, sit where you are, Kroll, I beg of you.

KROLL: What is this? I don't understand you. Be straight with me.

ROSMER: There is come a new summer in my soul. I see with the eyes of youth again. And so, where I stand now…

KROLL: Where…? Where do you stand?

ROSMER: There, where your children stand.

KROLL: You? You! But that's not possible. You stand where, you say?

ROSMER: On that same side as your son and daughter.

KROLL: (*With drooping head.*) A deserter. John Rosmer, a deserter.

ROSMER: I should have felt so glad of heart, so intensely happy, in my what you term desertion. But that it caused me torment too. I knew well, that this would grieve you bitterly.

KROLL: Rosmer… Rosmer! I'll never live with this. (*Looking sadly at him.*) Oh, that you as well could want to join and lend your hand in the work of perverting and disrupting this unhappy country.

ROSMER: What I will be about, is freedom's work.

KROLL: Oh I know that. So say they all, seducers and deceived alike. The ethos of our time is poisoning our entire society, and you believe that we can look to that for any freedom?!

ROSMER: I don't identify myself with the prevailing ethos. Nor with any party to the present strife. I want to try to gather people together, of every persuasion. As many and as sincerely as I can. I want to live, and devote all my life's powers, to this one end: the creation of true Government by the People in this country.

KROLL: You don't think then that we've had 'government by the people' enough already? What I see is every manjack of us bidding fair to be dragged down into the mire, where only the rabble can thrive.

ROSMER: And there I say democracy's true mission is.

KROLL: What mission?

ROSMER: To raise all people in the land to a nobility.

KROLL: All people?

ROSMER: At least as many as can be.

KROLL: By what means?

ROSMER: By setting their minds free, and cleansing their will: that's my belief.

KROLL: Rosmer, you're a dreamer. You, free them? You, cleanse them?

ROSMER: No, my dear friend...all I would, is seek to awaken them to that. The doing...has to be for them.

KROLL: And you believe them capable?

ROSMER: Yes.

KROLL: By their own powers you mean?

ROSMER: Yes indeed, by their own powers. There is no other.

KROLL: (*Rising.*) A man of God, and you say that?

ROSMER: I am man of God no more.

KROLL: No, but...the faith into which you were born...

ROSMER: That, I no longer have.

KROLL: You no lo –

ROSMER: (*Rising.*) I have set it aside. No choice for me, Kroll, but to set it aside.

KROLL: (*Shaken but controlled.*) I see… Yes, yes, yes. The one will go with the other… So that was the reason, then, you stepped down from the ministry?

ROSMER: Yes. Once I'd come to a clear knowledge of myself…once I knew beyond all question, here was no passing flirtation with doubt, but a cause that I could not, would not abandon ever: then I left.

KROLL: All this while, there's been this ferment in you. And we…your friends, have known no hint of it. Rosmer, Rosmer…how could you hide from us the grievous truth?

ROSMER: Because it seemed to me a matter for myself alone. Also I wanted not to cause yourself and my other friends a needless pain. I thought I could go on living here as always, in peace, joy, happiness. I would read, and immerse myself in all those works that had been closed books to me before. Enter with all my being in, to that great world of truth and freedom that now has been revealed to me.

KROLL: Deserter. Your every word's a testament to that. But why confess at all to this secret defection of yours? And of all times why tonight?

ROSMER: Because you yourself compelled me to it, Kroll,

KROLL: I? I compelled you…?!

ROSMER: When I came to hear of your violent manner at the public meetings…when I read of all the ugly speeches you were making there…all your effusions of loathing for those of other persuasion…your bigoted contempt for all opposed to you… Oh Kroll…for you, you, to have become such a man! I saw my duty there; and I must not say no. This factional strife that's current now is bringing out the evil in everyone. What's needed here is peace, and joy in our hearts, and a meeting of minds. It's for that reason I now step forward and openly declare myself for what I am. I too would put my powers to the test. Could you not find it in you…from where you stand…Kroll, to be with me in this?

KROLL: Never so long as I live shall I bargain with the forces that work for the destruction of our society.

ROSMER: If fight we must, at least let us do so honourably armed.

KROLL: Who is not with me on the critical issues of life, I no longer know. And I owe him no consideration.

ROSMER: That extends even to me?

KROLL: Rosmer, it is you who have broken from me.

ROSMER: Broken, you call it?

KROLL: I do. You have broken from all who were your allies till now. Now you must take the consequence.

REBECCA: (*Comes in right, throwing wide open the door.*) There, now: off is he gone to tender his great sacrifice. And we can proceed to supper. Principal, please.

KROLL: (*Taking up his hat.*) Good night, Miss West, I have no further dealing here.

REBECCA: (*Quickened.*) What's this? (*Shuts the door and comes to them.*) You've told him…?

ROSMER: He knows now.

KROLL: You're not lost to us for ever, Rosmer. We'll win you back to us perforce.

ROSMER: I come your way no more.

KROLL: That we shall see. You haven't it in you, to stand your ground alone.

ROSMER: I am not so alone as all that. There are two of us here to bear the loneliness.

KROLL: Ah… (*We see a suspicion occur to him.*) That as well. Beäta's very words –

ROSMER: Beäta – ?

KROLL: (*Abjures the thought.*) No, no…foul thought… Forgive me.

ROSMER: What? Forgive you what?

KROLL: Leave it. Oh, foul! Forgive me. Goodbye to you. (*He leaves by the porch door.*)

ROSMER: (*Following after him.*) Kroll! It must not end between us in this way! I'll come and look in on you tomorrow.

KROLL: (*In the porch, and turning.*) Never you step in at my door. (*He takes his stick, and is gone.*)

ROSMER: (*Stands a moment in the open doorway, then he shuts it, and comes to the table.*) Rebecca my dear, it is nothing. We shall survive this. We two loyal friends together. You and I.

REBECCA: What do you think was the notion he'd had, he thought so foul?

ROSMER: My dear, don't bother your head about it. He didn't believe it himself, the thought he had. Tomorrow, though, I will look in on him. Good night.

REBECCA: Tonight again, away to your bed so early? After this?

ROSMER: Tonight like any other. I feel such a relief now, that it is done. Rebecca my dear, you can see: I am quite tranquil. You too, take it in tranquillity. Good night.

REBECCA: Good night, dear friend! And sleep well.
(*ROSMER goes out through the door into the porch; soon he is heard climbing a stair. REBECCA goes and pulls a bell-cord by the stove. Soon MRS HELSETH comes in right.*)
If you'd clear the table again, Mrs Helseth. His Reverence won't be wanting anything… And the Principal has gone home.

MRS HELSETH: The Principal gone? Whatever was amiss with him?

REBECCA: (*Gathers up her crochetwork.*) He warned us, that some mighty storm is on its way.

MRS HELSETH: That was strange of him. There's not a fleck of cloud to be seen tonight.

REBECCA: So long as he doesn't meet the white horse. I'm afraid we could be hearing from some such phantoms very soon.

MRS HELSETH: God forgive you, Miss! Never say such a frightful thing!

REBECCA: Well, well…

MRS HELSETH: (*In a lower voice.*) Does Madam really think then, someone here will soon be taken?

REBECCA: I think no such thing. But there are so many kinds of white horse in this world, Mrs Helseth… Anyway, good night to you. I'm away in to my room now.

MRS HELSETH: Good night, Miss.

(*REBECCA goes with her crochetwork out right. MRS HELSETH turns the lamp low, shaking her head and murmuring to herself.*)
Lord above, Lord above. That Miss West. The things that she can say.

End of Act One.

ACT TWO

JOHN ROSMER's study. In the wall to our left, the door. In the background, curtains drawn aside reveal a doorway to the bedroom. A window to our right, and before this a writing desk, spread with books and papers. Bookshelves and cupboards along the walls. Frugal furnishing. An old fashioned sofa with a table before it, downstage left.

JOHN ROSMER, in his housecoat, sits in a high-backed chair at the desk. He is cutting the pages of a journal, leafing through it and glancing into it here and there.

A knock at the door to our left.

ROSMER: (*Without looking round.*) Just come in.
    (*REBECCA WEST comes in, in morning-coat.*)
REBECCA: Good morning.
ROSMER: (*Browsing through the journal.*) Good morning, my
    dear. Is there something you want?
REBECCA: I only wanted to know, were you able to sleep?
ROSMER: Oh, such a beautiful deep sleep. Not a dream.
    (*Turns.*) And you?
REBECCA: All right, thank you. Toward day.
ROSMER: I don't know when I last felt so light of heart as
    now. Oh, it's really good, to have all that said.
REBECCA: Yes John, you were silent too long.
ROSMER: I can't understand how I could have been such a
    coward.
REBECCA: Well, I wouldn't call it cowardice so much…
ROSMER: Oh yes, oh yes, Rebecca. Now I see it for what it
    is, some cowardice was there.
REBECCA: The braver of you then, to break and have done.
    (*Sits beside him, in a chair at the desk.*) But now I want to tell
    you something I have done…and it is not to make you
    cross with me.
ROSMER: Cross? My dear, how could you imagi –
REBECCA: Well, I might have taken matters rather into my
    own hands, but…

ROSMER: Well, tell me.

REBECCA: Last night, as Ulrik Brendel was leaving, I gave him a little note to take to Mortensgård.

ROSMER: (*With some misgiving.*) Rebecca my dear, but… Well, what did your note say?

REBECCA: It said, that if Mortensgård were to interest himself a little in that unhappy man and help him as best he could, he would be doing you a service.

ROSMER: My dear, that was wrong of you. That way you've done Brendel nothing but harm. And Mortensgård's a man I want kept well away from my life. You know there's that old trouble we once had.

REBECCA: But don't you think you might be as well now to make it up with him?

ROSMER: Me? With Mortensgård? Why should you suppose that?

REBECCA: Well, because your position can't be too safe now…with this, coming between yourself and your friends…

ROSMER: (*Looks at her, and shakes his head.*) You can't seriously believe that Kroll or any of the others could want to be vindictive? That they're any of them capable –

REBECCA: In the first heat of their rage, my dear: there can be no telling… I would say, if Kroll's reaction is anything to go by…

ROSMER: Oh, you should know him better than that. Kroll is a gentleman to the core. I shall go into town this afternoon and talk with him. I shall talk with them all. Oh, there'll be nothing to it, just you see…

(*MRS HELSETH comes in at the door left.*)

REBECCA: (*Standing.*) What is it, Mrs Helseth?

MRS HELSETH: Doctor Kroll is downstairs in the hall.

ROSMER: (*Stands quickly.*) Kroll!

REBECCA: The Principal! Fancy that – !

MRS HELSETH: He's asking if he might come up and have a word with Your Reverence.

ROSMER: (*To REBECCA.*) What did I tell you! Yes, of course he may! (*Goes to the door and calls down the stairs.*) Come on up, dear friend! I couldn't be more glad to see you!

(*ROSMER stands and holds open the door. MRS HELSETH goes. REBECCA draws the curtains to, across the doorway to the bedroom within. Then she tidies and straightens here and there. KROLL enters, hat in hand.*)

ROSMER: (*Quiet, moved.*) I knew that yesterday could never be the last…

KROLL: Today I see the matter in quite a different light.

ROSMER: I knew it, Kroll. Of course you do! Now that you've had time to reflect…

KROLL: You quite mistake my meaning. (*He puts down his hat on the table by the sofa.*) I must insist I speak with you alone.

ROSMER: Why may not Miss West…?

REBECCA: No, no, Mr Rosmer, I'll leave you.

KROLL: (*Looking her up and down.*) And I must crave the lady's pardon, for my calling so early in the day. That one surprises her, before she has had time to…

REBECCA: (*Astonished.*) What? You take exception, to my wearing a morning-coat about the house?

KROLL: Lord preserve us! How am I to tell what is the practice now at Rosmersholm?

ROSMER: But Kroll…my friend, this isn't at all the man I know.

REBECCA: If the Principal will excuse me…
(*She goes out left.*)

KROLL: If I may…
(*He sits on the sofa.*)

ROSMER: Of course, dear man, let's sit the two of us in confidence, and talk this through.
(*He sits on a chair, facing KROLL.*)

KROLL: Since yesterday I haven't had one wink of sleep. I've lain awake thinking and thinking, all night long.

ROSMER: And what do you say today?

KROLL: It'll take a while, Rosmer. Let me open with an introduction, as it were. I've a little news for you about Ulrik Brendel.

ROSMER: He's been to see you?

KROLL: No. He billeted himself in some low dive. In the lowest company, as you'd expect. Drinking and standing drinks all round, till he'd spent what he had. Then he started berating the whole pack of them for rabble and scum. Not that he was far wrong there. Whereat they gave him a trouncing and slung him in the gutter.

ROSMER: So there's no redeeming him after all.

KROLL: The coat, moreover, he had put in pawn. But that'll have been bought back for him of course. Can you guess by whom?

ROSMER: By yourself presumably?

KROLL: No. By our splendid Mr Mortensgård.

ROSMER: Ah.

KROLL: I am given to understand, our low-born imbecile was the first that Mr Brendel honoured with a call.

ROSMER: It was lucky for him he did.

KROLL: Very much so. (*Leans forward across the table, facing ROSMER a little more closely.*) Which brings us to a matter that our long – our erstwhile friendship obliges me to disclose to you.

ROSMER: Dear friend, whatever can that be?

KROLL: Namely, that in this house something or other is going on behind your back.

ROSMER: How can you credit that? Is it Re – Are you alluding to Miss West?

KROLL: Precisely. I can see it only too well from her point of view. Long used as she now is to being the authority in this house. Nevertheless…

ROSMER: Dear Kroll, you're totally mistaken there. She and I…there's nothing in the world that we keep hidden from each other.

KROLL: She will have admitted to you then, that she has entered into correspondence with the editor of *The Signalling Flame*?

ROSMER: Ah, you mean the note she had Ulrik Brendel take him.

KROLL: You're in the picture then. And you approve, of her making contact so with that scandalmonger, who week after week sets out to pillory me for my teaching and my political activities?

ROSMER: Dear friend, that aspect of it will never have occurred to her. Besides which of course, she's free to act entirely as she chooses, no less than I am.

KROLL: Indeed? Yes, it's all part no doubt of this new trend you're following now. Where you then stand, I take it Miss West stands alike?

ROSMER: She does. The two of us have worked our way forward together in mutual trust.

KROLL: (*Looks at him, and slowly shakes his head.*) Oh, you bewitched, unseeing man.

ROSMER: I am? How can you say that?

KROLL: Because I dare not – I will not think the worst. No, no; I must speak plainly. Rosmer…do you value my friendship at all? Or my high opinion? Do you?

ROSMER: That question needs no answering.

KROLL: Well, questions however there are that cry for answer: and full clarification on your part… Will you bear with me, if I examine a little as it were?

ROSMER: Examine?

KROLL: Yes, if I question you on a matter or two, you could find painful to recall? Because you see…this defection from your faith – well, your liberation as of course you call it: that is all of a piece with so much else, for which for your own sake you must account to me.

ROSMER: Dear friend, you ask anything. I have nothing to hide.

KROLL: Then tell me: in your honest opinion, for what reason ultimately did Beäta go out and end her life?

ROSMER: Can you be in any doubt there? Rather, are reasons at all to be sought, for the action of someone sick, unhappy, and unbalanced?

KROLL: Are you sure Beäta was so unbalanced as all that? The doctors anyway could not pronounce themselves so certain.

ROSMER: If the doctors had ever seen her as I so often saw her, night and day, they would have been in no doubt.

KROLL: Nor was I…at the time.

ROSMER: Oh no, I'm afraid there can be no doubting it at all, man. I've told you before of those frenzies of sensual abandon that would possess her…that she demanded I requite in kind. Oh, the terror she struck into me there! And then the utterly unjustified self-castigation that wasted her away, in her last years.

KROLL: Yes, once she had been told that she could never bear a child.

ROSMER: Well, you imagine… To be tortured by a cruel misery like that, for a plight she had done nothing to deserve. And she should be sane?

KROLL: Hm… Can you recall if at that time you had books in the house that treated of the purpose of marriage – according to the advanced opinion of our day?

ROSMER: I remember that Miss West did loan me one such work. She'd inherited old Doctor West's library, you know that. But, my dear Kroll, you don't for a moment believe we were ever so incautious as to let the poor sick woman learn of matters like that? You have my absolute assurance, we two are blameless. It was the nervous disorder in her own brain that set her faculties awry.

KROLL: One thing at least I can tell you now. Namely that the poor, tormented, overwrought Beäta made an end of her own life so that you could live happily…live in freedom and…after your desire.

ROSMER: (*Half-risen from the chair.*) What do you mean by that?

KROLL: Now you sit still and hear me, Rosmer. I can talk about this now. During the last year of her life she was at my house twice, bewailing her anguish and her despair.

ROSMER: On that subject?

KROLL: No. On the first occasion, she came in and asserted that you were on the way to becoming an unbeliever. That you were about to break with the faith of your fathers.

ROSMER: (*Heated.*) Kroll, that is not possible! Simply not possible! You have to be mistaken there.

KROLL: How so?

ROSMER: Because whilever Beäta was alive I was in
uncertainty still and conflict in myself. And all that fight,
I fought it through alone and in utter silence. I don't for a
moment think even Rebecca –

KROLL: Rebecca?

ROSMER: Well…Miss West, then. I call her Rebecca for
simplicity.

KROLL: I have observed.

ROSMER: So it is quite inconceivable to me, how Beäta
could have come by that notion at all. And why did she
not speak of it to me? That she never did. Never so much
as a word.

KROLL: Poor woman…she begged and entreated me, to
come and talk with you.

ROSMER: Then why did you not?

KROLL: Could I for a moment doubt it, but that she was
mentally disturbed? Making such accusation of a man like
you? …And then she came a second time: a month later,
it would be. On this occasion she seemed calmer. But as
she was leaving, she said: They can soon expect the White
Horse now at Rosmersholm.

ROSMER: Ay, yes, the White Horse; many a time she
mentioned that.

KROLL: And when I tried to wean her away from such
morbid thoughts, all she answered was: Time is short for
me now. John has to marry Rebecca right away.

ROSMER: (*All but speechless.*) What's that you say? Me,
marry – ?

KROLL: That was a Thursday afternoon… Saturday evening,
she threw herself from the footbridge into the millrace.

ROSMER: And you gave us no warning!

KROLL: You know well as I, the times she'd be hinting she
had not long to live.

ROSMER: I know that. All the same…you should have
warned us.

KROLL: I did think to do so. But by then it was too late.

ROSMER: But in all the time since, why haven't you…? Why
have you kept silent about all this?

KROLL: What good would I have done, coming here to pain and harrow you yet more? I truly took all that for vain deranged imagining of hers… Until last night.

ROSMER: And now no more?

KROLL: Beäta was lucid enough, was she not, when she said you were breaking with your faith into which you were born?

ROSMER: (*Gazing before him.*) Yes, that I do not understand. It's beyond all comprehension to me.

KROLL: Beyond comprehension or no, it is in this instance so. And Rosmer, now ask yourself this:…how much truth is there in what else she alleged? At the last, I mean?

ROSMER: Alleged? That was an allegation?

KROLL: You didn't observe perhaps the wording she used. She soon would be gone, she said… Because? Well?

ROSMER: Why, so that I could marry Rebecca…

KROLL: Her wording was not quite that. Beäta phrased it otherwise. She said: Time is short for me now. John has to marry Rebecca right away.

ROSMER: (*Looks at him a while; then stands.*) Now Kroll, I understand you.

KROLL: So? How do you answer?

ROSMER: (*Ever quiet, controlled.*) To so unspeakable a – ? There is no answer, but to show you the door.

KROLL: (*Standing.*) So be it.

ROSMER: (*Stands before him.*) Hear you me. For a year and more, ever since Beäta passed on, Rebecca West and I have lived by ourselves at Rosmersholm. All that while, you have known what Beäta alleged against us. Yet never have I for one moment observed your taking it ill, that Rebecca and I were living together in this house.

KROLL: I didn't know until last night, that we had an unbeliever here, co-habiting with a…an emancipated woman.

ROSMER: Ah…! You don't consider then, that where the unbeliever and the emancipated are, there can be chastity? You don't consider, they too can have a native impulse to morality?

KROLL: I wouldn't trust too much weight to a morality that hasn't its roots in religious faith.

ROSMER: And you include Rebecca and myself in that? And the relationship I and Rebecca have?

KROLL: I cannot in deference to the two of you depart from my conviction, that there'll be no great yawning gulf between Free Thinking and...hm.

ROSMER: And what?

KROLL: ...and Free Love...since you insist.

ROSMER: (*Softly.*) How you can say that to me! You, who have known me from my youngest days.

KROLL: For that very reason. I know how easily you let yourself be moulded by the company you keep. And this Rebecca of yours – Well, this Miss West – there is so little about her that we actually know. In a word, Rosmer: I'm not surrendering you. As to your part...you must strive to save yourself while you've yet time.

ROSMER: Save myself? How –

(*MRS HELSETH looks in at the door left.*)

What is it?

MRS HELSETH: Could I ask Madam please to come downstairs.

ROSMER: Madam is not up here.

MRS HELSETH: She's not? (*Looks about her.*) Well, that's strange.

(*She goes.*)

ROSMER: You were saying...?

KROLL: Now listen. Whatever took place in secret here while Beäta lived...and whatever is happening here now...I shall inquire into no further. No question but you were deeply unhappy in your marriage. Which goes some way in mitigation...

ROSMER: Oh, how little you know the man I am...

KROLL: Let me finish. What I do say is: if this ménage with Miss West is to continue, then it is absolutely imperative that you say nothing whatever of this sudden change in you...this grievous defection from your faith...into which she has seduced you. Let me speak! Let me speak! I tell you, if lunacy there must be, then for the Lord's sake subscribe to whatever views or tenets or beliefs you will, in the one sphere as in the other… Only keep your opinions to yourself. This is a purely private matter, after all. There is no need, for such things to be shouted the length of the land.

ROSMER: There is a need for me to come out from a position that is equivocal and false

KROLL: But you have a duty, Rosmer, to your heritage! Remember that! Since time beyond recall, Rosmersholm has stood as a bastion of discipline and good order; of respectful esteem for all those values upheld and sanctioned by the best in our society. The country all about has taken its character from Rosmersholm. It will provoke a tragic irremediable confusion, once it were put about that you of all men had broken with what I will call the Rosmer ethic.

ROSMER: Dear Kroll…I cannot share that view. I see before me a duty that I may not refuse: to touch to light and joy this place that the house of Rosmer has darkened and oppressed, these long long years.

KROLL: (*Looking at him with severity.*) Ay, there would be an apt ambition for that man, with whom his line dies out. I tell you, you leave well alone. Such a task is not for you. You were made for the quiet scholar's life.

ROSMER: Yes, could well be. But now I want into the turmoil of life for once, I too.

KROLL: Turmoil of life: you know what that will mean for you? It will mean a fight to the death, with all who have been your friends.

ROSMER: (*Quietly.*) I doubt if they're all such bigots as you.

KROLL: You're a naive being, Rosmer. A being unversed in the world, you are. You've no conception of the raging storm that will break upon your head.

(*MRS HELSETH glances in at the door left.*)

MRS HELSETH: Madam says I'm to ask you…

ROSMER: What is it?

MRS HELSETH: There's a man downstairs, wanting a word with Your Reverence.

ROSMER: The man who was here last night, I suppose?

MRS HELSETH: No, it's that Mortensgård.

ROSMER: Mortensgård!

KROLL: Ah! Far as that are we gone! Far already as that!

ROSMER: What does he want of me? Why didn't you send him on his way?

MRS HELSETH: Madam said I was to ask you if he might come up.

ROSMER: Tell him I'm with someone –

KROLL: (*To MRS HELSETH.*) Just let him in, Mrs Helseth.
(*MRS HELSETH goes. KROLL takes up his hat.*)
I quit the field…for now. The battle itself is yet to come.

ROSMER: Kroll, as I live…I have no dealings with Mortensgård.

KROLL: I don't believe you any more. Not on any matter. From now in whatever connection, your word is of no worth with me. From this day on, the knives are out. We'll do our best that's all, to make you harmless.

ROSMER: Oh, Kroll: how deep…how low you are fallen.

KROLL: I? You should speak for yourself. Remember Beäta!

ROSMER: Ever harking back to that.

KROLL: No. The mystery of the millrace is for you to fathom: after your own conscience. If such a faculty you still possess.
(*At the door left, MORTENSGÅRD enters softly and without a sound. He's a slight little man, with thin reddish hair and beard. KROLL visits on him a look of loathing.*)
So our *Signalling Flame,* no less… Alight at Rosmersholm. (*Buttoning his coat.*) Yes, no doubting now, what course I shall adopt.

MORTENSGÅRD: (*Conciliatory.*) *The Signalling Flame* shall always light the Doctor home.

KROLL: Ay, and evidence have we long seen, Sir, of your good will. There exists a Commandment, forbidding false witness against one's neighbour…

MORTENSGÅRD: I don't need our School Principal's instruction in the Ten Commandments.

KROLL: Not in the Seventh, even?

ROSMER: Kroll – !

MORTENSGÅRD: I'll come to His Reverence when I need that.

KROLL: (*With masked sarcasm.*) His Reverence? Oh yes, unarguably, in that regard His Reverence is very much your man. Enjoy a profitable meeting, gentlemen.
(*He goes out, and slams the door behind him.*)

ROSMER: (*Looks at the closed door a while, and speaks to himself.*) Well well…so that's that. (*Turns.*) Please say what it is, Mr Mortensgård, that brings you here.

MORTENSGÅRD: It was really Miss West I came to see. I felt I should thank her for her kind letter to me yesterday.

ROSMER: I know she wrote to you. You were able to speak with her?

MORTENSGÅRD: Briefly, yes. (*With a little smile.*) I'm told, one way and another, attitudes are changed out here at Rosmersholm.

ROSMER: My attitudes are very much changed. One might almost say…in every regard.

MORTENSGÅRD: So the lady said. For which reason she thought I should come up and have a word with Your Reverence about the matter.

ROSMER: About which matter, Mr Mortensgård?

MORTENSGÅRD: May I have your leave to announce in *The Signalling Flame,* that you have come to a different way of thinking…and that you now espouse Free Thought and the progressive cause?

ROSMER: That you certainly may. Indeed I urge you to announce as much.

MORTENSGÅRD: It'll appear tomorrow morning, then. It will be great, momentous news, that Parson Rosmer of Rosmersholm deems himself able to champion the cause of light, also in this other sense.

ROSMER: I don't know that I follow you, Sir.

MORTENSGÅRD: I'm saying, that it enhances our party's moral standing, every time we win a truly Christian spirit to our side.

ROSMER: (*Somewhat surprised.*) You don't know, then…? Has
Miss West not told you?

MORTENSGÅRD: What, Sir? The lady was in some hurry.
She said I must go on up and hear the rest from yourself.

ROSMER: Well, then I will tell you: that I have set myself
absolutely free. In every sense. I stand emancipated now
from all the teachings of the Church. They shall affect me
in the slightest not ever again.

MORTENSGÅRD: (*Looks at him in bewilderment.*) No…the sky
could fall in, and not surprise me m – … The Parson, no
less, declares himself free…!

ROSMER: Yes, my position now is, what your position long
has been. That also you may publish tomorrow in *The
Signalling Flame.*

MORTENSGÅRD: That too? No, my dear Parson Rosmer
I'm sorry: but that aspect of it is best not touched upon.

ROSMER: Not touched upon?!

MORTENSGÅRD: To begin with, I mean.

ROSMER: I don't follow…

MORTENSGÅRD: Well, you see, Sir… You'll not be so
familiar with all the implications as I am, it's fair to say. But
now that you've come over to the way of Free Thought…
and now that, so Miss West tells me, you wish to be active
in the movement…you do so presumably in the desire to
serve the cause and the movement in every way you can.

ROSMER: Yes, that is very much my wish.

MORTENSGÅRD: Well; then I can only tell you, Sir, if
you come into the open with this about your quitting the
Church, you'll be tying your own hands from the start.

ROSMER: You think so?

MORTENSGÅRD: Yes, I can tell you, Sir, there's not much
then that you'll be able to achieve in this part of the world.
Besides which…we've Freethinkers enough, Sir. I almost
said, we've far too many of their kind. No, what the party
needs are the Christian elements: something everybody
has to respect. There, we're desperately short. So your best
counsel, Sir, will be silence, on all except the public issues.
If you want my opinion.

ROSMER: I see. You'd be reluctant to involve yourself with me, as an avowed defector from the Church?

MORTENSGÅRD: (*Shakes his head.*) It's more than I dare, Sir. I've made it my working principle of late, never to support any anti-clerical cause or individual.

ROSMER: Are you yourself of late returned to the Church?

MORTENSGÅRD: That's quite another matter.

ROSMER: So, there's how it is. Yes, I take your meaning now.

MORTENSGÅRD: Your Reverence…you would do well to remember, that I…I, particularly…am not free to act entirely as I choose.

ROSMER: Why, what constrains you?

MORTENSGÅRD: What constrains me is the mark I bear.

ROSMER: Ah…of course.

MORTENSGÅRD: The mark I bear, Your Reverence. As you, of all men, would do best to remember. Since you it was, Sir, first and before any, had me marked as I am.

ROSMER: Had I stood then, where I stand now, I should have treated your trespass with better caution.

MORTENSGÅRD: I don't doubt. But the time's long gone for that. Your mark abides, Sir. I carry it all my days. Not that you've any conception Sir, what that can do to a man. Though I reckon Your Reverence could be feeling the sharp end himself before long.

ROSMER: I could?

MORTENSGÅRD: Yes. You don't believe for a moment, do you, that Principal Kroll and his circle will forgive you a defection such as yours? Their *County Newsletter* is threatening a pretty savage line, I'm told. Depend on it, Sir: from now, you'll find yourself a marked man in your turn.

ROSMER: Mr Mortensgård, I fear no assault on any aspect of my private life. My conduct is above reproof.

MORTENSGÅRD: (*With an arch smile.*) Your Reverence, you make a large claim there.

ROSMER: I'm sure I do. I have the right to claim as much.

MORTENSGÅRD: Even if you were to rake through your own conduct as thoroughly, as once you raked through mine?

ROSMER: You say that so curiously. To what might your allusion be? Is it something specific?

MORTENSGÅRD: Yes, it is one specific matter. Only the one. But that could spell trouble for you, should malicious opponents come to know of it.

ROSMER: Be so good as to tell me then, what this might be.

MORTENSGÅRD: Can Your Reverence not guess it for himself?

ROSMER: No, not at all. I have no idea.

MORTENSGÅRD: Well then, it seems I have to be direct with you... I have in my keeping a remarkable letter, that was written here at Rosmersholm.

ROSMER: The letter from Miss West, you mean? Is that so remarkable?

MORTENSGÅRD: No, that letter's not. But I did once receive an other letter from the Parsonage here.

ROSMER: Also from Miss West?

MORTENSGÅRD: No, Sir.

ROSMER: Well, from whom then? From whom?

MORTENSGÅRD: From the late Mrs Rosmer.

ROSMER: From my wife?! Had you a letter from my wife?!

MORTENSGÅRD: Yes, that is so.

ROSMER: When?

MORTENSGÅRD: It was toward the end of the late Mrs Rosmer's life. I'd say it was some eighteen months ago. And that is the letter that is so remarkable.

ROSMER: You are aware that my wife at that time was mentally unwell.

MORTENSGÅRD: Yes, I know that there were many who believed so. But I wouldn't say that was apparent from the letter. When I describe the letter as remarkable, I mean so in a different sense.

ROSMER: And what in the world could my poor wife have found to put in a letter to you?

MORTENSGÅRD: I have the letter at home. She begins to this effect, that she lives in terror and appalling fear. Because, she says, there are in these parts so many evil people. And those people Sir, intend you only hurt and harm.

ROSMER: Me?

MORTENSGÅRD: Yes, that's what she says. Now comes what's most remarkable of all. Shall I spell it out, Your Reverence?

ROSMER: Certainly. All of it. Keep nothing from me.

MORTENSGÅRD: The late Mrs Rosmer begs and entreats of me, to be large-hearted. She is aware, she says, Your Reverence it was, had me removed from my teaching-post. And she so passionately pleads with me, not to be vindictive.

ROSMER: In what way then did she think it possible for you, to be vindictive?

MORTENSGÅRD: It says in the letter, that should talk reach me, of sinful doing at Rosmersholm, I am to place no credence in a word of it; it would only be wicked people, spreading it about to cause yourself unhappiness.

ROSMER: The letter says that!

MORTENSGÅRD: Your Reverence may read it for himself, at any time.

ROSMER: But I don't understand…! What did she imagine then, these evil rumours were?

MORTENSGÅRD: First, to the effect that Your Reverence was about to renounce his childhood faith. To that, the lady quite categorically gave the lie…at the time. Next…hm.

ROSMER: Next?

MORTENSGÅRD: Well, next she writes – and this is somewhat confused – that there is to her knowledge no sinful relationship at Rosmersholm. That never has one single wrong been done against her. And if talk should emerge to that effect, then she implores me to make no mention of it in my paper.

ROSMER: Does she name any names?

MORTENSGÅRD: No.

ROSMER: Who brought you this letter?

MORTENSGÅRD: I have promised not to say. It was brought in to me one evening in the twilight.

ROSMER: If you'd made inquiries then and there, you'd have learned that my poor unhappy wife was not entirely in her right mind.

MORTENSGÅRD: I did so inquire, Sir. I have to say, such is
not the impression I received.

ROSMER: It's not?... Why though do you choose to
enlighten me now, as to this old demented letter?

MORTENSGÅRD: As a counsel to you, Parson Rosmer, to
take the utmost care.

ROSMER: In my private life, you mean?

MORTENSGÅRD: Yes. You need to bear in mind, you're out
of sanctuary now.

ROSMER: You persist in your opinion then, that there is
something to be hidden here?

MORTENSGÅRD: I see no reason, why a liberated man
should deny himself all possible fulfilment in his life. Only
as I say, take care from this day on. It needs but some talk
or other to set the reactionaries' teeth on edge, and you can
be sure the whole cause of liberation will be reaping the
cost. Goodbye, Parson Rosmer.

ROSMER: Goodbye.

MORTENSGÅRD: I'll be away then, straight to the printing
house, to put the great story in *The Signalling Flame*.

ROSMER: The whole story.

MORTENSGÅRD: As much of the story, as good people
need to know.

(*He bows, and leaves. ROSMER stands in the doorway,
waiting as the other descends the stairs. Sound of the closing of
the outer door.*)

ROSMER: (*In the doorway, calls quietly.*) Rebecca! Re – Hm.
(*Loud.*) Mrs Helseth, is Miss West not down there?

MRS HELSETH: (*Heard in the porch below.*) No, Your
Reverence, she isn't here.
(*The curtain at the back is drawn aside. In the doorway there,
REBECCA is revealed.*)

REBECCA: John!

ROSMER: (*Turns.*) What? You were in my bedroom? My
dear, what were you doing there?

REBECCA: (*Comes toward him.*) I was listening.

ROSMER: But Rebecca, how could you do that?

REBECCA: I could, that's all. He said that so detestably:
about my being not yet dressed...

ROSMER: Ah, so you were in there even while Kroll –

REBECCA: Yes. I wanted to know what he was up to.

ROSMER: I would have told you all that.

REBECCA: You'd hardly have told me everything. And certainly not in his own words.

ROSMER: So you heard it all.

REBECCA: Most, I think. I had to go downstairs a moment, when Mortensgård came.

ROSMER: And then back up again...

REBECCA: Don't let it make you cross, dear friend.

ROSMER: My dear, you must do as to you seems right and proper. You know you're free to do as you choose... But what do you say to it, Rebecca? Oh, I don't think I've ever had such need of you as now.

REBECCA: You and I have been long ready, for what one day had to come.

ROSMER: No, no: not for this.

REBECCA: Not for this?

ROSMER: I did expect, soon or late, our beautiful pure friendship might be misprised and misrepresented. Not by Kroll. I could never have imagined the like from him. From all the others I could, with their crude thinking and ignoble vision. Oh, Rebecca...I had indeed good cause, to shroud our bond so jealously from others' sight. Our secret had danger in it.

REBECCA: Oh, what should it trouble us, how all those other people judge us? We are sure in ourselves, we have no cause for guilt.

ROSMER: I? No cause for guilt? Ay, so I truly believed: up to this very day. But now, Rebecca, now...

REBECCA: Yes, now what?

ROSMER: How am I to account for Beäta's appalling indictment?

REBECCA: (*In outcry.*) Oh, don't talk about Beäta! Don't think about Beäta! You had left her quite behind you, with the dead!

ROSMER: But now I know this, and she seems eerily alive again.

REBECCA: Oh no...you mustn't think that, John. You must not!

ROSMER: Well, I'm telling you. We have to delve to the truth of this. How could her thinking take so wrong a turn, and she so tragically misunderstand?

REBECCA: So you're beginning to doubt it yourself, that she was virtually insane?

ROSMER: Oh, Rebecca…that is just what I can not be so sure of any more. In any case…suppose she were…

REBECCA: Suppose? Yes, well?

ROSMER: I'm saying: where are we to look for the cause itself, that provoked her morbid state into insanity at all?

REBECCA: Oh, what good can it do now, to waste yourself in such broodings as these?

ROSMER: I cannot help it, Rebecca. The doubt is gnawing at me, and for all I yearn to, I cannot leave it be.

REBECCA: Oh, but it can be dangerous to do, this ceaseless circling around the one same deathly thought.

ROSMER: (*Pacing restless and thoughtful about the room.*) I must have betrayed myself somehow. She must have noticed, from the time you came to us, how happy I began to be.

REBECCA: Yes, my dear, but even so…!

ROSMER: You'll see; Rebecca, it won't have escaped her, that we would read the same books. That we would seek each other's company, and discuss all the new thinking. But I do not understand it! Such pains I took, to shield her from it all. Now I think back, I'd say I went out of my way to keep her quite apart from everything we shared. Or am I wrong, Rebecca?

REBECCA: No, no, of course you did.

ROSMER: And you the same. And yet, for all that… Oh, the thought of this is appalling! How she must have gone about here: sick in her love…with never, never a word…watching us…observing all we did, and…and misconstruing all of it.

REBECCA: (*Wringing her hands.*) Oh, I should have never come to Rosmersholm.

ROSMER: Imagine only, the silent suffering hers must have been. All that ugliness, that she in her sick brain was able to amass and build around the two of us… She mentioned nothing to you ever, that might have given you a glimpse of that?

REBECCA: (*As though one startled.*) To me? Do you believe I would have stayed here one more day?

ROSMER: No, no, it goes without saying... Oh, what a fight must she have fought. And fought, Rebecca, alone. Despairing and utterly alone... Till at the last that cruel... accusing victory: in the millrace there.

(*He hurls himself down in the chair at the desk, rests his elbows upon its surface, and covers his face in his hands.*)

REBECCA: (*Approaches carefully behind him.*) John, now you listen to me. If it stood in your power to call Beäta back: to you; to Rosmersholm...would you do so?

ROSMER: Oh, how do I know, what I would or would not do? I can be thinking of this and this only: what is gone beyond recalling.

REBECCA: John, you should have been beginning now to live. Already you had begun. You had set yourself free: in every sense. You were feeling so joyous, so easy....

ROSMER: Ay, Rebecca, that I was... And now this crushing weight is come.

REBECCA: (*Resting her arms upon the chairback behind him.*) How lovely it was, when we would sit in the room down there in the twilight. And we'd help each other plan our new lives. You were to take hold on real living: the real life of our time, you said. You would make your way from household to household, a guest that comes to set all free. Winning their minds and their will to your cause. Raising all about us to nobility. Wider yet and wider the circle would reach. Nobility.

ROSMER: A nobility of joy.

REBECCA: Yes, joy.

ROSMER: For joy it is, Rebecca, that raises our spirit to nobility.

REBECCA: Do you not think...pain too? Great pain?

ROSMER: Surely: when once we win through it. Vanquish it. Transcend it.

REBECCA: It's that, you must.

ROSMER: (*Sadly shaking his head.*) This I can never transcend…entirely. There'll always be some doubt remaining. A question. Never again shall I come to exult in that, that makes of life so wonderful a loveliness to live.

REBECCA: (*Leaning over the chairback, softly speaking.*) What, John, do you say that is?

ROSMER: (*Looks up at her.*) Our quiet, joyful innocence.

REBECCA: (*A step back.*) Yes. Innocence.

(*A short silence.*)

ROSMER: (*Elbows on the desk, rests his head upon his hands and gazes before him.*) And the way her logic connected it all. So methodical, how she put it all together. First she begins to nourish doubt, how sound my faith. How could that thought have come to her so early on? Yet come it did. And it grew to a certainty. From there… Ay, she'd easily find the rest of it all too conceivable then. (*Sits up in the chair, and passes his hands through his hair.*) Oh, all these wild imaginings! I shall never be quit of them. I see that very clear. I know it. Out from nothing, they'll come charging to remind me of the dead.

REBECCA: Like the white horse of Rosmersholm.

ROSMER: Yes, like that. Seething in from the dark. In the stillness.

REBECCA: And all for this morbid web of fantasy, you'll let real living slip from you, no sooner than you had it in your grasp.

ROSMER: It's sad, you're right. Sad, Rebecca. But I've no choosing. How could I hope to transcend all this?

REBECCA: (*Behind the chair.*) By building new relationships.

ROSMER: (*With a start, looking up.*) New relationships?

REBECCA: Yes, new relationships with the world outside you. Life, work, activity. Not sitting here musing and brooding on unfathomable mysteries.

ROSMER: (*Standing.*) New relationships… (*Moves away across the room, pauses before the door, then comes back.*) A question does occur to me. Rebecca, have you asked yourself this question too?

REBECCA: (*Can barely breathe.*) Tell me…what question…it is.

ROSMER: How do you see our relationship shaping after
today?

REBECCA: Come what may, I believe our friendship has in
it to endure.

ROSMER: Yes, but I wasn't meaning quite that. Rather,
what it was in the beginning that brought you and me
together…what it is that binds us so intensely now: our
faith we share, in the life together a man and a woman can
lead in purity…

REBECCA: Yes, yes: so?

ROSMER: I mean, that a relationship such as that…like ours,
indeed: is not that the one best sorted to a quiet, happy,
peaceful existence…?

REBECCA: Go on.

ROSMER: Instead though, what's opening up before me
now is a life of conflict and unrest and powerful feelings.
For live my life I shall, Rebecca! I'll not allow sinister
possibilities to bring me down. I'll not allow my course
on earth to be dictated for me by the living or the…or by
anyone else.

REBECCA: No, no: you mustn't let that happen. John, you
have to be absolutely free!

ROSMER: But you know what I'm thinking, don't you? You
do see, how best I can win release from all these gnawing
memories; from all the miserable past?

REBECCA: Say.

ROSMER: By establishing against it a new, and living reality.

REBECCA: (*Groping for the chairback.*) A living… What do you
mean…by that?

ROSMER: (*Closer.*) Rebecca…if I were to ask you will you
be my second wife?

REBECCA: (*A moment speechless, lets out a shriek of gladness.*)
Your wife! Yours…! Me!

ROSMER: Fine. Let us try it. We two shall be one. The space
left by the dead here shall be empty no more.

REBECCA: I…in Beäta's place…

ROSMER: Then she's out of the story. Out altogether. For
ever and all time.

REBECCA: (*Softly, tremulous.*) John, do you believe that?

ROSMER: It has to be so. It has to be. I cannot – I will not go through life with a corpse on my back. Help me, Rebecca, cast it from me. And let us, in our freedom, our bliss, our passion, still all memories to rest. You'll be my only wife I ever had.

REBECCA: (*Controlled.*) Don't ever mention this again. I shall never be your wife.

ROSMER: What? Never? Oh, don't you think then, that you could come to love me? In our friendship already is there not a touch of love?

REBECCA: (*Stopping her ears as in terror.*) Don't say that, John! Don't ever talk like that!

ROSMER: (*Seizing her by the arm.*) Oh yes, oh yes: our bond does have in it the tender beginnings. I can see you feel as I do! Rebecca, don't you?

REBECCA: (*Secure and composed again.*) Now you listen. I'm telling you: you persist in this, and I leave Rosmersholm.

ROSMER: Leave? You? You can't do that. It's not possible!

REBECCA: It's even less possible for me to be your wife. Never in this world can I be that.

ROSMER: (*Looks at her in astonishment.*) 'Never can', you say. And say it in so strange a tone. Why can you not?

REBECCA: (*Seizes his hands.*) Dear friend…for your sake and for mine…do not ask why. (*Lets go of him.*) There's an end of it, John.

ROSMER: No other question can I ever ask from now but: why?

REBECCA: (*Turns and looks at him.*) Then it's finished.

ROSMER: Between you and me?

REBECCA: Yes.

ROSMER: It shall never be finished between us. You're never leaving Rosmersholm.

REBECCA: (*Her hand on the doorknob.*) No, I might well not. But you ask that of me once more…then it's none the less finished.

ROSMER: None the less finished? How?

REBECCA: Well, friend, because then I'll take the way Beäta went. Now, John, you know.

ROSMER: Rebecca…

REBECCA: (*In the doorway, slowly nodding.*) Now you know. (*She goes.*)

ROSMER: (*Staring bewildered at the closed door, and speaking to himself.*) What…is…this?

End of Act Two.

ACT THREE

The living-room of Act One. The window and the door to the veranda-porch stand open. Outside, the morning sun is shining.

REBECCA WEST, dressed as in Act One, stands at the window, watering and arranging the flowers. Her crochet shawl lies on the easy chair. MRS HELSETH goes around with a feather-duster, busying herself about the furniture.

REBECCA: (*After a short while.*) It's strange, His Reverence staying upstairs today so long.

MRS HELSETH Oh, he often does that. I expect he'll soon be down.

REBECCA: Have you seen him at all?

MRS HELSETH: A glimpse, when I went up with his coffee. He was moving about in his bedroom getting dressed.

REBECCA: I ask, because yesterday he wasn't too well.

MRS HELSETH: No, he didn't look it. I'm wondering, is there something not right between him and his brother-in-law.

REBECCA: Such as what, would you say?

MRS HELSETH: I can't tell. Perhaps it's that Mortensgård has set the two of them at odds.

REBECCA: It could well be, that. Do you know this Peter Mortensgård at all?

MRS HELSETH: I should say not. How can Madam think that of me? A one like him?

REBECCA: You mean, because he publishes that nasty paper.

MRS HELSETH: Oh, it's not only that… Madam must have heard, he had a child to a married woman whose husband had left her?

REBECCA: I've heard it said. But surely that was long ago, before I came here.

MRS HELSETH: Lord yes, he was only a lad at the time. And she should have shown the better sense. Married her, too, he would have done. Only he couldn't be allowed. So it cost him dear enough… My word though, how he's

160

made his way up in the world since then, that man. He's someone very much sought after now.

REBECCA: Most of the poorer folk do turn to him first, when they're in any trouble.

MRS HELSETH: Oh, not only the poor folk, either…

REBECCA: (*Casting her a covert glance.*) No?

MRS HELSETH: (*At the sofa, dusts and brushes vigorously.*) There'll be other folk too Miss, as you'd least expect.

REBECCA: (*Arranging the flowers.*) Oh, that's only a notion you have, Mrs Helseth. You now, could never be so certain of something like that.

MRS HELSETH: Does Madam think then, I can't know? I can, at that. Because – since I might as well tell you – I once delivered a letter to Mortensgård myself.

REBECCA: (*Turns.*) No…you did?!

MRS HELSETH: Yes, that I did. And that letter what's more had been written here at Rosmersholm.

REBECCA: Mrs Helseth, really?

MRS HELSETH: God's own truth, it was. And fine paper it was written on. And fine red wax on its outside to seal it too.

REBECCA: And you were entrusted to deliver it? Well, my dear Mrs Helseth, it's no great guess then, who the sender was.

MRS HELSETH: So?

REBECCA: It was obviously something the poor Mrs Rosmer, in her sickness –

MRS HELSETH: It's Miss West saying that, not I.

REBECCA: Then what did the letter say? Oh, I was forgetting: you could never know that.

MRS HELSETH: Hm, could be I might know it all the same.

REBECCA: She told you what she'd written?

MRS HELSETH: No, she didn't do that exactly. But that Mortensgård, when he'd read it, he started asking me questions all ways, till I had a pretty good idea of what the letter said.

REBECCA: What do you think then, the letter said? Oh, dear sweet Mrs Helseth, do tell me.

MRS HELSETH: Oh no, Miss. Not for the world.

REBECCA: Oh, but you can tell me. You and I are such good friends.

MRS HELSETH: God forbid Miss I should breathe a word to you about it. All I can say, it was something nasty they'd gone and made the poor sick lady believe.

REBECCA: Who had made her believe?

MRS HELSETH: Wicked people, Miss West. Wicked people.

REBECCA: Wicked…?

MRS HELSETH: Yes, and I say it again. Right wicked people they needed to be.

REBECCA: And who do you think they possibly were?

MRS HELSETH: Oh I know who I think, all right. Though the Good Lord seal my lips. Not that there isn't one lady I could mention, about in the town there…hm!

REBECCA: You obviously mean Mrs Kroll.

MRS HELSETH: Oh, that woman, she's a one. She's always been so uppity with me. And she's never had any time for you, ma'am.

REBECCA: Do you think, when Mrs Rosmer wrote Mortensgård that letter, that she was altogether in her right mind?

MRS HELSETH: You can never tell, Miss, with the mind. I wouldn't say though she was that far gone.

REBECCA: But it had quite unhinged her surely, learning she could never have a child. That was when the madness first broke out.

MRS HELSETH: Ay, poor lady, she took that very hard.

REBECCA: (*Takes up her crochetwork, and sits in the armchair at the window.*) In any case…don't you think Mrs Helseth, all told, for His Reverence it was just as well?

MRS HELSETH: What, Miss?

REBECCA: That here no child was born. What?

MRS HELSETH: Mm, I don't rightly know, what to answer to that.

REBECCA: Come on, you can trust me. It was best for him. Parson Rosmer's not a man to put up with the crying of children.

MRS HELSETH: At Rosmersholm Miss, the babies don't cry.

REBECCA: They don't cry?

MRS HELSETH: No. Here at the Parsonage the babies have never been ones to cry, not since folk can remember.

REBECCA: That would be strange.

MRS HELSETH: Yes, isn't it strange? But it goes in the family. And I tell you something else that's strange. Once they're grown up, they don't ever laugh. Don't ever laugh, in all their days.

REBECCA: Now that I can not believe…

MRS HELSETH: Has Madam ever heard or seen His Reverence once laugh?

REBECCA: No: now I think…you could well be right. But I'd say they none of them seem a people much for laughing in this part of the world.

MRS HELSETH: That they're not. People say, that that all started from this house. And then it spread from here, that too, I reckon, like a sort of contagion.

REBECCA: You're a deep-seeing woman, you are, Mrs Helseth.

MRS HELSETH: Oh, don't Madam sit and make a mock of me… (*Listening.*) Sh, sh…here's His Reverence coming down. He doesn't like to see the feather-brush in here.
(*She goes out through the door right.*
JOHN ROSMER, with stick and hat in hand, comes in from the porch.)

ROSMER: Good morning, Rebecca.

REBECCA: Good morning, my dear. (*After a moment, crocheting.*) You're away out?

ROSMER: Yes.

REBECCA: It is such a lovely day.

ROSMER: You didn't come up to see me this morning.

REBECCA: No: I didn't. Not today.

ROSMER: Won't you be doing that again, from now?

REBECCA: Oh I don't know yet, John.

ROSMER: Is there anything come for me?

REBECCA: The *County Newsletter* has come.

ROSMER: Kroll's paper…!

REBECCA: It's on the table there.

ROSMER: (*Sets hat and stick down.*) Is there anything…

REBECCA: Yes.

ROSMER: And you didn't send it on up –

REBECCA: You'll be reading it soon enough.

ROSMER: I see. (*He takes the paper, and reads it, standing at the table.*) …What? '…cannot counsel caution enough against spineless turncoats.' (*Looks across at her.*) They're calling me a turncoat, Rebecca.

REBECCA: No names are named.

ROSMER: Need there be? '…secret betrayers of what's good and true… Souls of Judas, who brazenly boast at their defection, as soon as they deem the moment timely and most advantageous.' '…Insensate onslaught on a venerable heritage…' … '…in expectation that those presently in power shall not come scant of due reward…' (*Rests the paper on the table.*) This they write of me. Those who have known me so long and so closely. This, that they themselves do not believe. This, that they know has in it not one word of truth…yet write it none the less.

REBECCA: There's more yet.

ROSMER: (*Takes up the paper again.*) … '…naivety of judgment some excuse…' … '…baleful influence… reaching perhaps into further areas of life, that we will not for the present expose to comment or censure…' … (*Looks at her.*) What's this?

REBECCA: An allusion to me, it would seem.

ROSMER: (*Puts the paper from him.*) Rebecca, this is the doing of dishonourable men.

REBECCA: Yes, I'd say they've not much cause to preach at Mortensgård.

ROSMER: (*Moves about the room.*) This has to be put straight. If this continues, everything good in people will be lost. But it shall not be so! Oh, the joy…the joy I should feel, if I could bring some little light to all this dismal ugliness.

REBECCA: Yes, John, that's right! In this can be your great and glorious life-cause!

ROSMER: Imagine, if I could waken them, to know themselves. Could bring them to remorse, and shame at what they are. Could have them draw toward each other in forbearance: in love, Rebecca…

REBECCA: Yes, pledge your powers only to that, and see, you shall prevail.

ROSMER: I'm sure it must be possible. Oh, what bliss would it be then to be alive. No strife of hatreds any more. Only the rivalry of friends. All eyes toward the one same goal. Each human will, each human mind urging forward… upward…each by the path that his own nature demands. The happiness of all: achieved by all. (*He's at the window, looking out. He awakens with a start, and sadly says.*) Ah! But not achieved by me.

REBECCA: No…? Not by you?

ROSMER: And not for me to know.

REBECCA: Oh, John, don't begin to doubt yourself so!

ROSMER: Happiness, dear Rebecca…happiness is, above and before all, that quiet, joyful certainty, we are guilt-free.

REBECCA: (*Gazing before her.*) Ay, all this about guilt…

ROSMER: Oh, little you know of it, to judge. But I…

REBECCA: You least of any!

ROSMER: (*Points out through the window.*) The millrace there.

REBECCA: Oh, John…!

(*MRS HELSETH looks in at the door right.*)

MRS HELSETH: Miss!

REBECCA: Later, later. Not now.

MRS HELSETH: Just a word, Miss.

(*REBECCA goes to the door. MRS HELSETH says something to her. They talk in whispers a moment. MRS HELSETH nods and goes.*)

ROSMER: (*Uneasy.*) Was that something for me?

REBECCA: No, just household matters. Now you should be going out in the fresh air, John dear. You ought to take a good long walk today.

ROSMER: (*Taking his hat.*) Yes, come on. We'll go together.

REBECCA: No, my dear. I can't right now. You must go by yourself. But you must shake all this morbid thinking from you. Promise me that.

ROSMER: I'll never shake free of it, I fear.

REBECCA: Oh, that something groundless as this can have you in its power so...!

ROSMER: Alas...it's not all that groundless, Rebecca. I've lain awake the night long, turning this over and over in my mind. Perhaps after all Beäta did see true.

REBECCA: True in what?

ROSMER: Saw true, in thinking Rebecca that I was in love with you.

REBECCA: Saw true in that?!

ROSMER: (*Rests his hat on the table.*) I'm tormented with this one question: whether the two of us have not all along been deceiving ourselves...in calling what we have a friendship.

REBECCA: You're not saying, it could as well be called –

ROSMER: – a love relationship. Yes, Rebecca, I do say that. Even while Beäta still lived, my thought was all of you. You only it was, I hungered for. It was in your company, I felt that quiet, rapturous joy, beyond all flesh. When we consider it, Rebecca, honestly...our life together began as a sweet sharing of secrets, like two little children falling in love. No urges, no dreams. Were not those your feelings too? Tell me so.

REBECCA: (*In conflict with herself.*) Oh... I don't know, how I am to answer you.

ROSMER: And this intensity of our living, each in the other and for the other, we have taken for friendship. No, Rebecca: what you and I have, has been a spiritual marriage...perhaps from the very first days. Therefore now this guilt in me. Because I had title to none of that: no right, because of Beäta.

REBECCA: No right to live in happiness? John, do you believe that?

ROSMER: She looked on the pair of us, as her own way of loving saw. Adjudged the pair of us, as her own way of loving was. How else? She could not judge us otherwise, than as she did.

REBECCA: But how can you chastise yourself, for Beäta's delusions?

ROSMER: For love of me – after her way of it – she went into the millrace there. That fact stands sure, Rebecca. I've no escaping that.

REBECCA: Oh, think of nothing but the great and beautiful task, to which you've pledged your life!

ROSMER: (*Shaking his head.*) That can never be achieved, Rebecca. Not by me. Not knowing as I now know.

REBECCA: Why not by you?

ROSMER: Because there can never be victory for a cause, that has its beginnings in guilt.

REBECCA: (*Crying out.*) Oh, all this is Rosmer doubt, Rosmer anxiety, Rosmer scruple. They say hereabouts the dead come back as white charging horses. I think this here is something such.

ROSMER: No matter what it is. What odds to me what, if I can never free myself from it? Believe you me, Rebecca. It's as I say. The cause that shall win through to lasting victory…demands for its champion a man joyful and free of guilt.

REBECCA: Is this joyfulness then so very essential to you, John?

ROSMER: Joyfulness? Oh yes, Rebecca…indeed it is.

REBECCA: For you, who never can laugh?

ROSMER: Even so. Believe me, I have a great capacity for joy.

REBECCA: Well, off you go now, my dear. A long walk… really far. You hear that? …Here is your hat, look. And here is your stick.

ROSMER: (*Taking both.*) Thank you. You're not coming then?

REBECCA: No, no, I can't just now.

ROSMER: Very well then. But you are with me nonetheless.
(*He goes out through the porch. REBECCA watches discreetly after him, through the open doorway. Then she goes to the door right.*)

REBECCA: (*Opens, and speaks in a low voice.*) All right then, Mrs Helseth. You can let him in now.
(*She moves away, toward the window.*
Soon Principal KROLL enters at the right. He bows in silence without a word, and keeps his hat in his hand.)

167

KROLL: He's gone then?

REBECCA: Yes.

KROLL: Is he out long usually?

REBECCA: Oh yes. But he's in such an unpredictable state today. So if you don't wish to meet him –

KROLL: I don't, I don't. It is yourself with whom I wish to speak. And quite alone.

REBECCA: Then it's best we make use of the time. Do be seated, Doctor Kroll Sir.

(*She sits in the armchair at the window. Principal KROLL sits on a chair to the side of her.*)

KROLL: Miss West…you can scarce imagine, how deep I am hurt in the heart: at this total change, that has befallen John Rosmer.

REBECCA: We were prepared for you to be so: at the first.

KROLL: At the first only?

REBECCA: John lived in the sure and certain hope, in time you would wish to join him.

KROLL: I would?!

REBECCA: You and all his other friends.

KROLL: Well, that shows you. How feeble his judgment, when it comes to people, and situations of real life.

REBECCA: In any case…now that he feels it a prime necessity to set himself entirely free –

KROLL: Yes but look: it's just that, that I do not believe.

REBECCA: What do you then believe?

KROLL: I believe it is yourself, the force behind all this.

REBECCA: You have that from your wife, Doctor Kroll.

KROLL: It's of no consequence from whom I have it. What is for sure, I entertain a profound suspicion – a most profound suspicion, I have to say – when I consider and weigh the sum of your conduct since your coming here.

REBECCA: (*Looks at him.*) Dear Principal, I seem to recollect, time was you entertained a most profound belief in me. An ardent belief in me, I could almost say.

KROLL: (*Subdued.*) On whom could your sorcery fail: once you were so minded?

REBECCA: So minded?

KROLL: Yes, as you were. I am not now the fool I was then, deluding myself that there was some emotion in the game you played. All you wanted was entry to this house. To establish yourself here. I was the help you needed to that end. I see it now.

REBECCA: You quite forget then, it was Beäta, who entreated and besought of me to come here to live.

KROLL: Yes, you'd worked your sorcery upon her too. Though is 'friendship' the word, for what she came to feel for you? It grew to an idolatry...an adoration. That in its turn became a – what am I to call it? – a desperate infatuation. Yes, that is the very word.

REBECCA: Do please recall the state of your sister's mind... As to my part, I doubt if I could be at all described as over-emotional.

KROLL: No, that you certainly can not. So much though the more dangerous you are, to those whom you would win into your power. You've such a gift for setting about things with premeditation, a full and thorough calculating, precisely because your heart is cold.

REBECCA: Cold? Are you so sure of that?

KROLL: Now I am convinced of it. How else could you persist year in year out in such unwavering pursuit of your own aims? Yes, yes: you have attained to what you desired. Dominion over him and all that's his. But to succeed in that, you haven't flinched from making him unhappy.

REBECCA: That is not true. It is not I. It is yourself Sir, that have made him unhappy.

KROLL: I have!

REBECCA: Yes, when you induced in him the notion, that he was to blame for the frightful ending to Beäta's life.

KROLL: So that has shaken him so deep?

REBECCA: You can be sure it has. A mind so sensitive as his.

KROLL: I'd thought a so-called liberated man had learned to grind all scruple underfoot... But there we are. Ah well; come to that, I should have expected as much. The scion of such men as gaze down upon us here: there'll be no tearing free for him from that unbroken heritage.

REBECCA: (*Looking thoughtfully down before her.*) John Rosmer has very deep roots in his lineage. That's sure and true.

KROLL: Yes, and you would have shown regard for that, if you'd had any feeling heart for him. But regard of that order I suppose is quite beyond you. Your background after all is poles apart from his.

REBECCA: How do you mean, background?

KROLL: I mean your family background. Your origins…Miss West.

REBECCA: Ah, that. Yes, it's true enough: I come from very poor circumstances. But even then…

KROLL: It isn't social standing that I have in mind. I'm thinking of the moral background.

REBECCA: Background…? To what?

KROLL: To your coming into this world at all.

REBECCA: What's that you say?

KROLL: I say it only, because of the light that casts on all your conduct.

REBECCA: I don't understand this. Explain your meaning!

KROLL: I wouldn't have thought that you needed it explaining. Or else it makes strange sense indeed, your agreeing to adoption by Doctor West…

REBECCA: (*Standing.*) So that's it. Now I understand.

KROLL: …and your assuming his name. Your mother's name was Gamvik.

REBECCA: (*Moving away across the room.*) Gamvik was my father's name, Doctor Kroll Sir.

KROLL: Your mother's occupation will have brought her time and again into the local doctor's company.

REBECCA: That is so.

KROLL: And then he takes you to his side…no sooner was your mother dead. He treats you harsh. And yet you stay with him. You know that he will leave you not one single shilling. You have from him only a crate of books. Yet you endure that life with him. Bear with him. Care for him until the last.

REBECCA: (*Away by the table, looking at him with contempt.*) And my doing all that, you ascribe to some immoral – some illicit aspect to my birth!

KROLL: What you did for him, I interpret as the instinctual reflex of a daughter. All your conduct in fact, I take for outcome of your origin.

REBECCA: (*Vehement.*) Not one word of what you say is true. And I can prove so. Doctor West had not yet come to Finmark, when I was born.

KROLL: Forgive me...Miss West. He arrived the previous year. I have established this.

REBECCA: You are wrong, I tell you. You are altogether wrong.

KROLL: You said in this room two days back, you were twenty-nine years old. Were into your thirtieth year.

REBECCA: Indeed? Did I say that?

KROLL: Yes, you did. And, counting from there...

REBECCA: Stop! Counting won't help you. I may as well tell you here and now: I am one year older than the age I give.

KROLL: (*With an unbelieving smile.*) Is that a fact? Here's something new. Why should this be?

REBECCA: By the time I was twenty-five, I was beginning to feel on the old side, unmarried as I was. So I took to pretending to one year less.

KROLL: You? A liberated woman? Cherishing received ideas concerning marriageable age?

REBECCA: Yes, it was foolish of me; ridiculous too. But there'll always be some trace or other cling to us, we cannot shake off. It's how we are.

KROLL: No matter. But my arithmetic can still for all that be correct. For the year before his appointment up there, Doctor West had briefly visited that way.

REBECCA: (*Cries out.*) That is not so!

KROLL: Is it not?

REBECCA: No. My mother never mentioned that.

KROLL: Did she not now?

REBECCA: No, never. Nor Doctor West either. Never a word.

KROLL: Might not that be, because the both of them had reason to discount a year? Exactly as you have done, Miss West? It's an hereditary quirk, perhaps.

REBECCA: (*Moving about, clenching and wringing her hands.*) It isn't possible. It's only something you want to make me believe. Never in the world is it true, what you say! It cannot be true! Never in all the – !

KROLL: (*Standing.*) But, my dear…in God's name how should this trouble you so? You have me quite alarmed. What am I to think or suppose from this…?

REBECCA: Nothing. You're to think or suppose nothing.

KROLL: Then really you must explain to me, why this fact…why this possibility can so distress you so deep.

REBECCA: (*Composing herself.*) It's all quite simple really, Doctor Kroll. I have no wish to be known for illegitimate.

KROLL: Indeed. Ah well, let us content ourselves with that account of it: for the duration. Though you retain then a certain…prejudice on this issue too.

REBECCA: Yes, I suppose I do.

KROLL: Well, I think with most of what you call your liberation, we'll find much the same story. You've schooled yourself in a whole host of new opinions and ideas. You've come to knowledge of a sort, of theories in various fields – theories, that seem largely to subvert all we'd held as irrefutable and unassailable till now. But all this has been no more than information to you, Miss West. A surface learning. It has not entered you in the blood.

REBECCA: (*Given thought.*) You could well be right in that.

KROLL: Yes, examine yourself only, you'll see that it is so. And if that's how it is with yourself, we can know for sure how it is with John Rosmer. It really is the purest, sheerest lunacy: a headlong plunge into ruin, for him of all men to stand forth openly and avow himself an unbeliever! Imagine: a man so retiring as he! Imagine him, abjured… hounded by that fraternity that had been his own till now. Exposed to pitiless onslaught, from the best in our society. He's never man enough to withstand all that.

REBECCA: He has to be. It's too late for him now to retreat.

KROLL: Not at all too late. By no means so. What already has occurred, need never be known…or at least can be presented as a temporary lapse, no more, albeit to be deplored. There is however one requirement that absolutely must be met.

REBECCA: And what might that be?

KROLL: You must prevail on him to legalize the relationship, Miss West.

REBECCA: The relationship in which he stands to me?

KROLL: Yes. You must be sure to see that he does that.

REBECCA: So you cannot at all be quit of the notion, that our relationship needs...what you call legalizing?

KROLL: I have no wish myself to go into the matter further. But I reckon right enough to have observed, that the sphere of life where so-called conventional morals are most readily set aside, is in the...hm.

REBECCA: Is in the relationship between man and woman, you mean?

KROLL: Yes; to be forthright: that is my belief.

REBECCA: (*Wandering the room, has come to the window, looking out.*) I could almost say...Principal Kroll, how I wish you were right.

KROLL: What do you mean? You say that in so strange a tone.

REBECCA: Oh nothing! Let's not talk about it any more... Ah: there he comes.

KROLL: Already! Then I'll be on my way.

REBECCA: (*Calls to him.*) No...stay. There's something you need to hear.

KROLL: Not now. I doubt if I can bear the sight of him.

REBECCA: I beg you, Sir: stay. You must. Or you'll rue it later. This is the last, that I shall ever ask of you.

KROLL: (*Looks at her in surprise, and puts down his hat.*) Very well, Miss West. As you wish.

(*A moment's silence. Then JOHN ROSMER comes in from the porch.*)

ROSMER: (*Sees KROLL; pauses in the doorway.*) What!... Are you here?

REBECCA: He didn't at all want to meet you, John.

KROLL: (*Involuntary.*) 'John', indeed!

REBECCA: Yes, Doctor Kroll. Rosmer and I...we are Rebecca and John to each other. It comes with the relationship we have.

KROLL: That's what you said I needed to hear?

REBECCA: That: and a little more.

ROSMER: (*Coming nearer.*) What is the purpose of this visit here today?

KROLL: I wanted to try one more time to stay you and to win you back.

ROSMER: (*Points to the newspaper.*) After what's printed in that?

KROLL: I didn't write it.

ROSMER: Did you make any move to suppress it?

KROLL: The cause I serve would not permit of that. Even supposing I could have done.

REBECCA: (*Tears the paper to pieces, crumples the shreds and throws them deep into the stove.*) There. It's out of sight now. So out of mind with it too. There'll be no more where that came from, John.

KROLL: Oh, yes, could you but see and make sure of that.

REBECCA: Come, let us sit, dear friends. All three of us. And I will tell you everything.

ROSMER: (*Sitting automatically.*) Rebecca, what is this, has come over you? This unnatural calm, whatever is it?

REBECCA: The calm of resolution. (*She sits.*) Principal, you be seated too. (*Principal KROLL takes his place on the sofa.*)

ROSMER: Resolution, you say. What have you resolved?

REBECCA: I want to give back to you, what it is you need to live your life. Your joyful innocence, dear friend, shall be restored to you.

ROSMER: Whatever do you mean?

REBECCA: I need only to tell. That's all it wants.

ROSMER: Well?

REBECCA: When I came down from Finmark here...with Doctor West...it was as though there opened up a new great wide world before me. The Doctor had given me the gist of an education. Scattered fragments, the only knowledge of life that I then had. (*Struggling and barely audible.*) And so...

KROLL: And so?

ROSMER: But Rebecca: I know all this.

REBECCA: (*Composes herself.*) Yes, yes; indeed you do. You know it too well.

KROLL: (*Looking hard at her.*) I think it's best I leave.

REBECCA: No, dear Principal, you shall stay as you are. (*To ROSMER.*) Yes John, it was like this, you see: I wanted to be part of that new age then dawning. To be part of all the new thinking... Doctor Kroll one day informed me, that Ulrik Brendel had been a powerful influence upon you once, while you were yet a boy. I thought, here must be something I could do, and take this up again.

ROSMER: You came here with a secret purpose...?

REBECCA: I wanted the two of us to go forward together in freedom. Ever further. Ever onward and ahead. But there was always that dismal, unscalable wall, between yourself and your becoming wholly, absolutely free.

ROSMER: What wall do you mean?

REBECCA: I mean, John, that you could never grow to be free but in the light of the Sun. And here you were, ailing and wasting in the darkness of a marriage like yours.

ROSMER: Never till this day have you spoken to me of my marriage so.

REBECCA: No, I did not dare to, else I should have frightened you.

KROLL: (*Nodding to ROSMER.*) You hear that?!

REBECCA: (*Ignoring this.*) But I saw well, what your deliverance must be. Your one deliverance. And so I set to work.

ROSMER: Set to work, how?

KROLL: Are you saying you –

REBECCA: Yes, John... (*She stands.*) Just sit and listen. You too, Doctor Kroll. It must into the daylight now. That was not you, John. You have no guilt. It was I, beckoning...who came in the end to beckon...Beäta out upon the twisted paths...

ROSMER: (*Leaping up.*) Rebecca!

KROLL: (*Rising from the sofa.*) ...the twisted paths!

REBECCA: Upon those paths...that brought her to the millrace there. Now you know it, both of you.

ROSMER: (*As in a stupor.*) But I'm not understanding this…
What is it she's saying? I'm not understanding a word

KROLL: Oh yes, John. I begin to understand.

ROSMER: But what is it you did?! What could you have said
to her at all? There was nothing to tell. Absolutely nothing!

REBECCA: She learned of your struggling to be free of all the
old morality.

ROSMER: Yes, but that wasn't happening then.

REBECCA: I saw that it was not far off for you.

KROLL: (*Nodding to ROSMER.*) Ah ha…!

ROSMER: And? Go on. Tell me the rest of it now.

REBECCA: Some while after…I begged and pleaded with
her, she had to let me go from Rosmersholm.

ROSMER: Why did you want to leave…then?

REBECCA: I didn't want to leave. I wanted to continue here,
where I was. But I said to her, really it were wisest for us
all if soon I did move on. I gave her to understand that,
should I continue here much longer, there could well…
there could well happen…what does happen.

ROSMER: So that, is what you said and did.

REBECCA: Yes, John.

ROSMER: That, is what you called setting to work.

REBECCA: (*In broken voice.*) I called it so, yes.

ROSMER: (*After a moment.*) Rebecca, is that your confession
done?

REBECCA: Yes.

KROLL: Not quite.

REBECCA: (*Looks at him, afraid.*) What more can there be?

KROLL: Did you not at the last give Beäta to believe, it was
imperative – not merely wisest: but in Mr Rosmer's interest
and yours, imperative that you move elsewhere…as soon
as possible?… Well?

REBECCA: (*Softly and indistinct.*) It might be I said something
of the sort.

ROSMER: (*Sinks low in the armchair at the window.*) And this
web of lies and deceit, that woman…the wretched suffering
woman, took for true! For sure and true! Rock sure! (*Looks
up at REBECCA.*) And never once did she turn to me. With

never a word! Oh, Rebecca...I can tell to look at you: you warned her not to speak.

REBECCA: She had it so fixed in her head, that...as a childless wife, she had no right to be here. And so she came to believe it her duty, to make way.

ROSMER: And you...you did nothing to disabuse her of that notion?

REBECCA: Nothing.

ROSMER: You confirmed her in it perhaps? Answer me! Didn't you?

REBECCA: It's possible she understood me so.

ROSMER: Yes, yes: and to your will she bowed in every matter. And so made way. (*Leaps up.*) How could you – how could you carry through such an appalling pretence?

REBECCA: I saw there was a choice here, John, to be made between two lives.

KROLL: (*With stern authority.*) It's not for you to make such choice as that!

REBECCA: (*Vehement.*) You think then, I set about this, cold and calculating and composed! I wasn't the woman then, I am now, telling you this. I should say rather, in any one person there are two sorts of will at work. I wanted Beäta gone. One way or other. But I never believed that it would really happen. With each step forward I ventured and dared, it was as though a terror in me cried: No further now! Not one step more! ...And yet I could not leave it be. Always I had to risk that one touch more. Only the one. And then one more...ever one more... And then it happened. That's how it goes, in a case like this. (*A short silence.*)

ROSMER: (*To REBECCA.*) What do you expect shall become of you now? After this you have done?

REBECCA: Let become of me, what will. It isn't all that great a matter.

KROLL: Not one word that speaks of remorse. Perhaps because you feel none?

REBECCA: (*Coldly dismissive.*) Pardon me, Sir: that's no concern to anybody else. I shall come to that in my own way.

KROLL: (*To ROSMER.*) And this, my friend, is the woman you have under your same roof with you. In intimate relationship. (*Looks up at the portraits.*) Oh…you that are gone: if you had eyes to look on this!

ROSMER: Are you going on into town?

KROLL: (*Takes his hat.*) Yes. I can't leave soon enough.

ROSMER: (*Takes his hat likewise.*) I'm coming with you.

KROLL: You are? Yes, I didn't think somehow we'd altogether lost you.

ROSMER: Come on, Kroll! Come on!

(*They go out through the porch without a look at REBECCA. After a moment, REBECCA discreetly makes her way over to the window, and peers out between the flowers.*)

REBECCA: (*Talks in a low voice to herself.*) Not over the footbridge today. He goes the long way about. He'll never cross that millrace. Never. (*Comes from the window.*) Ah well, ah well then.

(*She goes over and pulls on the bellcord. Soon MRS HELSETH enters right.*)

MRS HELSETH: What is it, Miss?

REBECCA: Mrs Helseth, would you be so good as to have my luggage-box fetched down from the loft?

MRS HELSETH: Luggage-box?

REBECCA: Yes, you know it, the brown sealskin one.

MRS HELSETH: Of course. But Lord take care of us: is Madam going on a journey then?

REBECCA: Yes…Mrs Helseth, I'm going on a journey now.

MRS HELSETH: What, this instant?

REBECCA: As soon as I've my packing done.

MRS HELSETH: I never heard the like. Madam will soon be back though, won't she?

REBECCA: I'll not be back ever again.

MRS HELSETH: Not ever? But Lord above, what shall become of Rosmersholm without Miss West here any more? No sooner than it's nice and comfortable again for His poor Reverence.

REBECCA: I know, but today Mrs Helseth something has frightened me.

MRS HELSETH: Frightened you? Dear Lord…whatever was that?

REBECCA: Well, I think you could say I saw a glimpse of white horses.

MRS HELSETH: White horses? In broad light of day?

REBECCA: Oh, they can be about at any hour, the white horses of Rosmersholm. (*Changes the subject.*) So…the luggage-box then, Mrs Helseth.

MRS HELSETH: Of course. The luggage-box.

(*They both go out right.*)

End of Act Three.

ACT FOUR

*The living-room of Acts One and Three. Late evening. On the table the
lamp, in its shade, alight.*

*REBECCA WEST stands at the table, stowing various small articles
into a travelling-bag. Her cape, hat and the white crochet shawl are
draped over the back of the sofa.*

MRS HELSETH comes in from our right.

MRS HELSETH: (*Subdued of speech and strained in manner.*)
Well, that's everything taken out now, Miss. It's in the
kitchen passage.

REBECCA: Good. The coachman knows to come?

MRS HELSETH: Yes. He's asking what time shall he be here
to fetch you.

REBECCA: I think about eleven. The steamer leaves at
midnight.

MRS HELSETH: (*Hesitating a little.*) His Reverence though?
What if he isn't home by then?

REBECCA: I still leave. If I don't manage to see him, you can
tell him I'll write to him. A long letter. Tell him that.

MRS HELSETH: Well, I suppose it's enough…to write it in
a letter. But, my poor lady…I do think you ought to try
talking with him one more time.

REBECCA: Perhaps. There again perhaps not.

MRS HELSETH: No…that I should live to see the day…I'd
never have expected this…

REBECCA: Why what did you expect, Mrs Helseth?

MRS HELSETH: Oh, I really expected Parson Rosmer to
have more man in him than that.

REBECCA: More man?

MRS HELSETH: My word I did.

REBECCA: But my dear, what do you mean?

MRS HELSETH: I mean no more Miss, than what's right and
true. He's wrong to be turning his back on it so, that he is.

REBECCA: (*Looking at her.*) Now you listen, Mrs Helseth. Tell
me honestly and truly…why do you think I am leaving?

180

MRS HELSETH: Lord above, because you have to, Miss. Oh ay-ai-ai. But I don't think His Reverence has acted decently at all. Mortensgård now, there was excuse for him. She had her husband still living. So those two could never have married, for all they might want to. But as for His Reverence...hm!

REBECCA: (*With a wan smile.*) You never expected such a thing of Parson Rosmer and myself?

MRS HELSETH: Never in the world. Well, I mean...not before today.

REBECCA: Today though...

MRS HELSETH: Well...after all the nasty things I hear there are about His Reverence in the papers, I mean...

REBECCA: Ah ha.

MRS HELSETH: What I say is, the man who can go over to Mortensgård's presuasion,* my word but you can expect anything of him.

REBECCA: Oh yes, that's true enough. Myself though. What do you say of me?

MRS HELSETH: Lord take care of us, Miss: I don't think there's all that much to be held against you. It can't be that easy for a single woman to resist, I'm sure... We're all of us only flesh and blood, Miss West.

REBECCA: You speak a true word there, Mrs Helseth. We're all of us flesh and blood... You're hearing something?

MRS HELSETH: (*Softly.*) Heavens... If he hasn't come home this very instant.

REBECCA: (*Starts up.*) So after all... (*Resolved.*) Ah well. Let come what must.

(*JOHN ROSMER comes in from the porch.*)

ROSMER: (*Sees the luggage, turns to REBECCA and asks.*) What's the meaning of this?

REBECCA: I'm leaving.

ROSMER: Right away?

REBECCA: Yes. (*To MRS HELSETH.*) Eleven o'clock then.

MRS HELSETH: Very well Miss.

(*She goes out right.*)

ROSMER: (*After a short pause.*) Rebecca, where will you go?

* *sic* represents a similar garble in the original

181

REBECCA: On the boat north.

ROSMER: North? What will you do up north?

REBECCA: It's from there I came.

ROSMER: But you've no call now up there.

REBECCA: Nor have I here.

ROSMER: How are you going to manage then?

REBECCA: I don't know. I want only to make an end of it.

ROSMER: An end of it?

REBECCA: Rosmersholm has broken me.

ROSMER: (*Alert suddenly.*) You say that?

REBECCA: Broken me asunder... When I came here, I had a will so fresh and brave. Now I am bowed beneath an alien law... I believe from this day, I shall venture nothing ever again.

ROSMER: Why not? What law is this, you say you –

REBECCA: My dear, let's not talk now of that... Between yourself and the Principal, how did it go?

ROSMER: We have concluded peace.

REBECCA: Ay well. So there it finishes.

ROSMER: He gathered all our old circle of friends together at his home. They've made it very clear to me: this task of raising a nobility of minds...it's not at all for me... And anyway Rebecca, it's in itself so hopeless a cause... I leave things as they are.

REBECCA: Yes, yes...that could well be the best.

ROSMER: That, you're saying now? That is your opinion now?

REBECCA: I have come to that opinion. These past two days.

ROSMER: Rebecca, that's a lie.

REBECCA: A lie...!

ROSMER: Yes, a lie Rebecca. You never did have faith in me. Never once did you believe I was man enough to advance the cause to any victory.

REBECCA: I did believe, the two of us together could succeed.

ROSMER: That is not true. You believed that you yourself had in you to achieve something great with your life. That you could utilise me, to help further your aims. That I could be an instrument to you, to your own end. That, you believed.

REBECCA: John, now listen…

ROSMER: (*Sits despondently down on the sofa.*) Oh leave it be! I'm seeing through to the truth of it now. I have been as a glove in your hands.

REBECCA: John, now listen. We have to confront this now. Once and for all. (*Sits in a chair by the sofa.*) I had intended writing to you about the whole of it, once I was home up north again. But it's probably best, you hear it from me now.

ROSMER: You've yet more to confess?

REBECCA: I've yet the greater part of it.

ROSMER: What greater part?

REBECCA: That, you have never once suspected. That gives to all the rest of it its light and shadow.

ROSMER: (*Shaking his head.*) I understand none of this.

REBECCA: It's perfectly true: I was at one time angling for admission here to Rosmersholm. Because it seemed to me, I must surely do well for myself here. One how or other… you understand me.

ROSMER: You certainly achieved what you wanted.

REBECCA: I think, I could have achieved anything, no matter what…at that time. For I still had that will of mine then, brave, free-born. No consideration gave me pause. I yielded to nothing… Till then came the onset of that, that has broken the will in me: and shrunken me in wretchedness for the rest of my days.

ROSMER: Onset of what? Tell me, in language I can understand.

REBECCA: When there came over me…this savage, ungovernable need… Oh, John…

ROSMER: Need? Rebecca…! For what?

REBECCA: For you.

ROSMER: (*Would leap up.*) What's this?

REBECCA: (*Staying him.*) My dear, sit and listen. There is more you have to know.

ROSMER: You mean to say…you loved me…in that way?

REBECCA: This must be what's called being in love – I thought at the time. I thought, this is Love. But it was not. It was as I tell you. It was a savage, ungovernable need.

183

ROSMER: (*With difficulty.*) Rebecca...is this really you...
you...you yourself you are describing here?

REBECCA: Yes, John, who else!

ROSMER: All for this...under the sway of this it was, you...
set to work, as you call it.

REBECCA: It came upon me like an ocean storm. It was like
one of those storms, our winter up there in the North can
bring. It seizes you...and carries you before it, John...far as
it will. Senseless to resist.

ROSMER: And swept the wretched Beäta out into the
millrace there.

REBECCA: Yes, such our struggle was, one or other must go
under.

ROSMER: Surely you were the strongest in this house.
Stronger than Beäta and myself together.

REBECCA: I knew you well enough to know: I could never
reach to you, until you were set free, in your outward
situation...and in your thought.

ROSMER: But I can't make sense of you Rebecca. You...you
yourself...everything you've done...are all unfathomable
mystery to me. Free now I am...in thought and situation.
You stand within a hand's-grasp of what was from the first
your goal. And yet you – !

REBECCA: Never have I stood further from my goal than now.

ROSMER: ...and yet I say, when yesterday I asked you...
begged of you: *Be my wife*...you shrieked out as in terror,
that could never be.

REBECCA: That John was a cry of my despair.

ROSMER: At what?

REBECCA: At how Rosmersholm has reft me of my powers.
Here has my brave will been grounded. And maimed.
That time's long gone for me, when I had in me to venture
anything. John Rosmer, my capacity to do is lost.

ROSMER: How has this happened, tell me.

REBECCA: It has happened through living with you.

ROSMER: How though? How?

REBECCA: When at last I was alone with you here... and
you were becoming your self...

ROSMER: Yes, yes?

REBECCA Because you'd never been wholly yourself, whilever Beäta was alive...

ROSMER: More's the pity, but that's true enough.

REBECCA: Once though I was living with you here at last: quietly...in solitude...and you were sharing your every, unreserved thought with me – each single emotion, be it so gentle or delicate, as it came to you...it's then the great change happened. Little by little, you understand. Barely perceivable...but at the last possessing all of me. To my deep core.

ROSMER: Oh, what are you telling me, Rebecca?

REBECCA: All that other...that ugly, drunken need, ebbed out so far, so far from me. All those troubled urges in me, sank into rest and were still. Over me there fell a peacefulness...like up at home there, that hush that stills a crag of seabirds at the midnight sun.

ROSMER: Tell me more about this. All, that you can put in words.

REBECCA: It's all of it near said now, John. There remains only this, that then a love came welling up in me. That great, renouncing love, that is content with a share in living with another: such as you and I have known.

ROSMER: Oh, if I had suspected but one whit of this.

REBECCA: It's best as it is. Yesterday...when you asked me, would I be your wife...the jubilation cried from me –

ROSMER: Yes, that it did, Rebecca! I felt it was that.

REBECCA: For an instant, yes. Of self-forgetting. Because that was my easier will of old, all for pulling free again. But that it has no power now...none that's enduring.

ROSMER: What do you say has done this to you?

REBECCA: It's Rosmer morality...or your morality, at least...that has blighted my will.

ROSMER: Blighted?

REBECCA: And made it sick. Bound it in thrall to a Commandment, that was of no weight with me before. Through you...living with you...I am a nobler soul...

ROSMER: Oh, if I could only be sure of that!

HENRIK IBSEN

REBECCA: You can be certain sure of it. The Rosmer ethic
does make nobler people of us. But… (*Shaking her head.*)
but…but…

ROSMER: But…? Yes?

REBECCA: But it's death to happiness, John.

ROSMER: Rebecca, you say that?

REBECCA: For me it has been.

ROSMER: Yes, but are you so sure you're right? If I were to
ask you again…? Beg and entreat you…

REBECCA: Dear one…don't ever speak about this any more.
It can never be possible…! Yes, for you have to know it
John, I have a…life I led before.

ROSMER: Something more, than you've already told?

REBECCA: Yes. Something more and something other.

ROSMER: (*With a faint smile.*) Isn't it strange, Rebecca?
Moments have been, when just such a suspicion did brush
my mind.

REBECCA: Did it? And yet you still…? In spite of that?…

ROSMER: I never gave it credence. I toyed with it only: in
my thoughts, you realize.

REBECCA: If you ask it, here and now I will tell you this too.

ROSMER: (*Declining.*) No, no. I'll not hear a word.
Whatsoever it be…I forget it.

REBECCA: But I do not.

ROSMER: Oh Rebecca…!

REBECCA: Yes, John…it's that that's so appalling: that now,
with all life's happiness beckoning to me in its abundance,
I should be so changed, my sense of my own past now bars
my way.

ROSMER: Your past is dead, Rebecca. It has no hold upon
you any more: no bearing on you…as you now are.

REBECCA: That's only rhetoric, my dear. What of freedom
from guilt, then? Where's that for me now?

ROSMER: (*Sadly.*) Ay, ay…freedom from guilt.

REBECCA: Freedom from guilt, yes. There happiness and joy
are. Wasn't that the teaching you wanted to make live in all
those joyous new nobility there were to be?

ROSMER: Oh, don't remind me. That was only a half-formed dream, Rebecca. An impetuous fancy, I don't myself believe in any more… A nobler way just cannot be impressed on people from without, my dear.

REBECCA: (*Softly.*) Even through the quiet power of love?

ROSMER: (*Given thought.*) Oh…that would be the miracle indeed. I should say, the greatest glory almost, life has to offer… If it at all be so. (*Restless and writhing.*) But how am I ever to know the truth of that? Myself see that?

REBECCA: Do you not believe me, John?

ROSMER: Oh, Rebecca…how can I have belief entirely in you now? You, who have dissembled and concealed so unspeakably much!… Now you come forward with yet more to confess. If you've some purpose underlying…tell me outright. Is there some end perhaps you seek thereby? I'll do for you gladly, all I can.

REBECCA: (*Wringing her hands.*) Oh, this murderous mistrust… John…John…!

ROSMER: Yes, appalling isn't it, Rebecca? But I'm helpless here. I can never free myself of the mistrust. Never know for certain, it is your love I have, all and unalloyed.

REBECCA: But is there nothing, nothing deep in yourself, to avouch for how changed I am? And that through you that change has come: only through you?

ROSMER: Oh Rebecca…my belief is gone, in my power to change anyone. My belief is gone, in myself altogether. My belief is gone, in myself and in you.

REBECCA: (*With a sombre look at him.*) How then can you live at all?

ROSMER: That's right, I don't myself know how. I can't conceive how. I don't reckon I can live on… Rather, there's nothing I know of in this world, could make my life worth living now.

REBECCA: But living…brings renewal with it. We have to hold on to it, John… It's over for us soon enough.

ROSMER: (*Leaps restlessly up.*) Then give me my belief again! My belief in you, Rebecca! My belief in your love! Evidence! Show me evidence of it!

REBECCA: Evidence? What evidence can I offer you…!

ROSMER: You must! (*He moves about the room.*) I cannot endure this desolation…this fearful emptiness… this… this… (*A loud knocking at the door.*)

REBECCA: (*Starts up from the chair.*) Oh you hear that! (*The door opens. ULRIK BRENDEL comes in. He's wearing a dress-shirt, black frock-coat and sturdy boots with his trousers tucked in. Otherwise, he is dressed as before. He looks disturbed.*)

ROSMER: Oh, Mr Brendel, is it you!

BRENDEL: John, my boy…I greet you: Farewell!

ROSMER: Where are you away to so late?

BRENDEL: Down the hill.

ROSMER: How's that…?

BRENDEL: Homeward for me now, my beloved disciple. I yearn for home in the mighty void.

ROSMER: Something has happened to you, Mr Brendel! What?

BRENDEL: So you observe the change? Ay…well you might. When last I set foot within these halls…I stood before you, a man of means, and patted my pocket.

ROSMER: What! I'm not quite with you…

BRENDEL: But the man you see before you tonight, is a king unthroned, on the heap of cinders where his castle was.

ROSMER: If there is any help that I can be…

BRENDEL: You've your heart of a child still, John. Can you advance me a loan?

ROSMER: Yes, yes, of course!

BRENDEL: Can you part with an ideal or two?

ROSMER: Whatever do you mean?

BRENDEL: A couple of ideals you'll not be wearing any more? You'll be doing a charity. I'm cleaned out, my dear boy. Quite skint.

REBECCA: Weren't you able to give your paper?

BRENDEL: No, alluring lady. What do you think! There I'm standing, ready to pour forth from my Horn of Plenty; and make the painful discovery that I am bankrupt.

REBECCA: But all your works you've yet to write!

BRENDEL: For twenty-five years I've squatted like the miser on his padlocked coffer. Then yesterday...I open it to bring my riches out: and there's nothing. The teeth of time had ground it to dust. There was *nichts* and nothing in the whole caboodle.

ROSMER: How can you be so sure?

BRENDEL: It admits of no doubt, dear child. The President has convinced me so.

ROSMER: The President?

BRENDEL: Oh well...His Excellency, then. *Ganz nach Belieben.*

ROSMER: Yes, but whom do you mean?

BRENDEL: Peter Mortensgård of course.

ROSMER: What!

BRENDEL: (*With mystery.*) Hush, hush, hush! Peter Mortensgård is Lord and Master of the Coming Age. Never did I stand before a mightier countenance. Peter Mortensgård has in him omnipotent powers. He can do everything he wants.

ROSMER: Oh don't you believe it.

BRENDEL: It's true, my boy! For Peter Mortensgård never aims after more, than what is possible. Peter Mortensgård is able to live without ideals. And that...you see...that is the great secret of action and victory. That is the sum of all the wisdom of the world. *Basta!*

ROSMER: (*Hushed.*) I see now...how you leave here poorer than you came.

BRENDEL: *Bien!* So let your old teacher be a lesson to you. Everything he printed in you, strike it out. Don't build your tower on shifting sand. And watch where you go... Test each step... For you build on this entrancing creature here, who sweetens your days.

REBECCA: Are you talking of me?

BRENDEL: Ay, my captivating mermaid.

REBECCA: Why should one not build on me?

BRENDEL: (*A step nearer.*) My understanding is, my pupil of old has a cause in life to bring to victory.

REBECCA: So...?

BRENDEL: His victory is assured him. But…note it well: there's one prerequisite that must be satisfied.

REBECCA: What?

BRENDEL: (*Takes her delicately by the wrist.*) That the lady who loves him, go joyfully out into the kitchen and chop off her dainty pink little finger…here…just here, at the middle joint. Likewise that the aforesaid loving lady, just as joyfully, slice off her peerlessly formed left ear. (*Leaves go of her and turns to ROSMER.*) My John the Conqueror, farewell.

ROSMER: You're leaving now? In this dark night?

BRENDEL: By dark of night is best. Peace be unto you. (*He goes. There is silence in the room a while.*)

REBECCA: (*Stifled.*) Oh, how heavy and close it is in here! (*She goes over to the window, opens it and stays standing there.*)

ROSMER: (*Sits in the armchair by the stove.*) There's nothing for it after all, Rebecca. I see now. It's right you go.

REBECCA: Yes, no other choice that I can see.

ROSMER: Let us use well this final hour. Come over here and sit beside me.

REBECCA: (*Comes away, and sits on the sofa.*) What do you want of me, John?

ROSMER: First to tell you, you've no need to be worrying about your future.

REBECCA: (*With a smile.*) Mm. *My* future.

ROSMER: I've seen ahead to all eventualities. Long since. No matter what happens, you are provided for.

REBECCA: Dear man, that too.

ROSMER: My dear you should not have needed telling.

REBECCA: It's more than a year now since I had any such thought.

ROSMER: Ay, ay…it must have seemed to you, how it was between the two of us could never alter.

REBECCA: Yes, I did think that.

ROSMER: I too. But if I were to be taken…

REBECCA: Oh John…you'll live longer than I shall.

ROSMER: It's in my power surely, to dispose of my own worthless life.

REBECCA: What are you saying! You're never thinking of –

ROSMER: Why, would that seem so strange to you? After this miserable heart-rending defeat that I have suffered! I, who was to lead my life's cause on to victory… And here I am, fled from it all…before the battle was itself begun.

REBECCA: John, take the struggle up again. Try it only: and see, you shall prevail! You shall raise hundreds. You shall raise thousands of souls to a nobility. Try only!

ROSMER: Oh, Rebecca… I, who believe no longer in my life's own cause.

REBECCA: But your cause has already been proven. One person at least there is, you have raised to a nobility. Myself, so long as I shall live.

ROSMER: Ay: if I could believe you there.

REBECCA: (*Clenching her hands.*) Oh, John…is there nothing you know of…nothing that could make you believe me?

ROSMER: (*Starts up in dread.*) Let be. Let well alone, Rebecca. Not one word more.

REBECCA: No, this above all we must go into now! Is there nothing you know of, that could quell your doubt? I can think of nothing at all.

ROSMER: Best for you, you can't… Best for us both.

REBECCA: No, no, no: I'm not accepting that! If you know of anything that could acquit me in your sight, then I demand it as my due, you name it me.

ROSMER: (*As one unwilling, driven onward against his will.*) Let us look then. You say, you have in you great love. That through me you have been ennobled in your soul. Is it true? Have you accounted aright, Rebecca? Shall we put your account to the reckoning? Do we?

REBECCA: I am ready for that.

ROSMER: At whatsoever the hour?

REBECCA: Whenever. And sooner the better.

ROSMER: Then show me, Rebecca…if you…for me…this very night… (*Breaks off.*) Oh no, no, no!

REBECCA: Yes, John! Yes, yes! Say it, and you shall see.

ROSMER: Have you the courage…the willing…in joy, as Ulrik Brendel said…for my sake, now tonight…in joy…to go that same road…Beäta went?

REBECCA: (*Rises slowly from the sofa and all but voiceless says.*) John...!

ROSMER: Yes, Rebecca...it's ever that question shall be haunting me when you have gone. Not one hour of the day but I'll be coming back to it. Oh, it's as though I see you, so lifelike before me. You stand out yonder on the bridge. Midway across. Now you lean out, over the rail! You sway, drawn down toward the raging water! No. You pull back. You don't dare it...what she dared.

REBECCA: But if I had that courage now? And that joy and willing? What then?

ROSMER: Then I could not other than believe you. Then I could not other than have the faith again in my life's cause. The faith in my own powers to raise the human spirit to a nobler way. The faith, that the human spirit has in it to be raised.

REBECCA: (*Slowly takes her shawl, draws it about her head and shoulders, and with composure says.*) You'll have your faith again.

ROSMER: Have you the courage and willing...for that, Rebecca?

REBECCA: You be judge of that tomorrow...or whenever after...when they fetch me up.

ROSMER: (*Claps his hands to his skull.*) There's a horror that's beckoning here...

REBECCA: For I'll not rest beneath that water. Any longer than it needs. See and be sure that I am found.

ROSMER: (*Leaping up.*) What are we doing...we're out of our minds! Leave now...or stay! This time too I'll take you at your word alone.

REBECCA: Rhetoric, John. No cowardice nor any running from it now, you see. After today, how can you take me at my mere word alone?

ROSMER: But I do not want to witness your defeat, Rebecca!

REBECCA: This shall be no defeat.

ROSMER: It shall. You've never it in you to go Beäta's way.

REBECCA: You think not?

ROSMER: Never. You're not as Beäta was. No twisted ethic has its power over you.

REBECCA But I answer to the Rosmer ethic now. For my transgression, I must expiate.

ROSMER: (*Looking hard at her.*) That's how you see it now.

REBECCA: Yes.

ROSMER: (*Resolved.*) Well then. While I answer to our liberated ethic now, Rebecca. We have no Judge above. And so, we must see justice done upon ourselves.

REBECCA: (*Misunderstanding him.*) That as well. That as well. My passing shall save what's best in you.

ROSMER: Oh, there's nothing in me left to save.

REBECCA: There is. I though…I from this day shall be only a troll of the sea, clinging to your ship and holding you back, where you must sail on. I must over the side. Or am I to continue here above, dragging my crippled life about the world? Pining and moping over the happiness my past has forfeit me? Out of the game with me, John.

ROSMER: If you go…I come with you.

REBECCA: (*With an almost imperceptible smile, looks at him and softly says.*) Yes, John, you come: and be a witness…

ROSMER: I come with you, I say.

REBECCA: To the footbridge, yes. That you never dare step upon.

ROSMER: You noticed that?

REBECCA: (*Sad and broken.*) Yes: for that, my love was ever hopeless.

ROSMER: Rebecca…I lay my hand upon your head. (*Does as he says.*) I take you to my true wife.

REBECCA: (*Seizes both his hands and bows her head upon his breast.*) Thank you, John. (*Leaves go of him.*) And I go now…in joy.

ROSMER: Husband and wife must go together.

REBECCA: Only to the footbridge, John.

ROSMER: And out upon it. Far as you go…I go with you as far. I dare that now.

REBECCA: Are you so firm and certain sure…this way is the best for you?

ROSMER: I know it is the only way.

REBECCA: What if you're deceiving yourself? If this be phantom only? One of these Rosmersholm white horses.

ROSMER: Could well be. We've no escaping those...none of us in this house.

REBECCA: Stay then, John.

ROSMER: The husband shall follow his wife, as the wife her husband.

REBECCA: Yes, first answer me that. Is it you that follow me? Or is it I that follow you?

ROSMER: That's more than we shall ever learn for sure.

REBECCA: Though I wish so much to know.

ROSMER: The two of us follow each the other, Rebecca. I you, you me.

REBECCA: I almost believe that.

ROSMER: Because we two are now one.

REBECCA: Yes. We are now one. Come then. Together joyfully away.

(*They go hand in hand out through the porch, and are seen turning left. The door stands open after they are gone. The room is for a moment empty. Then MRS HELSETH comes in at the door right.*)

MRS HELSETH: Miss...the coachman's here... (*Looks about her.*) Not in? Out together at this hour? Well then...I must say...! Hm! (*Goes out into the porch, looks about her and comes in again.*) Not on the bench there. Oh no, no. (*Goes to the window and looks out.*) Lord above! That white there...! Upon my soul, the two of them standing on the bridge! God forgive the sinners that they are. Not putting their arms about each other! (*Screams loud.*) Ah...out over...the two of them! Out into the millrace! Help! Help! (*Her knees trembling, she clings quaking to the back of the chair, and can hardly speak the words.*) No. No helping this... The dead wife took them.

The End.

WHEN WE DEAD WAKEN

Characters

ARNOLD RUBEK
sculptor

MAJA RUBEK
his wife

THE SUPERVISOR
at the spa

A LADY TRAVELLING

SISTER IN BLACK

WOLFHEIM
a landed squire

Staff and Guests at the spa

Children

Act One takes place at a coastal spa; Acts Two and Three near,
and in the vicinity of, a mountain sanatorium.

Hedda gabler - Trapped women - liberation by death

Death + life / life's Bitch

When We Dead Waken was first performed in this translation at the
Almeida Theatre in February 1990, with the following cast:

 # look at the relationships

IRENA, Claire Bloom

RUBEK, Espen Skøjnberg

WOLFHEIM, Miles Anderson

MAJA, Suzanne Burden

SUPERVISOR, Wolfe Morris

SISTER IN BLACK, Eve Pearce

Director, Jonathan Kent

Designer, Peter Davison

Violence + Physical Act. Chisells
Opposing
Not Subtle. Mentions breasts + Women in same Sentence.
Nora from Dolls House

Opposing

Anomalous Needs

I'm Free I'm Free Song 242 + end of act 3

Self realisation = Modernism: grows out of Realism

Art + Creations: Once created, no longer needed.
frustration - Humanity

- References to earlier work
- Stretches Realism
- Strindberg - poetic Symbolism
      - Setting difficult!
- Checked changed by stars
- Use of language - Suggests Realism
- Flesh + Stone
- Day of Resurrection

Mountain. Danger. Struggle. Freedom Promising
ACT 3 - Narrative Structure

- 'He Captured her Soul in Stone'

- 'Sexual Frustration?'
- Sister in Black/of Mercy - contrast to Irena - Symbolist Concern = Intentions of Character not made clear.
- Statue not seen all the way through
- Subjective conventions
- 'Dream like'

Contrast: High + Low Mountain (couple up). One couple Down.

198

ACT ONE

Before the spa hotel; its main structure part-showing to our right.
Open, parklike expanse with fountain, shrubbery, clumps of large
old trees. Left, a small pavilion all but overgrown with creeper and
wild vine. Before it, a table and one chair. Vista beyond, over the
fjord to the sea, with promontories and small islands afar. A summer
morning: stillness, in the warmth of the sun.

Professor RUBEK and his wife MAJA are seated in basket-chairs,
at a table set for them on the lawn before the hotel; they have
breakfasted. Now they are drinking champagne and seltzer; and have
each a newspaper. The Professor is an elderly man, of distinguished
appearance; he wears a black velvet jacket over light summer clothing.
MRS RUBEK is in full flush of youth: a lively face, merry and
mischievous eyes; but a touch of weariness there. She wears elegant
travel attire.

MAJA: (*Sits a while as though waiting for the Professor to speak;*
    then lowers her paper with a sigh.) Oh no, no…
RUBEK: (*Looks up from his paper.*) Yes Maja? What is
    bothering you, my dear?
MAJA: Just listen to how silent all this is.
RUBEK: (*With a tolerant smile.*) And you can hear that?
MAJA: What?
RUBEK: The silent?
MAJA: Yes, actually I can.
RUBEK: Well, dear child, perhaps you're right. Silence in fact
    is something one can hear.
MAJA: God, I should say. When it's so utterly suffocating as
    all this, so −
RUBEK: Here at the Spa, you mean?
MAJA: I mean everywhere back in this country of ours. Oh,
    in the town there was din and noise enough, I know. But
    even there…the very din and noise had somehow a touch
    of the dead.
RUBEK: (*Gives her a searching look.*) Are you not all that happy,
    Maja my dear, to be in your home country again?

MAJA: (*Looks at him.*) Are you?

RUBEK: (*Evasive.*) Me…?

MAJA: Yes. You have been away so much much the longer.
Are you honestly happy to be home again?

RUBEK: Well…I can't honestly say…so happy as all that…

MAJA: (*All life.*) You see! I was right!

RUBEK: Perhaps I've been too long abroad. I feel quite alien
now to all this…to this provincial atmosphere.

MAJA: (*Eager, draws her chair nearer to him.*) Well then, Rubek!
So what's to stop us being up again and on our way? As
soon as we can!

RUBEK: (*Somewhat testy.*) That is the intention, Maja my love.
You know that.

MAJA: But what's to stop us leaving, here and now? Just think
of all that comfort and ease we're missing, down south
there in our lovely new house –

RUBEK: (*With his tolerant smile.*) Our lovely new home, we
surely mean.

MAJA: (*Short.*) No, house I mean. Let's keep it that way.

RUBEK: (*A long look at her.*) You really are a strange little
character.

MAJA: Am I so strange?

RUBEK: I think you are.

MAJA: Why though? Because I've no great urge, you mean, to
be footering about up here…?

RUBEK: Which of us made it a matter of life or death, our
coming north this summer?

MAJA: Well that was me, I know.

RUBEK: Certainly not I.

MAJA: God Almighty, though, who could have expected
everything in this country to be so hideously changed?
And all in so short a time! Why it can't be more than four
years at most since I left –

RUBEK: Ay: newly-wed.

MAJA: Newly-wed? What has that to do with it?

RUBEK: (*Continuing.*) …to become *Frau Rubek, Professor's Wife,*
mistress of a splendid home – forgive me, magnificent
house it seems the word must be. Also a villa on Lake
Taunitz, where all the Quality are now to be found. Oh

yes: all very splendid and civilized my dear, no question of that. And ample space. No call for us to be forever under each other's feet –

MAJA: (*Making light of it.*) No, no indeed; house-room and so on, we've certainly no shortage there…

RUBEK: So it's altogether a superior and more spacious style of living that you now enjoy. And a society more cultivated than you were used to at home.

MAJA: (*Looks at him.*) Well; so you're thinking it is I that have changed?

RUBEK: Yes Maja, I do think that.

MAJA: I only? Not the people here?

RUBEK: Well, they have too. A little, maybe. And they're none the more amiable for it, I grant you.

MAJA: Yes, you have to grant me that.

RUBEK: (*Changes the subject.*) You know what I begin to feel, when I consider people's lives around me here?

MAJA: What?

RUBEK: I find myself thinking back to that night we were on our way up in the train.

MAJA: You sat in our compartment, the whole journey asleep.

RUBEK: Not entirely. I was noticing, at every little station, how silent it was. I was hearing the silence. As you can, Maja –

MAJA: Mm. As I can; yes.

RUBEK: That's how I knew we'd come over the frontier. Now were we well and truly home. Because at every little halt, the train would stop and wait…and no passenger traffic at all.

MAJA: Why *did* it wait and stand like that? And nothing happening?

RUBEK: No idea. No traveller stepped down, none came aboard. And yet that train stood waiting there so long, an eternity. And at every station I could hear two railwaymen walking the platform – one of them carrying a lantern – and they were talking to each other, murmuring, muted, meaningless out there in the dark.

MAJA: Yes, you're right. There's always a pair of men out there, walking and talking…

RUBEK: …about nothing. (*More lively suddenly.*) But just you wait till tomorrow. That lovely big steamship will be there in dock for us. On board we'll go, and sail the coast: to the far north: right up into the Arctic waters.

MAJA: Yet that way you'll see nothing of the country at all; nor its life. Your very reason for coming.

RUBEK: (*Terse, and with an ill grace.*) I've seen enough and more.

MAJA: You think a sea-trip will be better for you?

RUBEK: It always makes a change.

MAJA: Sure, sure, so long as it'll do *you* some good, then –

RUBEK: Me? Some good? There's nothing at all needs putting right with me.

MAJA: (*Stands, and goes to him.*) Oh Rubek, yes there is. Surely you yourself feel that.

RUBEK: But Maja, my dearest: what at all could that be?

MAJA: (*Behind him, leaning forward over the back of the chair.*) You tell me. You've started to wander aimlessly: restless, ill-sitting; finding no peace anywhere. At home, nor out of doors. Quite unsociable you're becoming, this last while.

RUBEK: (*A touch sarcastic.*) Really? Don't tell me you have noticed that.

MAJA: No one can fail to, who knows you, my dear. And what makes me so sad, is how you've lost all pleasure in your work.

RUBEK: That too?

MAJA: How you'd be working! Morning, noon and night, time was; and never weary.

RUBEK: (*Dark.*) Ay: time was.

MAJA: But ever since you finished that great piece of yours…

RUBEK: (*Nodding pensively.*) 'Day of Resurrection', yes…

MAJA: …and it's gone its journey round about the world. And made you so famous…

RUBEK: That, Maja, could well be what is wrong.

MAJA: How do you mean?

RUBEK: When my creation of that great work was done… (*With an impassioned sweep of the hand.*) For a great work 'Day of Resurrection' is! Or in the beginning it was. No: is yet. It has to be, it has to be, great work it has to be!

MAJA: (*Looks at him, surprised.*) Rubek, yes! Why, the whole world knows it is.

RUBEK: (*Curt, dismissive.*) 'The whole world' knows nothing! Understands nothing!

MAJA: But surely at least they can sense…

RUBEK: Something not present at all, oh yes. Some thought I never had. See? It's that that has them in their ecstasies. (*Growling away to himself.*) What's the good of it? Slogging one's guts out for the multitude. For 'the whole world'.

MAJA: You think it's better, then: more worthy of yourself, to do as you are now? Producing the odd portrait-bust once in a while?

RUBEK: (*With a smug smile.*) Those are not really portraits, Maja, I'm turning out there.

MAJA: Oh come on, of course they are… These past few years…ever since your big group was finished and taken from the house…

RUBEK: All the same, they're no mere portrait-busts, I tell you.

MAJA: What are they then?

RUBEK: There's more to those figures than meets the eye; a hidden meaning, covered, within:…a secret no public can see.

MAJA: So?

RUBEK: (*Definitively.*) I alone can see. And that amuses me no end. On the surface, they show this 'striking resemblance' so-called, that people stand gawping at so stupefied… (*Lowers his voice.*) But inwardly, at its true core, it is the lofty, lordly phizog of a horse; or the muzzle of a bigoted ass, the flop-eared brainless skullpan of a dog, the gorged chops of a pig: and there'll be the dumb and flaccid visage of a bullock in there somewhere too.

MAJA: (*Indifferent.*) The entire domestic circus, in fact.

RUBEK: The domestic circus, Maja, and nothing more. Every single creature that we have corrupted in our own human image. And that has corrupted us in turn. (*Drains his glass of champagne, and laughs.*) And these two-faced works of art are what our upright bourgeois insist on commissioning from me. And pay for: so trustingly, and through the nose. Worth its weight in gold, as they do say.

MAJA: (*Fills up his glass.*) Rubek, you should be ashamed. Drink up and be merry.

RUBEK: (*With a repeated stroking of his brow, leans away in his chair.*) Oh I am, Maja. Truly I am. In a sense. (*He's silent a moment.*) It is, after all, a certain happiness: to feel absolutely free; unbeholden to any. To be well supplied with all that one could ever think to want. One's outward self, that is. Maja, you do agree?

MAJA: Oh yes, indeed. All that's fine: so far as it goes. (*She looks at him.*) But do you remember what you promised me? The day we came to our agreement on that delicate matter...

RUBEK: (*Nods.*) ...that we should marry. Not an easy step that, Maja my dear, for you to take.

MAJA: (*Persisting unperturbed.*) ...and that I should leave the country with you, spend the rest of my days abroad, enjoy the good life? Can you remember what you promised me at that time?

RUBEK: (*Shaking his head.*) No, I can't say I do. Why, what did I promise you?

MAJA: You said you would take me with you up a high mountain and show me all the glory of the world.

RUBEK: (*Taken aback.*) Did I really promise *you* that as well?

MAJA: (*Looks at him.*) Me as well? Who else?

RUBEK: (*Casual.*) No no, I'm thinking only, did I promise to show you...?

MAJA: ...all the glory of the world. That's what you said. And all that glory would be mine and yours, you said.

RUBEK: It's a turn of phrase I was given to using, time long gone.

MAJA: No more than a turn of phrase?

RUBEK: Yes, from when I was at school. I used to say things like that to tempt the other children out with me into forest and mountain to play.

MAJA: (*A hard look at him.*) Perhaps all you wanted of me, was to come out playing too?

RUBEK: (*Laughing it off.*) Well Maja, the game has been quite pleasurable, you won't deny?

MAJA: (*Cold.*) I didn't come with you only to play.

RUBEK: No, no, possibly not.

MAJA: And you never took me with you up any high mountain, either, nor showed me –

RUBEK: (*Riled.*) – all the glory of the world? No: that I never. I have to tell you: you weren't exactly made for mountain-climbing, Maja my pet.

MAJA: (*With an effort to contain herself.*) Even though you gave me to believe, one time, you thought I was.

RUBEK: Yes. Four or five years ago. (*Stretches in his chair.*) Four, five years… That, Maja, is a long, long time…

MAJA: (*Looks at him, bitterness visible upon her.*) Has that time, Rubek, been all that very tedious to you?

RUBEK: It is beginning to drag a little. (*Yawns.*) Once in a while.

MAJA: (*Returns to her chair.*) Then I shall weary you no more. (*She sits in her chair, takes up her newspaper and starts leafing through. Silence from the two of them.*)

RUBEK: (*Leans forward on his elbows upon the table, and gives her a teasing look.*) Have we offended our Professor's Lady?

MAJA: (*Cold, without looking up.*) Not in the least.
(*Guests at the spa, mainly women, entering right, begin in ones and groups to cross the park and exit left. Waiters, bringing refreshments from the hotel, pass behind the pavilion. The SUPERVISOR, wearing gloves, and stick in hand, comes from his morning round in the park, meeting the guests, acknowledging them with deferential greeting, and a word or two exchanged with one or other of them.*)

SUPERVISOR: (*Coming forward to Professor RUBEK's table and courteously doffing his hat.*) Permit me to wish you a very good morning, Madam. Good morning, Professor, Sir.

RUBEK: Good morning, Supervisor, good morning.

SUPERVISOR: (*Addressing himself to MAJA.*) May one inquire of Sir and Madam if they enjoyed a restful night?

MAJA: Yes, thank you very much; quite outstandingly so: speaking for myself, that is. Come night, I sleep like a stone.

SUPERVISOR: And delighted I am to hear it. One's first
night in an unfamiliar surrounding can often be somewhat
disturbed. And the Professor, Sir…?

RUBEK: Oh, my sleep of a night is in a sorry way. Especially
of late.

SUPERVISOR: (*With a show of sympathy.*) Oh, it troubles
me to hear that. But a few weeks' stay with us, taking the
waters: and we'll soon have you right again.

RUBEK: (*Looks up at him.*) Tell me, Sir. Is there a patient of
yours who takes the waters by night?

SUPERVISOR: (*Surprised.*) By night? No, I've never heard
mention of that.

RUBEK: You've not?

SUPERVISOR: No; I've knowledge of no one here so sick
they need do that.

RUBEK: Is there someone here then who goes for a walk in
the grounds at night?

SUPERVISOR: (*With a smile and a shake of his head.*) No, Sir:
that would be against our regulations.

MAJA: (*Suddenly impatient.*) For God's sake, Rubek, I told you
this morning: you dreamed it.

RUBEK: (*Dry.*) Did I indeed? Thank you! (*Turns to the
SUPERVISOR.*) It so happens that I was up last night; I
wasn't able to sleep. I thought I'd take a glance at what
kind of weather it was outside…

SUPERVISOR: (*Alert.*) Yes, Sir? And?

RUBEK: So I look out of the windows: and there I see a pale
shape in among the trees.

MAJA: (*Smiling at the SUPERVISOR.*) And according to the
Professor, the shape was wearing a bath-robe…

RUBEK: …or something similar, I said. I wasn't near enough
to see exactly what. But something white is what I saw.

SUPERVISOR: Most extraordinary. Was it a gentleman or a
lady?

RUBEK: Oh, no question but it was a lady. But after her,
there came a second shape. And that was totally dark. Like
a shadow…

SUPERVISOR: (*With a start.*) Dark, you say? Even black maybe?

RUBEK: So far as I could make out, yes.

SUPERVISOR: (*Realization dawning.*) And coming after the white one? Following her…?

RUBEK: That's right. Some little way after.

SUPERVISOR: Ah! I think, Professor Sir, I can throw some light on the matter for you.

RUBEK: Well?

MAJA: (*In the same moment.*) You mean the Professor wasn't dreaming?

SUPERVISOR: (*Suddenly whispering, pointing toward the background right.*) Sh, Madam, Sir, if you please… Over there, look… If we could just lower our voices a moment… (*A slender lady, clad in fine creamy white cashmere, and followed by a deaconess in black with a silver cross hanging on a chain upon her breast, emerges from behind the hotel-corner, and makes her way across the park toward the pavilion in the foreground on our left. Her face is pallid, and her features as though petrified; eyelids down, and in her eyes a look that does not see. Her dress reaches to her feet, and fits closely about her body in straight perpendicular folds. Over her head, neck, breast, shoulders and arms is draped a short white shawl of crepe. Her arms she holds up, crossed before her breast. This attitude unyielding. Stiff steps, and measured. So too the sister's bearing: measured, and like that of a woman ministrant. Her brown piercing eyes gaze fixed upon the lady, and never stray from her. The waiters, with white napkins on their arms, emerge from the hotel doorway watching curiously after as the two strangers go. These pay no heed and, without looking about them, pass into the pavilion.*)

RUBEK: (*Can not help rising slowly from his chair, gaze fixed upon the shut pavilion door.*) That lady, who was she?

SUPERVISOR: She's a stranger here, renting the little pavilion yonder.

RUBEK: Foreign?

SUPERVISOR: It would seem so. Certainly the two of them arrived from foreign parts. A week or so since. They've not been here before.

RUBEK: (*Looks at him, convinced.*) She's the one I saw in the grounds last night.

SUPERVISOR: That's who it was, surely. That was my very first thought.

RUBEK: Tell me Sir, what is that lady's name?

SUPERVISOR: She has signed in as Madame de Satoff, and lady companion. We know nothing more.

RUBEK: (*Pondering.*) Satoff? Satoff…?

MAJA: (*With a sarcastic laugh.*) Rubek? What, is that the name of somebody you know?

RUBEK: (*Shakes his head.*) No, not at all… Satoff? It sounds Russian. Slavic, anyway. (*To the SUPERVISOR.*) What language does she speak?

SUPERVISOR: When the two ladies talk between themselves, it's in a language lost on me. Otherwise she speaks good honest Norwegian.

RUBEK: (*Cries out in surprise.*) Norwegian? You're sure of that?

SUPERVISOR: Oh yes, I can be sure of that.

RUBEK: (*Looks at him; tense.*) You've heard it yourself?

SUPERVISOR: Yes. I've actually spoken with her. On a few occasions. Though only a word or so. She's not at all forthcoming. But…

RUBEK: …but she spoke Norwegian?

SUPERVISOR: Good native Norwegian. Perhaps with a note of the Far North in her speech.

RUBEK: (*Gazes before him; he is moved, and whispers.*) That too.

MAJA: (*Somewhat put out and uneasy.*) Rubek? Perhaps the lady was a model for you once. Think back.

RUBEK: (*Casts her a cutting look.*) A model?

MAJA: (*With a mocking smile.*) Yes: in the days of your youth, that is. You must have had no end of women model for you. Time long gone, of course.

RUBEK: (*Adopting the same tone.*) Oh no, my pet. There was only ever the one real model for me. Only the one: for all that I have ever created.

SUPERVISOR: (*Has turned to pause looking out left.*) I'm very sorry, I must ask you to excuse me. I see someone yonder it's no particular delight to meet. Least of all with ladies present.

RUBEK: (*Looks out yonder too.*) That huntsman coming: who is he?

SUPERVISOR: That is Squire Wolfheim, from –

RUBEK: Squire Wolfheim indeed?

SUPERVISOR: The Bear-Slayer, as they call him.

RUBEK: That man I know.

SUPERVISOR: Ay, who doesn't?

RUBEK: Only very slightly, though. Come to take the cure, has he, at last?

SUPERVISOR: No, oddly enough; not yet. He stops over here once each season, on his way up to the hunting-grounds. If you'll excuse me for now…
(*Makes to enter the hotel.*)

WOLFHEIM: (*Off.*) Hold it a moment there! Hold it, damn you! Why do you always scuttle when I come?

SUPERVISOR: (*Pauses.*) Not scuttling, Squire Wolfheim, at all.
(*SQUIRE WOLFHEIM comes in from the left,* [*followed by a servant leading a pair of hunting hounds. WOLFHEIM is*] *in hunting-wear, with high boots and a felt hat with feather. He is a lean, tall, sinewy figure, with matted hair and beard, loud-voiced, of an age not easy to tell from his appearance; but no longer young.*)*

WOLFHEIM: (*Goes charging up to the SUPERVISOR.*) What way is that to welcome strangers, Sir? Slinking off with your tail between your haunches: as though you had the Devil panting after.

SUPERVISOR: (*Easy, not answering him.*) Did you come by steamer, Sir?

WOLFHEIM: (*Growling.*) Can't say I was vouchsafed a glimpse of any steamer. (*Hands on his hips.*) Don't you know I sail a cutter of my own? [(*To the servant.*) Lars, see to your fellow creatures' needs. But take care they're still ravenous after though. Fresh bones. But not too much meat on them, hear me? And see they're raw, the red blood reeking. And get something into your own belly too. (*Kicks at him.*) Oh get the hell out of here.
(*The servant goes off with the dogs behind the hotel-corner.*)]

SUPERVISOR: Would Sir like to take a seat in the restaurant for luncheon?

* Material in square brackets was cut in the Almeida production.

WOLFHEIM: Amid all those flies and guests with one foot in the grave? For all I thank you, no Sir.

SUPERVISOR: Very well, as Sir pleases.

WOLFHEIM: But have the maid fix up for me my usual hamper! No stinting with the food! And a decent supply of brandy…! Tell her from me else, my man Lars or I shall come and give her merry Hell –

SUPERVISOR: (*Interposes.*) We've not forgotten. (*Turns.*) Anything, Professor, I can ask the waiter to bring you? Or Mrs Rubek perhaps?

RUBEK: No thank you, nothing for me.

MAJA: Nor for me.

(*The SUPERVISOR passes into the hotel.*)

WOLFHEIM: (*Stares at them a moment, then raises his hat.*) Well I'll be damned! The bumpkin finds himself among the Quality.

RUBEK: (*Looks up.*) How do you mean, Sir?

WOLFHEIM: (*Humbler, and with better courtesy.*) If I'm not mistaken, I stand before master-sculptor Rubek himself.

RUBEK: (*Nodding.*) We did meet socially once or twice. That autumn I was last at home.

WOLFHEIM: But that was years ago! You were not the celebrity then you must be now. Why, even a miry hunter of the bear might venture near you then.

RUBEK: (*Smiles.*) I don't bite, even today.

MAJA: (*Looking at WOLFHEIM with interest.*) Are you a real actual bearhunter?

WOLFHEIM: (*Sits at the neighbouring table, between them and the hotel.*) For preference, lady, I hunt the bear. Though I'll settle for whatever wildlife comes my way. Eagle, wolf, woman, elk, reindeer… And if it's young, lively, full-blooded…well then…! (*He quaffs from his hip-flask.*)

MAJA: (*Cannot take her eyes from him.*) But for preference the bear.

WOLFHEIM: For preference, yes. There's always the knife, then, at hand if things turn tricky. (*A little smile.*) We work with an obdurate matter, the two of us, Lady: your husband and I. He hews away at his marble, I dare say; I hew at the taut and quivering sinews of the bear. But his matter or mine, we each end up on top of it. Make ourselves master and lord of it. We will not yield, until we've triumphed over what resists us so.

RUBEK: (*His thoughts afar.*) That you say is true enough.

WOLFHEIM: I do: for stone too has its cause, I know. It is dead and withstands, with all its weight and power, its own hammering into life. The bear is exactly the same, when someone comes poking at him in his lair.

MAJA: Are you on your way there now, up hunting in the forests?

WOLFHEIM: Way up the mountain I will go. I suppose my lady's not been up the mountain, has she?

MAJA: No, never.

WOLFHEIM: You damn well see you make it up there, then, before the summer's out. You can come with me. I invite yourself and the Professor both, and welcome.

MAJA: Thank you. But Rubek has a sea-trip in mind for this summer.

RUBEK: Along between the islands and the coast.

WOLFHEIM: Ugh, up that damnable festering open drain? What in hell's name are you thinking of? The idea! Crawling along that ditch of sewage? Spewage, it'll be, I say.

MAJA: Rubek, you hear that?

WOLFHEIM: No, you're best coming with me up the mountain. No touch nor taint of humanity there. You can't imagine what that means to me. Though a lady so delicate...

(*He pauses.*
The SISTER IN BLACK comes out from the pavilion and passes into the hotel.)

WOLFHEIM: (*Follows her with his eyes.*) Look at that one, will you. Black crow there. Who's for the grave?

RUBEK: I don't know that anyone here is...

WOLFHEIM: Well, there's one of us hereabout gasping his last. In some nook or cranny. The sick and the ailing should show the grace to have themselves put six feet under: and waste no time.

MAJA: Squire Wolfheim, were you yourself ever sick?

WOLFHEIM: Never. Or I wouldn't be sitting here now. Those closest to me though…those poor wretches, they've been sick.

MAJA: So, and what did you do for them?

WOLFHEIM: Shot them, of course.

RUBEK: (*Looks at him.*) Shot them?

MAJA: (*Jerking her chair away.*) Shot them dead?

WOLFHEIM: (*Nods.*) Lady, I don't miss.

MAJA: But what can possess you to go around shooting people?

WOLFHEIM: I'm not talking about people –

MAJA: You said those closest to you –

WOLFHEIM: Those closest to me I'd say were my dogs there.

MAJA: Your dogs?

WOLFHEIM: I've no one closer. My honest, trusty, steadfast comrades of the chase… When one of those takes sick and failing…pkh! There's him, good friend, sent speeding on his way. Over to the other side.
(*The SISTER IN BLACK comes out from the hotel with a tray, on which milk and bread; sets this down on the table before the pavilion, and passes on within again.*)
(*With a scornful laugh.*) See that? You call that food for a body? Milk-and-water, mushy pappy bread? Oh, my lady should see my comrades at their feeding. [Fresh meaty bones. Raw, and the red blood reeking.]* Would Madam like to come and watch that?

MAJA: (*Smiles across at the PROFESSOR, and rises.*) Yes, I rather would.

WOLFHEIM: (*Standing too.*) You're an adaptable lady, Madam, I can see. Come with me, then. Huge great knuckles of meat they gobble whole. Belch them up, then gobble down again. Oh, the sight of it's a glory to behold. Come along and I'll show you. And we can talk a little further, about this trip up the mountain…
(*He exits round the hotel-corner. MAJA follows after him. In almost the same moment, the strange LADY emerges from the pavilion and sits at the table.*)

* Material in square brackets to be inserted here when character of Lars is cut.

LADY raises the glass of milk, about to drink, but pauses, and looks out at RUBEK with blank expressionless eyes.)

RUBEK: (*Remains seated at his table; his gaze upon her, grave and fixed. At last he stands, takes a step toward her, pauses, and in a hushed voice speaks.*) I recognize you well, Irena.

LADY: (*In a toneless voice, putting down her glass.*) Tell who I am, can you, Arnold?

RUBEK: (*Not answering.*) And you recognize me too, I see.

LADY: With you it's quite a different matter.

RUBEK: What's that…? With me…?

LADY: You're living still.

RUBEK: (*Not understanding.*) Living…?

LADY: (*After a moment.*) Who was that other? She you had with you: at your table there?

RUBEK: (*A little reluctant.*) She? It was…it was my wife.

LADY: (*Nods slowly.*) Ah yes. As well, Arnold. Someone who doesn't concern me, then.

RUBEK: (*Uncertain.*) No, of course not…

LADY: …Someone you found yourself, after my lifetime.

RUBEK: (*Suddenly stares at her.*) After your…? What are you saying, Irena?

IRENA: (*Not answering.*) And the child? Our child of course will be thriving. After me, our child lives on. In glory and esteem.

RUBEK: (*Smiles as at a distant memory.*) Our child? Yes, we did call it that…at the time.

IRENA: In my lifetime, yes.

RUBEK: (*Essays a lighter note.*) Yes, Irena: you can be sure, round all the world our child is famous now. You'll have read about it, I know.

IRENA: (*Nods.*) And has made its father famous too… You dreamed of that.

RUBEK: (*In a voice hushed with emotion.*) It's to you I owe all of it, Irena, all of it. Thank you for that.

IRENA: (*Sits on a while, pondering.*) If I had done at that time, Arnold, as I had right…

RUBEK: Yes? What?

IRENA: I should have killed that child.

RUBEK: Killed it, you say?

IRENA: (*In a whisper.*) Killed it: before I left you. Smashed it. Smashed it to dust.

RUBEK: (*With a reproachful shake of the head.*) Irena, that's something you had not in you to do. You hadn't the heart for that.

IRENA: No, I hadn't then that heart it needs.

RUBEK: Afterwards, though? Since?

IRENA: Since, I have killed it times without number. Killed it in hatred... Vengefulness... Agony.

RUBEK: (*Goes up to her table and asks quietly.*) Irena...tell me now at last...after all these years...why did you go from me when you did? Forsake me so and leave no trace...never to be found again...

IRENA: (*Slowly shaking her head.*) Oh Arnold... Why tell you now? ...now that I am on this other side.

RUBEK: Was there someone else that you had come to love?

IRENA: There was one who had no use for the love I had to give. Use for my life no more.

RUBEK: (*Would change the subject.*) Hm... Let's leave off this talking of what's past and done...

IRENA: No, no, be sure we talk no more of the other side. Of what is now the other side for me.

RUBEK: Where did you go to, Irena? For all my seeking, you were as one vanished from the earth.

IRENA: I passed into the dark: while there the child stood in transfiguring light.

RUBEK: Have you journeyed much about the world?

IRENA: Yes. Journeyed in many lands and countries.

RUBEK: (*Looks at her with compassion.*) And how have you managed for yourself, Irena?

IRENA: (*Looks directly at him.*) Bide a moment. Let me see... Ay, now I recollect. I've posed on the music-hall revolve. Posed as a naked statue in living tableaux. Pulled in a deal of money. Not something I much did with you: you had none... Also I have gone with men that I could drive demented. Again not something Arnold I much did with you. More your own master, you always were.

RUBEK: (*Anxious to pass that issue by.*) And you, too, have married?

IRENA: Yes; one of them.

RUBEK: Who is your husband?

IRENA: He was a South American. High-ranking diplomat. (*Gazes out with a smile of stone.*) I lost him his wits altogether. Crazed him; beyond all curing, crazed him; beyond redeeming, crazed him. Great sport, while in the making, believe you me.

RUBEK: And now where's he living?

IRENA: Down below in a churchyard somewhere. And a tall impressive statue on top of him. Also a clattering bullet of lead in his skull.

RUBEK: He killed himself?

IRENA: Yes. He had the grace to be that step ahead of me.

RUBEK: You feel no grief for him, Irena?

IRENA: (*Uncomprehending.*) For whom should I grieve?

RUBEK: Why for Herr von Satoff.

IRENA: Satoff was not his name.

RUBEK: No?

IRENA: Satoff is my second husband's name. He's a Russian…

RUBEK: And where in the world is he?

IRENA: Far away in the high Ural mountains. Amid all his mining for gold.

RUBEK: He's living *there*…?

IRENA: (*Shrugs her shoulders.*) Living? Living? Truth to tell, I have killed the man.

RUBEK: (*With a start.*) Killed him?

IRENA: Killed him with a fine sharp dagger I have always with me in my bed…

RUBEK: (*Crying out.*) I don't believe you, Irena!

IRENA: (*With a gentle smile.*) Oh Arnold you can well believe me.

RUBEK: (*Looks at her with compassion.*) Did you have no children ever?

IRENA: Oh yes, I have had a number of children.

RUBEK: And where are those children away to now?

IRENA: I killed them.

RUBEK: (*Severe.*) Now there you go lying to me again!

IRENA: I tell you, I have killed them. And how my heart was in it as I murdered them. No sooner, no sooner had they come into the world. No, long before then, long before. The one and then the next.

RUBEK: (*Laden and grave.*) There's hidden meaning in all this you're telling me.

IRENA: How can I help that? Each word I speak to you is whispered in my ear.

RUBEK: It's for me alone, I think, to sense your meaning.

IRENA: So should it be for you alone.

RUBEK: (*Leans upon his hands on the table and looks into her, deep.*) There are strings within you that are snapped asunder.

IRENA: (*Easy.*) That's sure to happen, when a young full-blooded woman dies.

RUBEK: Oh Irena, put all these warped notions behind you... You are still alive! Alive...alive!

IRENA: (*Stands slowly from her chair and speaks, trembling.*) Long years I was dead. They came and bound me. Laced together my arms behind my back... Then lowered me into a tomb, shut and fast with iron bars. The walls were padded...for no one on the earth above to hear my shriekings from the grave... But I'm beginning now to stand, half-risen; from the dead. (*She sits again.*)

RUBEK: (*After a moment.*) I am the one you blame?

IRENA: Yes.

RUBEK: Blame for that...you call your dying?

IRENA: To blame for leaving me no choice but die. (*Suddenly in a tone quite neutral.*) Arnold, why don't you sit?

RUBEK: I may?

IRENA: Yes. No need to fear you'll catch your death of cold. I don't think I'm entirely ice just yet.

RUBEK: (*Brings a chair and sits at the table.*) There, Irena. Here we are sitting together as in days gone by.

IRENA: A little apart from each other. Also as in days gone by.

RUBEK: (*Draws nearer.*) That's how it had to be, then.

IRENA: Had to be?

RUBEK: (*Absolute.*) There had to be distance between us...

IRENA: Really Arnold there had to be?

RUBEK: (*Going on.*) Do you remember, when I asked if you would come with me out far into the world, the answer you gave?

IRENA: I held up my hand, on oath, and swore to follow you to the ends of the earth so long as I should live. To serve you absolutely –

RUBEK: As model for my art –

IRENA: …in free and utter nakedness…

RUBEK: (*Moved.*) …and serve me you did Irena, open, and joyful, and unashamed.

IRENA: Yes, with all the throb of my young living blood, I served you!

RUBEK: (*Nods, with a thankful look.*) There's no denying that.

IRENA: Fell at your feet and was your servant, Arnold! (*Raising a clenched hand at him.*) But you, you…you…

RUBEK: (*Parrying.*) I did you no wrong, Irena, none!

IRENA: Oh but you did! You did wrong to my inmost being –

RUBEK: (*Draws back.*) I…

IRENA: You, yes! Naked and entire I showed myself before you, for your beholding… (*Voice softer.*) And never once did you lay hand upon me.

RUBEK: Irena, did you not see, days on end I was like a man out of his mind, you were such a loveliness to me?

IRENA: (*Persists regardless.*) And yet…if you had laid hand on me, there and then I do believe I would have killed you. I had a sharp needle about me. Hidden in my hair… (*A brooding stroking of her brow.*) And yet… No: for all that…for all that…that you were able…

RUBEK: (*Looks at her assertively.*) Irena, I was a creative artist!

IRENA: (*Dark.*) Precisely. Precisely.

RUBEK: Before and above all else, a creative artist. And I was diseased there with wanting to achieve the supreme work of my life. (*Lost; remembering.*) 'Day of Resurrection', was its name to be. An image, in the likeness of a young woman, waking from the sleep of death…

IRENA: Our child, yes…

RUBEK: (*Goes on.*) The noblest, purest, ideal vision of woman on earth it was to be: she, the awakening. And that's when I found you. You were everything I needed for it. And you

217

gave of yourself with such willing and joy! You left go of your mother and father, and followed after me.

IRENA: To follow you, was resurrection for the child I was.

RUBEK: Precisely for that above all were you of use to me. You and no other. You became for me a hallowed being, never to be touched but in adoring thought alone. Irena, I was still a young man then. And an irrational dread had possessed me: if I should touch you, want you after the way of the flesh, then would my vision be defiled: and I could never hope after, to bring to final form what I was striving to achieve. And I feel still there is some truth in that.

IRENA: (*Nodding, with a touch of scorn.*) First the sculpture; afterward, the human child.

RUBEK: Judge how you will. But I was utterly in thrall then to my creative purpose! And I felt so exultant and fulfilled in that.

IRENA: And you triumphed in your purpose.

RUBEK: All thanks and blessing be to you. Yes, I triumphed in the purpose. My wish was to create the pure woman, as I envisioned her awakening on Resurrection Day. Not in astonishment at something new, unknown or unconceived till now. But flooding with a hallowed joy, to find herself not changed at all – she, woman of earth…in these loftier, freer, gladder realms: after the long dreamless sleep of death. (*Speaking more softly.*) And I created her so… In your image, Irena, I created her.

IRENA: (*Lays her hands flat upon the table and leans away against the back of her chair.*) And that was your need of me done…

RUBEK: (*Reproachfully.*) Irena!

IRENA: …your use for me, all at an end…

RUBEK: You can say that!?

IRENA: …time for you now to cast about, for images of other perfection…

RUBEK: I found none; none after you.

IRENA: And no others to model for you, Arnold?

RUBEK: You did not model for me. You were my creation's source.

IRENA: (*Is silent a moment.*) And since: what poetry have you done? In marble, that is. Since that day I went from you?

RUBEK: Since that day, I've done no poetry at all. I've pottered about with portraits only.

IRENA: And that woman with whom you're living now…?

RUBEK: (*Breaks passionately in.*) Oh don't be talking of her now! It cuts to the heart.

IRENA: Where are you thinking to go with her next?

RUBEK: (*Listless and weary.*) Oh I look like making some dreary sea-trip, northward up the coast.

IRENA: (*Looks at him, with an almost imperceptible smile, and whispers.*) Journey upward, rather, high among the mountains. The highest you can go. On upward, on upward… Arnold: ever upward yet.

RUBEK: (*Tense, in expectation.*) Up there is where you're going?

IRENA: Have you the courage to encounter me a second time?

RUBEK: (*Struggling, unsure.*) If we could… Oh, if we could…

IRENA: Why can't we, where we have the will? (*Looks at him, and whispers entreatingly, clasping her hands.*) Oh Arnold, come away, come away. Oh, come away above to me…! (*MAJA emerges from behind the corner of the hotel, flushed with pleasure, making straight for the table where she and RUBEK had earlier been sitting.*)

MAJA: (*As she rounds the corner, before she sees them.*) Well Rubek, you can say what you like, I… (*Her eyes light on IRENA and she pauses.*) Oh, do excuse me… You've introduced yourself, I see.

RUBEK: (*Terse.*) Re-introduced myself. (*Standing.*) What was it you wanted of me, my dear?

MAJA: I only wanted to tell you… You can suit yourself what you do: but I'm not coming with you on that horrid steamer.

RUBEK: Why not?

MAJA: Because I'm going up the mountain and into the forests, that's where. (*Wheedling.*) Oh Rubek, you have to allow me to go. I'll be so nice to you, so nice to you after!

RUBEK: Who's put that notion in your head?

MAJA: He has. That frightful Bear-Slayer man. Oh, the tales he has about the mountain are amazing, you can't imagine! And about the life up there! They're hideous, frightful, ghastly and revolting, the lies he tells, most of them.

I'm sure they have to be lies. Yet for all that, strangely
enticing… Oh may I be allowed to go with him? Only to
see for myself, you realize, if what he says is true. Rubek,
may I…?

RUBEK: Yes, my dear, but of course you may go. Off with
you, up among the mountains: away as far and for as long
as you want. I could be coming the same journey myself.

MAJA: (*Quickly.*) Oh no no no, don't think you have to do
that! Not just because of me!

RUBEK: I choose to go to the mountains. Decision's already
made.

MAJA: Oh thank you, thank you! May I go and tell Bear-
Slayer now?

RUBEK: You tell your Bear-Slayer all you like.

MAJA: Oh thank you, thank you, thank you! (*Makes to seize his
hand; he'll none of that.*) Oh Rubek how sweet and kind you
are today!
(*She runs into the hotel. At the same moment the pavilion door
gently and soundlessly opens a little way. In the aperture, the
SISTER IN BLACK is standing, observing, on the watch,
herself unseen.*)

RUBEK: (*Resolved, he turns to IRENA.*) We meet, then, there
above?

IRENA: (*Standing slowly.*) Ay, we meet indeed… I have been
in search of you so long.

RUBEK: Irena, when did you set out in search of me?

IRENA: (*With a touch of bitter joking.*) From that moment I first
saw it clear, that I had made a gift to you, Arnold, of what
is not for anyone to give. That we do wrong to let be taken.

RUBEK: (*Bows his head.*) Ay, and the thought of it eats at me.
You gave me three, four years of your young life.

IRENA: That was not all, not all I gave you. Squanderer I
was…

RUBEK: Yes, you were free with your giving. You offered me
all your lovely nakedness…

IRENA: …to gaze upon…

RUBEK: …and celebrate…

IRENA: Ay, win celebration for yourself. And for the child.

RUBEK: Irena, and for you.

IRENA: But you've forgotten the rarest gift of all.

RUBEK: The rarest…? What gift was that?

IRENA: All my young and living soul, I gave to you. And I
stood on there, after: hollowed within. All soul in me gone.
(*Stares fixedly at him.*) Arnold, it's of that I died.
(*The SISTER IN BLACK draws open the door full ajar, and
stands aside for her. She passes into the pavilion.*)

RUBEK: (*Stands gazing after her; then in a whisper.*) Irena!

End of Act One.

ACT TWO

*High, near a mountain sanatorium. Landscape, a wild flat upland,
bare and measureless, reaching away toward a long mountain-lake.
Beyond that, rising, a range of mountain-peaks; in their crevasses, the
snow seems tinged with blue. In the foreground to our left, a rippling
stream divides and tumbles down over a steep face of rock, to flow
its even way across the wild, and out to our right. Scrub, vegetation,
boulders mark the course of it. In the foreground to our right, a knoll;
stone bench atop it there. A summer evening; sunset near.*

*Some way away, on the barren wild beyond the stream, a group of
little children are singing as they play and dance. Some are town clad,
some in traditional dress. The sound of their happy laughter will be
heard, muted, throughout the opening scene.*

*Professor RUBEK sits up there on the bench, a rug about his
shoulders, looking down upon the children's playing.*

*After a moment, his wife MAJA comes making her way between some
bushes on the wild land midground to our left, scanning afar, hand
shading her eyes. She's wearing a flat tourist-cap, a three-quarter
length skirt, gathered half-way up her shin, and high, stout, lace-up
boots. In her grasp, a long vaulting-stock.*

MAJA: (*At last catches sight of RUBEK, and calls.*) Hallo-o!
    (*She makes her way across the wild toward him; with the aid
    of the vaulting-stock she clears the stream, and comes climbing
    up the slope of the knoll.*)
    (*Panting for breath.*) Rubek, I've been chasing high and low
    for you.
RUBEK: (*Nods without interest, and asks.*) Have you come up
    from the Sanatorium Hotel?
MAJA: Yes, that fly-trap, I was there just now.
RUBEK: (*Looks at her a moment.*) You didn't put in an
    appearance at lunch, I noticed.
MAJA: No, the two of us had ours served in the open air.
RUBEK: 'Two of us'. Which two would these be?
MAJA: Myself, and that frightful bearslayer man, of course.

222

RUBEK: Ah: him.

MAJA: That's right. And tomorrow early we're off out again.

RUBEK: After bear.

MAJA: That's right. A-hunting Bruin we will go.

RUBEK: Have you and he found trace of one?

MAJA: (*Superior.*) You won't find bear up here above the tree-line, will you?

RUBEK: Where then?

MAJA: Way down below. On the wooded slopes beneath. Deep in the forest's heart. Where ordinary urban people could never enter.

RUBEK: And you and he are off down there tomorrow?

MAJA: (*Flings herself down in the heather.*) That's right, that's the plan. Though we could be making a start tonight even… So long of course as that's all right by you?

RUBEK: By me? Far be it from me…

MAJA: (*Adds hurriedly.*) Lars will be coming as well. Naturally… And his dogs.

RUBEK: I've not the least interest in Master Lars nor in his dogs. (*Changing the subject.*) Don't you want to come and sit properly up here on the bench?

MAJA: (*Drowsily.*) No thanks. It's so lovely and soft here, lying in the heather.

RUBEK: I can see to look at you, you are tired.

MAJA: (*Yawns.*) Think I'm beginning to be.

RUBEK: It comes on after, does that. Once the excitement is over…

MAJA: (*In a sleepy voice.*) That's right. I'll rest and shut my eyes. (*A brief pause.*)
(*Impatient suddenly.*) Oh Rubek… How can you abide to sit there and listen to those children shrieking?! And watch them acting the goat like that?

RUBEK: Once in a while…in that rough-and-tumble there… something like a harmony is happening…almost musical. Midst all that clumsiness. And those rare moments are good to sit and watch for…when they come.

MAJA: (*With a snicker.*) That's right, Rubek, forever the artist.

RUBEK: And long may I continue so.

MAJA: (*Turning over onto her side, her back to him.*) There's not a trace of artist in him.

RUBEK: (*Alert.*) Who's that is no artist, you say?

MAJA: (*In sleepy voice again.*) Him; that other man, of course.

RUBEK: Our marksman of the bear, you mean?

MAJA: That's right. No trace of the artist in him. Not a trace.

RUBEK: (*With a smile.*) No, I'd say you have the measure of him there.

MAJA: (*Violent, without stirring.*) And he's so ugly! (*Tugs up a tuft of heather and flings it from her.*) So ugly, so ugly! Ugh!

RUBEK: Is it for that you can set out with him so easy? Into the wild?

MAJA: (*Abrupt.*) I don't know. (*Turns to face him.*) Rubek, you're ugly too.

RUBEK: Only now you notice that?

MAJA: No, I saw that long ago.

RUBEK: (*Shrugs his shoulders.*) Age, Mrs Rubek. Age.

MAJA: That's not at all what I mean. But I'm noticing a look in your eye so wearied, so despairing… That is, when you so much as sneak a glance at me. Once in a while.

RUBEK: You reckon do you to have noticed that?

MAJA: (*Nods.*) Little by little you've taken on this mean look. You could almost be plotting me some harm.

RUBEK: Indeed? (*Amicable, but grave.*) Come up here and sit beside me, Maja. And we can have a little talk.

MAJA: (*Half-rising.*) Will you let me sit on your knee then? As we did at the beginning?

RUBEK: No you may not. People can see us from the hotel down there. (*He shifts a little.*) You can come and sit here on the bench… Beside me.

MAJA: No, in that case thank you I'll stay lying as I am. I can hear just as well. (*Casts him an inquiring look.*) So. What was it to be about, this little talk?

RUBEK: (*Begins slowly.*) When I agreed to our coming here this summer, why really do you think that was?

MAJA: Well… You were pretty insistent for one thing on the world of good it would do *me*… But…

RUBEK: But…

MAJA: But I don't believe at all now that was why.

RUBEK: Why then, would you say now?

MAJA: I believe now it was because of that white lady.

RUBEK: Mrs von Satoff...!

MAJA: Yes; that woman on our tail wherever we go. Last night she surfaced even here.

RUBEK: But why on earth should I –

MAJA: Well, you've known her so very intimately, that is why. Long before you knew me.

RUBEK: And had forgotten her... Long before I knew you.

MAJA: (*Sits up.*) Rubek, what, can you forget so easy?

RUBEK· (*Curt.*) Exceedingly easy. (*Adds harshly.*) When I wish to forget.

MAJA: A woman even who has been a model for you?

RUBEK: (*Dismissive.*) When she's of no more use to me, that's right...

MAJA: One who has stripped herself quite naked for you?

RUBEK: Means nothing. To those of us who paint and sculpt. (*Changes his tone.*) Besides...how, if I dare ask, was I to tell that she was in this country here?

MAJA: You could have read her name in a passenger-list. In one of our papers.

RUBEK: Yes but I'd no notion what name she's using now. Hadn't ever heard of any Herr von Satoff.

MAJA: (*With a show of weariness.*) For God's sake, then you must have had some other real reason for wanting to come.

RUBEK: (*Serious.*) Yes, Maja... I did have another reason. Altogether a different reason. And that's what the two of us must bring into the open for once.

MAJA: (*Stifling laughter.*) Lord above, you're looking so solemn.

RUBEK: (*Eyeing her closely with mistrust.*) Ay, a little more solemn perhaps than I need.

MAJA: Why should –

RUBEK: And as well, for us both.

MAJA: Rubek, you arouse my curiosity.

RUBEK: Curiosity only? Not some slight unease?

MAJA: (*Shakes her head.*) No trace of that.

RUBEK: Splendid. So hear you me. Down at the Spa that day you were saying how edgy you thought I'd recently become...

MAJA: Yes and you certainly are.

RUBEK: And what do you think could be causing that?

MAJA: How am I to know…? (*On an impulse.*) You're probably fed up with being forever with me.

RUBEK: Forever? More like for ever and ever.

MAJA: Every day, then, with me. We've been going around in that world down there, the pair of us with none but each other, four, nearly five whole years now, and hardly one hour apart. The pair of us, utterly alone.

RUBEK: (*This interests him.*) And? Go on…

MAJA: (*With some difficulty.*) Rubek, you're not a man for human company. You go your own solitary road, your struggle is all in yourself. And I can't talk to you properly about what occupies you. All this about art and everything… (*A sweep of the hand there.*) And God in Heaven, much I want to, either.

RUBEK: Indeed so. Hence, more often than not we're sitting at the chimney-corner, chatting about what occupies you.

MAJA: God in Heaven, I've nothing occupying me to chat about!

RUBEK: Well, nothing serious, possibly. Though Maja that too does help us while the time away.

MAJA: You're so right. While the time away. Rubek, time is passing you by! And it's really that, I suppose, that's making you so restless –

RUBEK: (*Nods emphatically.*) And so unsettled! (*Writhes on the bench.*) No, I shan't be able to keep up this miserable life much more!

MAJA: (*Rises, and stands a moment, looking at him.*) If you want quit of me, you have only to say.

RUBEK: What way is that to talk? Want quit of you?

MAJA: Yes, if you want rid of me, you tell me straight. And I'm away, here and now.

RUBEK: (*An almost imperceptible smile.*) Maja, is that intended as a threat?

MAJA: There's surely nothing of a threat to you in that.

RUBEK: (*Standing.*) No, you're absolutely right. (*A moment later, adds.*) We can't possibly continue, you and I, living together in this way…

MAJA: Well then…

RUBEK: Well then nothing. (*With emphasis upon the words.*)
That we cannot continue living with only each other…does
not at all mean we must part.

MAJA: (*With a scornful smile.*) Merely separate a little while,
you're saying?

RUBEK: (*Shakes his head.*) Nor any need for that.

MAJA: What then? Let's be hearing what you want to do with me.

RUBEK: (*Feeling his way.*) What need I have now…desperate
in me, searing…is of someone about me of my own, truly
close to me in my inward life…

MAJA: (*Interrupting him in her anxiety.*) Rubek, am I not that?

RUBEK: (*Brushing her aside.*) Not in the sense I mean. I need
my life sharing with another person: who could as it were
complete me…make me whole…be one with me in all I do.

MAJA: (*Slowly.*) True, I could never serve a need in you so
deep as that.

RUBEK: Indeed not, Maja: there you're better leaving well alone.

MAJA: (*Cries out.*) And Lord knows, Rubek, I never felt the
least desire to, either.

RUBEK: As is painfully clear. Not that I attached you to me,
with a view to your being a helpmate of that order.

MAJA: (*Observing him.*) You've someone else there, I can see,
in mind.

RUBEK: Really? I hadn't noticed you'd clairvoyant powers.
See that then, can you?

MAJA: Yes I can. Oh I read you like a book, Rubek, like a
book!

RUBEK: Perhaps you can also see then, who it is I have in
mind?

MAJA: Yes actually I can.

RUBEK: Really? Be good enough to tell me…

MAJA: You're thinking of that…that woman who used to be
your model for… (*Suddenly lets the thought drop.*) You know
people in the hotel down there think she's deranged?

RUBEK: Do they? And what do people in the hotel down
there think of you and your bear-slayer then?

MAJA: That's not the point. (*Resumes her earlier thought.*) But
it is that white lady you had in mind.

RUBEK: (*Frank.*) Precisely she. When her use to me was done… And when she left me anyway… Vanished… Was simply gone…

MAJA: …You made do with me as a poor substitute, I suppose?

RUBEK: (*With less regard for her feelings here.*) Something like that, Maja my pet, to be quite frank with you. Eighteen months or so I'd gone, alone and brooding…putting the last touches, the very last, to that piece of mine. 'Day of Resurrection' went out across the world and brought me fame…and all the pomp that goes with that. (*More feelingly.*) But my love for my own work was gone. The public brought garlands and incense: and as good as had me retching, and despairing; hounded deep into the forest's heart. (*Looks at her.*) And there what thought occurred to me, you with your clairvoyant powers, can you guess?

MAJA: (*Indifferent.*) Sure, you thought of doing portrait-busts of gentlemen and ladies.

RUBEK: (*Nods.*) To commission, yes. Masks, over faces of beasts. Those they had, thrown in; on the house, you understand me. (*With a smile.*) No, I wasn't referring quite to that.

MAJA: What then?

RUBEK: (*Serious again.*) This: the whole to-do about the artist's calling, artistic activity… All that… I began to see for what it is: so empty, hollow, void utterly of meaning.

MAJA: What would you do instead?

RUBEK: Live, Maja.

MAJA: Live?

RUBEK: Because isn't it of altogether greater worth to live amid beauty in the light of the Sun? Than go on and on till the end of one's days, in a chill damp catacomb, slogging away until exhausted unto death, at lumps of clay and blocks of stone?

MAJA: (*With a little sigh.*) Well, that's certainly always been my feeling.

RUBEK: After all, I had the means now: to a life of abundance in the indolent shimmering beams of the sun.

To have built for me that villa on Lake Taunitz, and that palace in the capital. And all the rest of it.

MAJA: (*Takes up his tone.*) And then, to set the seal on all, you had means to acquire me too. And gave me leave to make use of all your hoard.

RUBEK: (*Jokingly, to steer their talk away.*) I promised you, didn't I, to take you with me up a high mountain and show you all the glory of the world?

MAJA: (*With a gentle expression.*) You might have taken me with you, Rubek, up a high enough mountain; but you haven't shown me all the glory of the world.

RUBEK: (*With an irritated laugh.*) Oh Maja, there's no satisfying you. No satisfying you at all. (*In passionate outcry.*) But do you know what causes me the most despair? Can you make a guess?

MAJA: (*Quietly defiant.*) Sure: what else but that you're coupled to me now: for life.

RUBEK: I wouldn't word it quite so heartlessly.

MAJA: What it amounts to is heartless as that.

RUBEK: You've not any real clear notion, how it feels to be an artist.

MAJA: (*Smiles, shaking her head.*) Lord above, I've not the first notion how it feels to be myself.

RUBEK: (*Ignoring that.*) Maja, I live so driven. For us creative people, that's how living is. I myself, I have lived a whole lifetime through, in these few years we two have known each other. I have come to see now, any hope of a happy life of idle pleasure is not for me. Myself and my kind aren't made that way. Mine must be an unremitting toil – bringing work after work into being – up till the very day I die. (*This last not easy.*) For which reason, Maja my dear, I can't go on any longer, with you. Not any longer, with only you.

MAJA: (*Easy.*) Are you saying in effect that you are tired of me now?

RUBEK: (*Flaring up.*) Yes I am saying that! I am tired now… Tired beyond endurance, weary, will-less, living with you. You know now. (*Taking control of himself.*) These are ugly, cruel words I'm saying to you, my dear. They hurt me just as much. And none of this is any fault at all of yours: I freely acknowledge that. It is I, and I only…in this new revolution I have undergone… (*Half to himself.*) …in this awakening to where my living truly is.

MAJA: (*In spite of herself, clasps her hands in entreaty.*) Why on earth can we not leave each other then?

RUBEK: (*Looks at her in surprise.*) You could agree to that?

MAJA: (*Shrugs her shoulders.*) Well…if there's nothing else we could do –

RUBEK: (*Eager.*) But there is something else we could do. There is another way out from this –

MAJA: (*Wagging her finger at him.*) Now you're thinking of the white lady again!

RUBEK: Ay, truth to tell, she must be ever in my thinking now. Since that moment I met her afresh. (*Drawing nearer.*) Because I have a secret, Maja, I will share with you now.

MAJA: Well?

RUBEK: (*With beat of the hand upon his breast.*) Here within, you see, I've a small little treasure-casket with a singular lock. And in this casket's keeping, all my images repose. But when she went from me as she did and left no trace, that lock sprang shut. And she had the key…and that, she took with her… You, Maja my little one, you had no key, not you. So everything lies on within and all unused. And the years pass! No way for me to reach my treasure now.

MAJA: (*Trying to fight down a devious smile.*) Then have her open it for you again…

RUBEK: (*Not understanding.*) Maja…?

MAJA: …now that she is here. No doubt it's in the casket's cause she's come.

RUBEK: I've never breathed one word of this to her.

MAJA: (*Looks at him, all innocence.*) But Rubek my sweet…does it really merit all this stir and commotion, for a want so utterly simple?

RUBEK: You think it simple as all that?

MAJA: Yes actually I do. Just go with whomever you most need. (*Nods at him.*) I know I can always find somewhere to put myself.

RUBEK: Such as where?

MAJA: (*Offhand, evasive.*) Well…I can always move out to the villa if need requires. But it shan't. After all, in the town, somewhere surely in all that great house of ours, given a little good will…there could prove space for three.

RUBEK: (*Doubtful.*) And you would expect *that* to last?

MAJA: (*Lightly.*) God in Heaven, if it doesn't work out, it doesn't work out. There's no more to be said.

RUBEK: But Maja if it didn't work out, then what do we do?

MAJA: (*Undismayed.*) Then we simply go our separate ways. For good. I can always find myself a new life somewhere or other. Something free! Free! Free! Don't you worry about me, Professor Rubek! (*Points suddenly out right.*) There, look! There comes our lady.

RUBEK: (*Turns.*) Where?

MAJA: Out across the moorland yonder. Step on step…like a statue in marble. She's making this way.

RUBEK: (*Stands and gazes yonder, his hand shading his eyes.*) Oh does she not seem the Resurrection itself made flesh? (*To himself.*) That I could have moved her aside… Could stand her in the shadow! Alter her… Oh, fool I was!

MAJA: What's all that about?

RUBEK: (*Brushing her question aside.*) Not a thing. Not something you can ever understand.

(*IRENA advances from our right across the wild. The playing children have already long caught sight of her, and have run to meet her. Now she is ringed about with the company of them; some seeming at ease and secure, others shy and tense. She talks quietly to them, then gestures that they should go down now, in the direction of the sanatorium; she herself would rest a while by the stream. The children run off over the slope, in midground left. IRENA makes her way on toward the face of mountain-rock, and lets the waterfall's divided streams play coolingly upon her hands.*)

MAJA: (*Speaking low.*) Go down and speak with her, Rubek; you and she.

RUBEK: And where will you go the while?

MAJA: (*Visits on him a look charged with meaning.*) From this day on, I've my own road I go. (*She goes down the hill, and vaults on the stock over the course of the stream. Before IRENA she pauses.*) Professor Rubek is up there, Lady, waiting for you.

IRENA: What does he want?

MAJA: He wants your help with a treasure-casket whose lock is sprung shut on him.

IRENA: I can be of help with that?

MAJA: He's of a mind you are the only one who can.

IRENA: Then I shall go and try.

MAJA: Lady, you must.

(*She goes down the path towards the sanatorium. After a moment, RUBEK makes his way down the slope toward IRENA, but stays his side of the stream from her.*)

IRENA: (*After a short pause.*) She there, that other, says you have been waiting for me.

RUBEK: Year after year I have been waiting for you…and myself not known it.

IRENA: Wasn't able to come to you, Arnold. Lying down there, you see: sleeping the long sleep, deep and dreaming.

RUBEK: But now Irena you are awake.

IRENA: (*Shakes her head.*) I have the heavy deep sleep yet upon my eyes.

RUBEK: You'll see the daylight dawn again for both of us.

IRENA: Don't you believe it.

RUBEK: (*Insistent.*) I do believe it! I know it! Now, that I have found you once more –

IRENA: Arisen.

RUBEK: Transfigured by light!

IRENA: Arnold, arisen only. Transfigured by no light.

(*He balances his way across stepping stones beneath the waterfall towards her.*)

RUBEK: Irena, where have you been to all the day?

IRENA: (*Points away.*) Far, far beyond, in those vast regions of the dead…

RUBEK: (*To draw her from this theme.*) You haven't your…your sister friend with you today, I see.

IRENA: (*With a smile.*) My sister friend, for all that, is keeping a good eye on me.

RUBEK: She can?

IRENA: (*Glancing about her.*) Be sure she can. Wheresoever I go. Never lets me from her sight. (*In a whisper.*) Until one fine sunny morning I kill her.

RUBEK: You would?

IRENA: With all my heart. Give me only the chance.

RUBEK: Why would you wish to do that?

IRENA: She exerts dark powers. (*With mystery.*) Arnold, imagine: she has transformed herself into my shadow.

RUBEK: (*Seeking to soothe her.*) Well, well…shadow we must all of us have.

IRENA: I am my own shadow. (*Cries out.*) Not that you understand that!

RUBEK: (*Sad.*) Oh yes Irena, oh yes, I understand that well enough.
(*He sits on a rock before the stream. She stands away before him, leaning against the wall of rock.*)

IRENA: (*After a while.*) Why do you sit there so, eyes turned away from me?

RUBEK: (*Hushed, shaking his head.*) Dare not…dare not look at you.

IRENA: Why daren't you any more?

RUBEK: You have a shadow that's a torment to you. I have my consciousness that weighs me down.

IRENA: (*With a joyful cry of deliverance.*) Now at last!

RUBEK: (*Leaping up.*) Irena? What is it?

IRENA: (*Fending him from her.*) Easy there, easy, easy…
(*Breathes deep; then speaks, as though a burden shed.*) There, you see? They've let go of me. For the while. Now we can sit and talk with each other as we did, time was…when we were living.

RUBEK: Oh, if only we could talk as we did, time was.

IRENA: Sit where you were. And I sit here beside you. (*He sits again. She sits on a separate rock next to him.*)
(*After a brief silence.*) Now Arnold am I come back to you, from the ends of the earth.

RUBEK: Ay, from a journey infinitely far, that's sure.

IRENA: Come home to my master and lord –

RUBEK: To what is ours… To what, Irena, is our own.

IRENA: Have you hoped for my coming? Each and every day?

RUBEK: How dared I hope?

IRENA: (*Glancing aside at him.*) No: how dared you hope indeed? When you understood nothing.

RUBEK: Was it really not for someone else, you all a sudden left me as you did?

IRENA: Arnold, could it not as well have been for you?

RUBEK: (*Looks at her, uncertain.*) What are you saying…

IRENA: When my service to you was done: with my soul and with my body…and the image in stone stood finished: our child, as you called it…then I placed at your feet the most precious offering of all. To banish myself for ever from the earth.

RUBEK: (*Bows his head.*) And laid my life waste.

IRENA: (*Suddenly flares up.*) I wanted precisely that! You, never never to create again, after you'd created that one child of ours.

RUBEK: It was jealousy you were feeling at that time?

IRENA: (*Cold.*) I think it came closest to hatred.

RUBEK: Hatred? For me?

IRENA: (*Impassioned again.*) Yes, for you. For the artist, who so utterly uncaring and undismayed could take a body warm with blood, a young human life and rend the soul from it: because it was of use to you in fashioning a work of art.

RUBEK: And you can say that…? You who aflame with joy, and in all-hallowed yearning, yourself took part in my creative labour? That labour, about which each morning the two of us would gather as for a sacramental act.

IRENA: (*Cold, as before.*) I'll tell you this much, Arnold.

RUBEK: What?

IRENA: I never did love your art before I met you. Nor have I since.

RUBEK: But the artist Irena?

IRENA: The artist I hate.

RUBEK: Even the artist in me?

IRENA: In you most of all. When I bared myself to the flesh and stood there before you, oh Arnold then I hated you…

RUBEK: (*Vehement.*) Irena you did not! That is not true!

IRENA: I hated you because you could stand there so unmoved…

RUBEK: (*Laughs.*) Unmoved? You think?

IRENA: …or so insufferably self-controlled. Because you were an artist, an artist only: not a man. (*Suddenly in tones of warmth and tenderness.*) But that image in wet, living clay: that, I loved…as out from those raw unshapen masses came a child emerging, human and with soul… Because that, was creation of ours; child of ours. Mine and yours.

RUBEK: (*Laden.*) That it was, in spirit and in truth.

IRENA: I tell you, Arnold…it's for that child of ours, I've taken up this weary pilgrim's quest.

RUBEK: (*Alert suddenly.*) For that image in marble…?

IRENA: Call it what you please. I call it our child.

RUBEK: (*Uneasy.*) And now you want to see it? The finished work? In marble that you always thought so cold? (*Eager.*) You don't know, maybe, it's standing in one of the great museums now, away out far in the world?

IRENA: Some such story had reached me.

RUBEK: Though of course you always had an aversion to museums. You called them tombs…

IRENA: I will go a pilgrimage there, to where my soul lies entombed, and the child of my soul.

RUBEK: (*Uneasy and in dread.*) You must never set eye on that sculpture again! Irena, you hear me? I beseech you…! Never, never set eye on it again!

IRENA: For fear I might die of it a second time?

RUBEK: (*Wringing his hands.*) Oh I don't know myself what I fear. But how was it even to occur to me you would bond and fasten on that image so? You, who had gone from me…before it stood full-born.

IRENA: It stood full-born. That set me free to go. And leave you be.

RUBEK: (*Sits, elbows rested on his knees, rocking his head, hands before his eyes.*) It was not what it was later to become.

IRENA: (*Takes soundlessly, lightning-swift, half out from her breast a fine sharp knife, and asks, in a hoarse whispering.*) Arnold… have you done our child some harm?

RUBEK: (*Evasive.*) Some harm? I'm not so sure at all what you would say it is I've done.

IRENA: (*Breathless.*) Tell me here and now what you have done to our child!

RUBEK: I shall tell you, if you will sit and listen quietly to what I say.

IRENA: (*Hides the knife.*) I shall listen quietly as any mother can, who…

RUBEK: (*Interrupting.*) And I'll not see your eye upon me while I'm telling you.

IRENA: (*Moves away, to a rock behind his back.*) I'll sit behind you here… So tell me.

RUBEK: (*Takes his hands from his eyes, and gazes before him.*) When I found you, I knew immediately the use that I must make of you in my great work.

IRENA: 'Day of Resurrection' you called your great work. I call it our child.

RUBEK: I was young then. I had learned nothing of living. My idea then was, for the Resurrection to be best and most beautifully symbolised, it must be as a young untainted woman – innocent of all experience of the earthly life – awakening to light and glory with nothing ugly in her nor impure to shed.

IRENA: (*Quick.*) Yes: and that is how I'm standing surely in our great work today?

RUBEK: (*Hesitates.*) Not altogether quite like that, Irena.

IRENA: (*In mounting tension.*) Not qu – …? I'm not standing how I stood for you?

RUBEK: (*Not answering her.*) Irena, in the years that came after, I learned about this world. 'Day of Resurrection' began to grow, became a more complex presence in my thought. The little round base on which your image stood upright and alone…that was proving no longer sufficient, for all the further imagery I was needing to add…

IRENA: (*Gropes for the knife, but lets it be.*) What further imagery? Tell me!

RUBEK: Imagery of what with my own eyes I was seeing about me in the world. I had to include that too. No choice, Irena. I extended the base…till it was large and spacious.

Then on it I laid a section of the arching, bursting earth.
And up through the cracks in its crust came swarming new
humanity, with animal faces, if you could but see. Women
and men...exactly as I knew them from reality.

IRENA: (*Breathless in expectancy.*) But amidst the throng
the young woman is standing, light's rapture upon her?
Arnold, I am still so?

RUBEK: (*Evasive.*) Not quite in their midst. I'm afraid I had to
take that figure somewhat back. For the effect of the whole
piece, you understand. Else that would have dominated far
too much.

IRENA: But my face is illumined as ever, transfigured in my
rapture at the light?

RUBEK: It is, Irena. In a sense. A little muted, perhaps. As
required by the change in my thinking.

IRENA: (*Stands with not a sound.*) That image, Arnold,
expresses the reality that you see now.

RUBEK: One could say that.

IRENA: And in this image you have demoted me, somewhat
dimmed, to a background figure...one of a group.
(*She draws out the knife.*)

RUBEK: Not a background figure. At best a shape in the mid-
ground, let us say. Or something such.

IRENA: (*In a hoarse whisper.*) There you have spoken your
sentence of death. (*About to lunge forward.*)

RUBEK: (*Turns to look up at her.*) Death?

IRENA: (*Hurriedly hides the knife and speaks in a voice choking as
in pain.*) All my living soul...you and I...the two of us, of
us, of us and our child were in that one shape of stone.

RUBEK: (*Eager, tearing his hat from him and wiping the sweat
from his brow.*) Yes, but hear how I have pictured myself
in the group. Down front, before a spring of water, as in
this place, a man is sitting, laden with guilt, who cannot
quite pull loose from that crust of earth. Remorse, I call
him, for a life misused. There he sits, trailing his fingers
in the rippling water – to cleanse them – and he is eaten
and racked with knowing he can never, never make them
clean. Not all his straining upward through eternity shall

bring him free, arising from the dead to live again. He sits
on, ever, in his hell.

IRENA: (*Hard and cold.*) Poet!

RUBEK: Poet how?

IRENA: Because you are sloppy and slovenly and fat with
self-forgiving for all you've ever done in your life and all
you've ever thought. You have dealt death to my soul:
and now you mould an image of yourself in remorse,
contrition, self-accusing… (*She smiles.*) And thus you reckon
your account made good.

RUBEK: (*Defying.*) Irena, I am a creative man! And I'll yield
to no shame for whatever failing might attach to me. I was
born a creator; understand that. And nothing else that I
could ever be.

IRENA: (*Looks at him with a smile of veiled malevolence, and
mildly and gently says.*) Poet, Arnold, is what you are…
(*Strokes gently the hair of his head.*) You great beloved aging
child. Not to see that…

RUBEK: (*Nettled.*) Why will you insist on calling me poet?

IRENA: (*With knowing eyes.*) Because that word strikes some
excusing note, my friend. Self-justifying: and draws a cloak
over all your failing. (*A sudden change of tone.*) But I was a
human being: then! And I too had a life to live…and a
human destiny to fulfil. Look how I left go of it all: gave
it away, to make myself your underling. Oh there was a
suicide. A deadly wrong against my self. (*Half whispering.*)
And that wrong can I never make good.
(*She sits near him before the stream, passing an observing eye
on him unseen, and starts as though inwardly elsewhere a
plucking of blossoms from the bushes round about them.*)
(*With a semblance of self control.*) I should have brought
children into the world. Many children. Actual children.
Not the kind that lie unseen in tombs. There was my
calling. Not at all to be servant to you… Poet.

RUBEK: (*Lost in rememberings.*) Yet, they were beautiful times,
Irena. Wondrously beautiful times. Now I think back –

IRENA: (*Looks at him with a gentle expression.*) Can you call to
mind one little word that you said…once you were done…

done with me and with our child? (*Nods at him.*) Arnold, can you call that little word to mind?

RUBEK: (*With a questioning look at her.*) I said a little word that time, you still remember?

IRENA: Yes, you did. Can you not recollect that now?

RUBEK: (*Shaking his head.*) No, I can't say that I do. Not this instant, that's for sure.

IRENA: You took my two hands and pressed them warm between your own. And I stood there, not daring to breathe, awaiting… And you said: 'I thank you, Irena, with all my heart. This has been,' you said, 'a miraculous episode for me.'

RUBEK: (*Looks dubious.*) I said episode? That's not a term I'm given to using.

IRENA: You said episode.

RUBEK: (*With feigned assurance.*) Well…come to that, essentially an episode is what it was,

IRENA: (*Terse.*) For that one word, I left you.

RUBEK: Irena, you take things always so painfully to heart.

IRENA: (*Stroking her brow.*) You could be right. Let's shake ourselves free of what's heart-sore and sad. (*She plucks the petals of a mountain rose and strews them in the stream.*) There, Arnold, look, Our birds are swimming.

RUBEK: What birds are they?

IRENA: Can't you see? Flamingoes, of course. If they're pink.

RUBEK: Flamingoes don't swim. They wade only.

IRENA: They're not flamingoes then. They're seagulls.

RUBEK: Seagulls with red bills they could well be… (*He pulls up broad green leaves and throws them after.*) There, I send my ships out after them.

IRENA: There must be no huntsmen on board though, to trap them.

RUBEK: No, there'll be no huntsmen to trap them. (*Smiles at her.*) Can you remember that summer we sat like this, outside the little farmhouse by Lake Taunitz?

IRENA: (*Nods.*) Saturday evenings, yes… When our work for the week was done…

RUBEK: …and we'd travel out there by train. And stay there the Sunday…

IRENA: (*With a malicious glint of hatred in her eye.*) It was an episode, Arnold.

RUBEK: (*As though not hearing.*) Then too you sent birds swimming on the stream. They were water-lilies, and you –

IRENA: White swans, were those.

RUBEK: Swans I mean, yes. And I remember coupling a great downy leaf after one of the swans. Water-dock, I suppose it was.

IRENA: That was for Lohengrin's boat…with the swan before.

RUBEK: You were so happy, Irena, playing at that.

IRENA: We were forever playing that.

RUBEK: Each and every Saturday, I do believe. All summer long.

IRENA: You said I was the swan that drew your boat after.

RUBEK: Did I say that? Ay; could well have done. (*Caught up in the game.*) Our gulls there, swimming away down river, look…

IRENA: (*Laughs.*) And all your ships have run aground.

RUBEK: (*Places more leaves upon the stream.*) I've ships a-plenty in store. (*Follows the leaves with his eyes; launches more petals; and soon he says.*) Irena? …I've bought the little farmhouse on Lake Taunitz.

IRENA: You've bought it now? You were always saying you'd buy it if ever you had the means.

RUBEK: Since then I have come by means enough. And so I bought it.

IRENA: (*With a look askance at him.*) Is that where you're living now…in that old house of ours?

RUBEK: No, I've had that torn down long ago. And built myself a splendid great comfortable villa in its place, with parkland all around. And it's usually there that we – (*Pauses, and corrects himself.*) …usually there that I spend the summer…

IRENA: (*Containing herself.*) So you and…and that other go out to stay there now?

RUBEK: (*A touch of defiance.*) That's right. When my wife and I aren't travelling: as this year we are.

IRENA: (*Gazing afar.*) A beautiful life, beautiful that was, by Lake Taunitz.

RUBEK: (*As though looking back within himself.*) And yet, Irena…

IRENA: (*Completing his thought.*) …and yet the two of us let all that beautiful way of living slip from our grasp.

RUBEK: (*Softly, needful.*) Is our repentance come too late?

IRENA: (*Does not answer him, but sits a while in silence; then points away, across the mountain waste.*) Arnold, look there. Behind the mountain peaks, the sun is going down. Just look at that: in the slant of its light, how red it tinges all those tufts of heather there.

RUBEK: (*Looking yonder too.*) It's a while since I saw a sunset from the mountain.

IRENA: And since a sunrise, longer?

RUBEK: A sunrise I think I have never seen.

IRENA: (*Smiles, as though lost in a remembering.*) I once saw a wondrously beautiful sunrise.

RUBEK: You did? Where was that?

IRENA: Away up high, high on a giddying mountain-top… You lured me with you up that height with promise I should see revealed there all the glory of the world; if I would only – (*She stops short.*)

RUBEK: If you would only…? What?

IRENA: I did as you said. Followed you, up to the height above. I fell there to my knees… And adored you. And served you. (*Is silent a moment, then speaks softly.*) Then it was, I saw the sunrise.

RUBEK: (*Bringing the conversation round.*) You wouldn't wish at all to come south with us and live in our villa there?

IRENA: (*Looks at him with a smile of scorn.*) Live with you…and that other lady?

RUBEK: (*Urging.*) Live with *me*…as in the days of our creation. Unlocking all that is seized and stunted in me! Irena, could you not find it in you to do that?

IRENA: (*Shaking her head.*) Arnold, I don't have the key to you now.

RUBEK: You have the key! You and only you! (*Entreating, begging.*) Oh bring me help...and I can be again the living man I was.

IRENA: (*Immovable as before.*) Empty dreams. Fatuous, dead dreams. Our way of sharing has no resurrection after.

RUBEK: (*Abruptly breaking off.*) On with our playing then.

IRENA: Ay: playing, playing...playing, only!

(*They sit, strewing leaves and petals upon the stream, to swim and sail there.*

Up over the steep slope to our left in the background SQUIRE WOLFHEIM and MAJA come in hunting-gear. [*The man follows after, with the brace of hounds, and leads them on out to our right.*])

RUBEK: (*Catching sight of them.*) Oh look, little Maja, off and away with our marksman there.

IRENA: Your lady, yes.

RUBEK: Or his.

MAJA: (*Looking out across the mountain landscape as she goes; catches sight of the couple at the stream and calls over.*) Good night, Professor! Dream of me! I'm away now, on my great adventure!

RUBEK: (*Calls back to her.*) What adventure shall that be?

MAJA: (*Coming nearer.*) To put living in place of all else.

RUBEK: (*Wry.*) Indeed, you too, my little one?

MAJA: Oh yes! I've made a rhyme about it. Like this: (*Sings and exults.*)

> I am free! I am free! I am free! — *Re awakened*
> The cage has sprung open for me! *...life of sexuality*
> I am free now! I fly away free!

That's right: because I feel I've woken up: at last.

RUBEK: So it would seem.

MAJA: (*Breathes full and deep.*) Oh...to waken is like floating in Heaven with no weight at all!

RUBEK: Good night, Mrs Rubek...and good luck to your –

WOLFHEIM: (*Calls out to silence him.*) Hush there! To Hell with your dark summonings! Can't you see we're off shooting?

RUBEK: Maja, what shall my trophy be, you bring me from the hunt?

MAJA: Yours shall be a hawk you can model. I'll wing and bring one down for you.

RUBEK: (*With a mocking and bitter laugh.*) Ay, wing him…and not know it… Long been the way with you, has that.

MAJA: (*With a toss of her head.*) Just let me stand on my own two feet from now, you'll see…! (*Nods and laughs roguishly.*) Goodbye then! And a good and quiet summer night to you on the high wild land!

RUBEK: (*Jovial.*) Thank you! And I wish the pair of you and your hunting the filthiest luck on earth!

WOLFHEIM: (*Bellows with laughter.*) That's more like it, we can do with some of that!

MAJA: (*Laughing.*) Thank you, thank you, thank you, Professor!
(*They have both come over what of the wild can be seen, and pass on out to our right.*)

RUBEK: (*Silence a moment; then.*) Summer's night on the high wild land. Ay: that's what living could have been.

IRENA: (*Suddenly, a crazed look in her eyes.*) You want that? A summer's night on the high wild land: you and I?

RUBEK: (*Reaches to her.*) I will, I will… Come away!

IRENA: Oh my love, my master and my lord!

RUBEK: Oh Irena!

IRENA: (*Hoarse, smiling, and fumbling in her breast.*) It's still nothing but an episode… (*Quickly, in a whisper.*) Sh… Arnold, don't look behind you…

RUBEK: (*Softly likewise.*) What is it?

IRENA: A face there, staring at me.

RUBEK: (*Can't help turning.*) Where? (*With a start.*) Ah…
(*The head of the SISTER IN BLACK is half-visible, amid the bushes on the pathway downward to our left. Her gaze is on IRENA, fixed, unwavering.*)

IRENA: (*Stands and says, sotto voce.*) We must come away from each other. No, you stay sitting. You hear me?! You mustn't follow me. (*Bows over him, and whispers.*) Till later tonight. On the high wild land.

RUBEK: Irena, you will come?

IRENA: For sure I shall. Wait for me here.

RUBEK: (*Repeats, dreamily.*) Summer's night on the high wild land. With you. With you. (*His eyes meet hers.*) Oh Irena… that life was there for us to live… And we have forfeit it, the two of us.

IRENA: We see what's lost for ever, only when –
(*She stops short.*)

RUBEK: (*In a questioning tone to her.*) When…?

IRENA: When we dead waken.

RUBEK: (*With a melancholy shaking of his head.*) Ay, and what then do we see?

IRENA: We see that we never were alive.
(*She makes her way over toward the knoll, and passes down the path. The sister steps aside for her, and follows after. RUBEK sits on before the stream, unmoving.*)

MAJA: (*Heard singing exultant amid the mountains above.*) I am free, et cetera.

End of Act Two.

ACT THREE

Wild cloven mountain, with plunging precipice beyond. Rightward, snowclad rearing peaks, lost in driven clouds above. Leftward, amid a scree of shattered rock, an old hut, half collapsed. Early morning. Dawn greying. Sun not yet up.

Mrs MAJA RUBEK comes down over the scree, left, furious and blushing red. SQUIRE WOLFHEIM follows, half wrath, half laughter – he has her fast by the arm.

MAJA: (*Trying to pull free.*) Let go of me! Let go of me, I say!

WOLFHEIM: Well well... The lady'll be biting me next. She's quite the she-wolf when aroused.

MAJA: (*Hits him on the hand.*) You let me go I tell you! Calm down –

WOLFHEIM: So help me: never.

MAJA: All right, then I'm not going with you one step further. You hear me? Not so much as one step!

WOLFHEIM: Ho ho! And how will you escape from me on this wild mountain?

MAJA: I'll make a run for it, over and down that rockface there if I have to –

WOLFHEIM: And smash and mash my Lady up for dog-food: all luscious with gore... (*Lets go of her.*) Off you go then. Take a run down the rockface if that's what you want. It's that steep, you'll be reeling. One narrow track, and next to useless.

MAJA: (*Brushes her skirt with her hand, and looks at him with fury in her eyes.*) Ay. A fine and lovely specimen you are, to take a woman out hunting.

WOLFHEIM: Go after game with her, you mean.

MAJA: Game, you call this?

WOLFHEIM: I do, I permit myself that liberty. The class of game I relish most of all.

MAJA: (*Tosses her head.*) Well... I have to say! (*A moment: then she gives him a quizzical look.*) Why did you release the dogs up there?

245

WOLFHEIM: (*With a wink and a smile.*) For them to do a little hunting of their own, what else?

MAJA: That isn't true at all. You weren't thinking of them when you let the dogs go.

WOLFHEIM: (*Still smiling.*) Why did I let them go then? Do tell us…

MAJA: You let them go because you wanted rid of Lars. He was to chase after and catch them again, you said. And meanwhile we… Oh, very charming of you Sir!

WOLFHEIM: And meanwhile we…?

MAJA: (*Cutting him short.*) No matter.

WOLFHEIM: (*In confidential tones.*) Lars won't find them. You can bet your word on that. He'll not be back with them before the proper time.

MAJA: (*With a furious look at him.*) No, that's for sure.

WOLFHEIM: (*Grabbing after her arm.*) Because Lars…he knows my…my way with game, you see.

MAJA: (*Eludes his grasp, and casts over him an appraising eye.*) Squire Wolfheim, you know what you look like to me?

WOLFHEIM: I reckon I must look most of all like myself.

MAJA: You're absolutely right. Because you are the living image of a faun.

WOLFHEIM: A faun…?

MAJA: That's it exactly, a faun.

WOLFHEIM: A faun…isn't that some kind of monster? A class of forest-devil, you might say?

MAJA: Yes, that's the very thing you are. Bearded like a billy-goat, and the legs of a billy. Yes, and the faun has his horns!

WOLFHEIM: Hey, hey…has *he* horns too!

MAJA: A pair of frightful horns, yes, just like yours.

WOLFHEIM: You can see my sad little horns?

MAJA: Oh, I think I can see them very clear.

WOLFHEIM: (*Draws out the dog-leash from his pocket.*) I reckon it's best then that I truss my Lady up.

MAJA: Are you out of your mind? Truss me up…?

WOLFHEIM: If devil you would have me, devil let me be. I should say so! See my horns then, can we?

MAJA: (*To calm him.*) There there now… Squire Wolfheim, do show some manners… (*Breaks off.*) So where's this hunting-

lodge of yours, then, you were bragging about so grandly?
You said it was surely somewhere here.

WOLFHEIM: (*Points out the hut to her.*) You see it, Lady,
before your very eyes.

MAJA: (*Looks at him.*) That old pigsty?

WOLFHEIM: (*Laughing into his beard.*) It's sheltered more
than one king's daughter in its time.

MAJA: Was it there, you were telling me the revolting fellow
came in upon the princess in the shape of a bear?

WOLFHEIM: That's right, good mistress comrade of the
chase… The scene of the crime. (*With an inviting flourish of
the hand.*) If my Lady will please to step within…

MAJA: Ugh! I'm not so much as setting foot in that… Ugh!

WOLFHEIM: Oh, but a couple can drowse a summer's night
away quite cosily in there. A whole summer, come to that.

MAJA: Thank you! They'd need a taste for it. (*Losing patience.*)
But I'm tired now, of you and this hunting. I want to go
down to the hotel…before people start waking down there.

WOLFHEIM: How d'you think you're going to find your way
back down?

MAJA: It's you Sir must see to that. There has to be some way
or other down from here, I'm sure.

WOLFHEIM: (*Points away beyond.*) Bless you, of course there's
way down, of a sort: straight out across the rock face
yonder…

MAJA: There, you see? All it needs is a little good will…

WOLFHEIM: …but take a look, is it a path you'd dare.

MAJA: (*Given pause.*) You think not?

WOLFHEIM: Never in all the world. Unless I help my Lady
there…

MAJA: (*Uneasy.*) Well come and help me then. Else why are
you with me?

WOLFHEIM: Which would my Lady rather, I sling her on
my back…

MAJA: Nonsense.

WOLFHEIM: …or carry her in my arms?

MAJA: We had enough of that foolery before.

WOLFHEIM: (*Anger suppressed.*) I took one time the huzzy of a lass... Lifted her up from the filth of the street and carried her on my arms. With kid gloves I handled her. Wanted to carry her so, life long...lest she should dash her foot against a stone. For when I first found her, she had shoes so very thin...

MAJA: But you took her up though, and handled her gently as that?

WOLFHEIM: I took her up from the mire and carried her, high and carefully as I was able... (*With a growling laughter.*) And you know the thanks I had for it?

MAJA: No. What?

WOLFHEIM: (*With a look at her, smiling and nodding.*) I grew the horns. The horns my Lady can see 'very clear'. Isn't that a funny story to tell our lady the bear-sticker's wife?

MAJA: Ay; amusing enough. I know a story even more amusing.

WOLFHEIM: How does that story go?

MAJA: Like this. Once there was a silly little girl: she had father and mother both living; but in rather deprived a home. Along came a mighty great lord of a man, entering in on all that deprivation. And he took up the girl in his arms – as you did – and went off with her far, far away...

WOLFHEIM: She wanted all that much to be with him?

MAJA: Yes, because she was silly you see.

WOLFHEIM: And he of course was such a fine and lovely figure of a man.

MAJA: Oh no, he wasn't so particularly lovely at all. But he gave her the notion that she'd be coming to live with him, on top of the highest mountain, amid sunshine and light beyond compare.

WOLFHEIM: Mountaineer then, this man, was he?

MAJA: Yes he was: after his fashion.

WOLFHEIM: And he took the wench away up with him?

MAJA: (*Tosses her head.*) Oh sure. He took her with him, gloriously above, believe you me. Oh no: he lured her into a chill, damp cage, with neither sun nor fresh air...or so it was for her... Gold-lining on the walls about her, that was all, and colossal ghosts of men and women turned to stone.

WOLFHEIM: Serve her damn well right.

MAJA: But it's still a really amusing story, don't you find?

WOLFHEIM: (*Looks at her a moment.*) Now listen to me, good comrade of the chase…

MAJA: Well? What is it this time?

WOLFHEIM: Should not the two of us be stitching one to other these two poor tatters that we are?

MAJA: The squire fancies himself with needle and thread now, does he?

WOLFHEIM: He does. Couldn't the two of us try cobbling the odd rag together here and there? And come up with some rough resemblance of a human life?

MAJA: And when the poor rags are utterly worn through, what then?

WOLFHEIM: (*With an expansive gesture.*) Why, then we're left standing, frank and free…as Nature made us.

MAJA: (*Laughing.*) You with your billy-shanks, yes!

WOLFHEIM: And my Lady with her – Well, enough of that.

MAJA: That's right, come on: enough of *this*.

WOLFHEIM: Stop! Where's the hurry, friend?

MAJA: Down to the hotel of course.

WOLFHEIM: And what after?

MAJA: Then we bid each other a fond farewell and thanks for the company.

WOLFHEIM: We can part now, you and I? You think that possible now?

MAJA: Well, you never did manage to truss me up, remember.

WOLFHEIM: I have a castle I can offer you…

MAJA: (*Points to the hut.*) The like of that?

WOLFHEIM: It's not yet quite collapsed.

MAJA: And all the glory of the world, I suppose?

WOLFHEIM: One castle, I tell you…

MAJA: Thanks! I've had as much of castles as I want.

WOLFHEIM: …with splendid hunting land for miles around.

MAJA: Are there works of art in that castle too?

WOLFHEIM: (*Slowly.*) No; actually it hasn't any works of art. But –

MAJA: (*Relieved.*) Well, that's something.

WOLFHEIM: You're coming with me then? Away as far and for as long as I ask of you?

MAJA: There is a tame hawk, sits and keeps me ever in his sight.

WOLFHEIM: (*Savage.*) Maja: we shall shoot him a bullet in his wing!

MAJA: (*Looks at him a moment; then speaks, resolved.*) Come on, then; and carry me away below.

WOLFHEIM: (*Flings his arms about her waist.*) And not a moment too soon! The mists are gathering above our heads!

MAJA: Is it fearfully perilous, the pathway down?

WOLFHEIM: The mists of the mountain are peril worse.
(*She tears free, goes over to the crevasse and looks below, but pulls sharply back. WOLFHEIM goes laughing to meet her.*) What's this, a little dizzying for Madame?

MAJA: (*Weak.*) That too. But you go and look over. Those two, coming up…

WOLFHEIM: (*Goes yonder, and leans out over the precipice.*) It's only that hawk of yours…and his strange lady.

MAJA: Can't we slip past them: without being seen?

WOLFHEIM: Not possible. The track is far too narrow. And here there is no other way below.

MAJA: (*Musters herself.*) Very well… Then let's confront them here.

WOLFHEIM: There speaks one born to slay the bear, my friend.
(*PROFESSOR RUBEK and IRENA ascend into view from the chasm beyond. He has his rug about his shoulders, she a fur cape loosely cast about her white dress, and a hood of swansdown on her head.*)

RUBEK: (*Still only half-seen beyond the mountain's sloping edge.*) What's this, Maja? The two of us meet yet again?

MAJA: (*With an assumption of confidence.*) Your servant, Sir. Do come on up.
(*RUBEK comes up fully into view, and reaches his hand to IRENA, who also now comes fully up onto the height.*)

RUBEK: (*Coldly to MAJA.*) You've been all night on the mountain too then, have you? Like us?

MAJA: I've been out hunting, yes. You did give me leave to go.

WOLFHEIM: (*Points towards the chasm.*) Did you come up Sir by that pathway there?

RUBEK: As you well saw.

WOLFHEIM: And the strange lady too?

RUBEK: Goes without saying. (*With a glance at MAJA.*) The strange lady and I don't mean to be taking separate paths from now.

WOLFHEIM: You didn't know then that's a deathly path you've come?

RUBEK: Well, the two of us tried it nonetheless. There seemed nothing to it at the start.

WOLFHEIM: No, at the start there is nothing to it. But then you can find yourself on a foothold so tight, you've no way forward you can see, nor back. And there you stand stuck, Professor Sir. Climb-locked, as we huntsmen say.

RUBEK: (*Looks at him with a smile.*) Are these words of wisdom, Sir, you're offering us?

WOLFHEIM: God forbid I should traffic in words of wisdom. (*Urgently, pointing up toward the height.*) But can't you see Sir that the storm is on us? Aren't you hearing the shocks of the wind?

RUBEK: (*Listens.*) It sounds like the overture to Resurrection Day.

WOLFHEIM: It's a storm-squall, man, from the peaks up there! Just look at the clouds, rolling in and sinking low. They'll be wrapping about us any moment like a winding-sheet.

IRENA: (*With a start.*) That sheet I know.

MAJA: (*Drawing him to her.*) Let's be on our way down.

WOLFHEIM: (*To RUBEK.*) I can help only the one. Wait in the hut there the while...until the storm is past. Then I'll send people up to fetch you both.

IRENA: (*With a shriek.*) Fetch us? No! No...

WOLFHEIM: (*Harsh.*) Bring you by force if so need. It's a matter of life or death, this place. You know now. (*To MAJA.*) Come on then, Lady: trust in your friend's strong arms.

MAJA: (*Clinging about him.*) Oh, if I make it down there in one
piece, shall I rejoice and sing!

WOLFHEIM: (*Begins the descent, and calls to the others.*) You
wait then in the bothy there, till the men come with ropes
and fetch you.
(*WOLFHEIM, with MAJA in his arms, clambers, with
urgency but care, down into the chasm.*)

IRENA: (*Looks a while at RUBEK with terror in her eyes.*)
Arnold, you hear that? There'll be men on their way up to
fetch me! A party of men on their way up here...

RUBEK: Irena, just be calm now!

IRENA: (*In mounting terror.*) And that one...she in the black...
she'll be with them. She must have long noticed I am gone.
And Arnold she'll seize hold of me! She'll put me in the
straitjacket. Oh yes, she's brought one with her in her box.
I myself have seen it...

RUBEK: No one shall be let lay hand upon you.

IRENA: (*With a crazed smile.*) No indeed... I do have answer of
my own to that.

RUBEK: What answer, my dear?

IRENA: (*Draws out the knife.*) This.

RUBEK: (*Grabs for it.*) You've a knife!

IRENA: All the time, all the time. Day and night. And in my
bed.

RUBEK: Give me that knife, Irena!

IRENA: (*Hides it.*) You're not having it. I could well be
needing it for myself.

RUBEK: What use will it be to you here?

IRENA: (*Fixes her gaze on him.*) Arnold. It was intended for
you.

RUBEK: For me!

IRENA: When we were sitting by Lake Taunitz down there
yesterday evening...

RUBEK: By Lake –

IRENA: In front of the farmhouse. Playing with swans and
water-lilies...

RUBEK: And...? And...?

IRENA: …and I heard you say, in voice of ice, chill as the grave…that I had been nothing but an episode in your life…

RUBEK: It was you who said that, Irena. I did not.

IRENA: (*Continuing.*) …then I had the knife out. I was going to plunge it in your back.

RUBEK: (*Dark.*) So why then did you stay your hand?

IRENA: Because I saw all a sudden, horribly clear, you were already dead…these long years gone.

RUBEK: Dead?

IRENA: Dead. Dead; you as I am. There we sat, before Lake Taunitz, the two of us, clammy corpses, playing a children's game with one another.

RUBEK: I wouldn't call that being dead. But you don't understand me.

IRENA: Where then is that burning want for me, you strove and struggled against, when I stood frank and openly before you as the woman risen from the grave?

RUBEK: Irena, that love between us is assuredly not dead.

IRENA: That love, that was of our earthly being…of our earthly being of beauty and of wonder; of our earthly being, so deep with mystery…for both of us, that love is dead.

RUBEK: (*Impassioned.*) Well you know, it is that very love… seething and burning in me now with all the fire it ever did before!

IRENA: But I? Have you forgotten who I now am?

RUBEK: Be who you will, or whatever; to me, all one. You are to me the woman I look at and I dream I see.

IRENA: I have stood on the revolving stage…naked…made a show of my body to men by the hundred…since with you.

RUBEK: It was I that drove you up onto that stage. Blind eyes of mine that would not see! To set as I did the dead image of clay so high, above the joy of life and of love.

IRENA: (*With downcast eyes.*) Now too late. Now too late.

RUBEK: Not by the breadth of one hair has all that's happened in the years between made you any the lesser in my sight.

IRENA: (*Raising her head.*) Nor in my own.

RUBEK: Well then! So we are free now. And there is time for us yet Irena, to be alive and living.

IRENA: (*Says sadly to him.*) Arnold, the desire for living died in me. I am arisen now. I search for you. I find you. And I see you, and all that's living, lying there like – lying there as I have been.

RUBEK: Oh my love how mistaken you are! The life within us and around us is in a ferment and a raging as it ever was!

IRENA: (*Smiles, shaking her head.*) Your young woman has risen, and can see all livingkind laid out for dead.

RUBEK: (*Seizes her in powerful embrace.*) Then these two dead we are must live this one moment utterly alive – before we each sink back into our graves!

IRENA: (*With a cry.*) My love!

RUBEK: But not in this half-darkness here. Not here, with this hideous wet gravecloth beating about us…

IRENA: (*In transport of passion.*) No, no… Up into the light, amid the splendour and the glory. Up to the promised mountain peaks above!

RUBEK: There shall we hold our wedding feast, Irena…oh love of my heart!

IRENA: (*Proud.*) Dear husband, now the sun may gladly look on us.

RUBEK: All the Powers of Light may gladly look on us. And all the Powers of Darkness too. (*Seizes her hand.*) So will you come with me there, my ransomed bride?

IRENA: (*As one transfigured.*) Readily and freely, I come with my master and lord.

RUBEK: (*Drawing her with him.*) First we must up through the gathering mist, Irena, and then…

IRENA: Ay, up through all the gathering mist. And so, to the topmost towering pinnacle above, aflame there in the rising of the Sun.

(*The clouds of mist sink dense and denser about the landscape. RUBEK with IRENA, hand in hand, set off upwards across the snowfield to our right, and soon are lost amid the lower clouds. Sharp squalls of wind flail and whine through the air.*

*The SISTER IN BLACK emerges, ascending the rockfall to
our left. She pauses there, and looks about her, making no
sound, scanning for a sight of them.*)

MAJA: (*Heard rejoicing and singing in the chasm far below.*)

I am free! I am free! I am free!

The cage has sprung open for me!

I am free now! I fly away, free!

(*Suddenly from up on the snowfield a thunderous roar is
heard: it's slipping and swirling in raging onrush down.
RUBEK and IRENA are obscurely glimpsed, swirled about in
the masses of snow, and buried in them.*)

SISTER IN BLACK: (*Lets forth a cry, and reaches out toward the
fallen, calling.*) Irena! (*She stands silent a while, then traces the
Sign of the Cross in the air, and says.*) Pax vobiscum.

(*MAJA's rejoicing and song are heard from yet farther off
below.*)

The End.

Endnotes

PEER GYNT

Act One

Aase almost as 'awesome' without the final 'm' sound (*aa* throughout represents the Nordic *å*).

Peer like 'pair' and **Gynt** as German *Günt* would be; but the traditional Anglicized pronunciation is now established, and should be preferred.

Gjendin *Yen*deen.

Lunde better heard on the English stage as *Loo*nde.

Likewise **Hegstad** *Heg*stahd, and the *st–* must not be Germanized.

Mads Moen Mahss *Moo*en.

Hedal *Hey*dahl.

Solveig *Sol*veh.

Out over the grass the Scandinavian farmstead is traditionally built squarely around a rectangular area of sward.

Kitchenmaster Master of Ceremonies at a country wedding.

The dance, or 'fling', is strictly a *halling*.

We're his mother lit. a peasant idiom *Aase-and-I*.

Act Two

Baard, Kaare Bawrd, *Kaw*ra.

Snap of a pike the Norwegian here means 'He's like childrens' eyes (*barne-øyne*) from the blackest tarn', which taken literally makes no sense. I've read that *barne-øyne* is a dialect usage for a mountain-water perch or pike, but cannot trace the reference to acknowledge it.

She-in-the-green is not 'doubled' with Ingrid. She *is* Ingrid, differently experienced and perceived. (Likewise later the **Hag**.)

Yourself be enough obscure, but that's how Ibsen intends it. The motto is a riddle, and presented as such, its meaning to be pondered. The play itself explores it. It is nothing to do with self-sufficiency: that makes moral nonsense of the play. There *is* an element of parochial self-satisfaction: enclosed communities both yearn for escape, and resent the success of those who achieve it. The real moral danger in the troll ethos is its *solipsism*.

The **Böyg** *öy* (= Norwegian øy) as in French *–euil*. He was a legendary mountain monster, coiled around you, invisible in the mist or dark. However clear you leapt of him, he was always there, inertly in your way. The word is now a common Norwegian term for obstacle. He is some deep inertia in Peer's nature that he cannot transcend.

Silver prayerbook *lit.* 'claspbook'. The clasp on Solveig's prayerbook is silver, and has made a deep impression on Peer's mind. It seems to image her maidenhead, which he will not violate. In translating this (very Freudian) moment, I've risked the purposeful sort of fusion that happens in a dream.

Clegg a horsefly. Standard Ulster, Scots, and Northern English. Standard Norwegian too.

Act Three

Soria Moria Castle a fairytale castle set on an island in the Red Sea. I add *in Araby land* to make its mythic location clear; also to prepare an echo (unconscious on Peer's part) when he plans his scholarly journey in Act Four.

My back's the Devil an Ulsterism, chosen to enhance the echo of the Hag's remark about her bad labour in the preceding scene.

Act Four

Trumpeterstraale (*–pe–* as 'pay', *–straa–* as 'straw') the name means Trumpetshriek – a preposterous attitudinising, void of heroic content. All the names are burlesque: **Cotton**, staple material of the English Industrial Revolution;

Ballon, presumably a bag of Gallic hot air; **Eberkopf**, Ebonyhead. Gynt never dignifies any of these four by addressing him by name. French and German phrases are in the original (where Cotton has some English as well). I've added a touch of Swedish for Trumpeterstraale, and dotted some extra burlesque French and German about the scene for the other two.

Oppressorsh not drunkenness. Some Swedish people, speaking English, confuse y and j; their native *–rs* sound, pronounced *–rsh*, persists as well.

(Which *language* are these people speaking, anyway?) The whole scene I have very much condensed. Also, where Ibsen's Trumpeterstraale seems obsessed with Sweden's faded glory, especially a historic insult done to Charles XII by the Turks, I have generalized the portrait: a sentimental chauvinist, diligently polite – and opportunist.

The Eternal Feminine not Norway's but *Germany's* great Goethe says nothing of the sort. Faust's *Ewig-Weibliche* 'draws us upward'. (Peer has already garbled Scripture likewise, and will continue to do so, to the end.)

Milk beneath cold northern sky *lit.* a reference to goat-milk cheese, a great Scandinavian institution, but hardly elegant in English song.

Solveig's song my model here, as in Act Five, has been the traditional Ulster air *She Moved Through the Fair.*

Sea-route to Athens in the original, Peer seems to expect this to take him through the Pass of Thermopylae. A sad truth, but a modern audience has even less 'grounding' in Scripture and the Classics than Peer, so his more recondite howlers are better omitted now. In any case, it's the man's tragic superficiality that does the work on stage.

Repressed anxiety Ibsen says 'unease', but, since it's a stage-direction and not spoken text, I honour his 'Freudian' insight with a Freudian term.

Pure Reason not, I think, intended in Kantian sense; rather, absolute unarguably valid Sanity itself.

Whom shall I choose? In the original, he singles out an inmate called Huhu. This character is obsessed with the loss of his native Malabari language that imperialism has cost him. Ibsen was conscious of a Danish literary chauvinism that relegated Norwegian to the lowly status of a brogue, fit only for folksong and fishermen; and Huhu's anguish finds parallels today. He is, of course, a distorted refraction of Peer in his Norwegian aspect (as are 'King' Apis and Husain, of Peer in other aspects); for all that, Huhu's contribution to the play's total scheme is tenuous and marginal. Also, Ibsen has written for him no proper climax. Huhu is my one actual excision from the play (apart from some sections of the play's very first scene – see *Foreword*).

Es lebe hoch this line is in German in the original, and all the Keepers say it.

Act Five

HallingsSkarv printed so, to help the actor divide the name correctly. *Skarv* means stony mountainland, but has homonyms that mean cormorant and rogue. The Halling region gave its name to the peasant 'fling' danced at the Wedding in Act I, soon to be darkly recalled in the Auction Scene below. I add *Ridge of him* for clarity.

Jökel as German *Jökl* would be pronounced.

Still presumably 'as all those years ago when I left'.

FolgeFonn *Fo*lle-fawn. These mountains are variously grouped around the Hardanger Fjord, and from Peer's point of view Folgefonn's the nearest. (The ship seems to be making for Bergen.)

Dovre *lit.* the Ronde, Peer's home mountainscape. But it faces the Dovre mountain, Dovre is the one significant name that we have heard, and for a non-native audience all geographical references must be kept simple and meaningful. (Likewise with the Pastor's reference to Gudbrandsdal below.)

Lower the stern-boat strictly, 'stern-boat' if in davits astern, 'quarter-boat' if on the stern-quarter.

Guilt and terror Norwegian *angst*, which Ibsen here means, as I understand it, in Kierkegaardian sense – an awareness of being damned. The texture of the Norwegian dialogue here is congested and baroque. The translator's choice is bleak: over-simplify, or remain obscure.

Peer Gynt can't die in the middle of Act Five. The most audacious alienation-effect I know.

And where *does* Peer die? In the asylum? Earlier in the shipwreck? Here? A vexed question – for some. By this drastic stroke, I think Ibsen disabuses us: the question is irrelevant. It's the greater death that matters.

Valley near Dovre *lit.* Gudbrandsdal.

I peel ye bare It would not be natural for Peer's lost native speech to reassert itself any earlier than this. (Even now, it should only intermittently recur: as and where my spelling indicates.) The device is my own; but takes its cue from certain echoes in Ibsen's text.

Threadballs This notoriously 'unstageable' scene ideally calls for a filmic solution along Disney Gothic lines – and none the worse for that. In most staging, we will have to content ourselves with a stumbling Peer beset by voices. The *nøster* are wound balls of cotton or thread, that I assume are coming unwound as they trundle about Peer's feet.

Cross roads in the Ulster idiom adopted for this translation, 'cross roads' is two words with the stress on the second. So is 'cross road', which also the Buttonmoulder will use, in the same sense.

His Maker's purpose the original refers to craftsmen's 'escutcheons' that, in some European streets, still hang outside their shops.

Out with it the Skinny One actually says (in German) Raus! That would have confusing connotations now.

I must fly South in the original, a stage-direction *Exit, making South.* The most exquisite instruction dramatist ever gave character, and I enshrine it as a spoken line.

The Processional Hymn My underlying model here was *Come Down, O Love Divine* (itself a translation) and to the Vaughan Williams tune. In practice, the words will not be clearly heard; the tune and the singing must do the emotional work. It is a Whitsuntide hymn, alive with joy and a sense of salvation, from which Peer feels excluded.

Waiting where dark begins Ibsen asks for the Buttonmoulder to be merely heard, speaking from behind the hut. Staged thus in our modern theatre, the final image would be in moral and emotional imbalance.

ROSMERSHOLM

Unlike *Peer*, which enjoys a rich and experimental performance-tradition in English-language theatres, *Rosmersholm* is almost unknown. My translation was in fact commissioned for a company in Canada where it had never been staged at all. In such circumstances a translator owes a responsibility to the letter of the text. Also, the play itself, coming some twenty years later (1886), represents an advanced development in Ibsen's dramaturgical technique. Its narrative progression is so compacted, there's not a spoken phrase to spare. It is imperative to render strictly. Also, I have here translated Ibsen's stage-settings in full – unfashionable though they are – for they define onstage the drama's inner world made visible: a modern stage-designer must discern and express their essentials (why, for instance, a stove *and* flowers?) I have tended to distil Ibsen's stage-directions for the characters, or leave them implicit. In practice, actors ignore all playwrights' stage directions, and arrive at them through the spoken text. What is, I think, more useful to an actor, and this I have faithfully done, is to reproduce Ibsen's punctuation rhythm – the surest indication as to how he himself 'heard' the energy running through a line or a speech.

Norwegian social etiquette For a translator, some difficulties arise in matters of styles and terms of address – particularly as shadings and shiftings in these can express the inner narrative process:

His Reverence For *pastoren* 'the Pastor' would seem the natural rendering, and is traditional; but a Pastor, to us, is a figure of non-conformist Dissent. In the Norwegian context, he is a figure of Establishment. So I have risked the rather Anglican-sounding *Parson*, and somewhat more Irish-sounding *His Reverence*. Less quaint, more Protestant-sounding (and accurate, in a production that suggests an English or Ulster context) would be '(the) Rector'. In a Scottish context, he'd be the 'Minister'. But it's a matter of discretion, and in performance 'Pastor' can always be preferred. (Rebecca, in conversation with Mrs Helseth, always takes strategic care to respect and echo the more conventional woman's mode of address for Rosmer.)

Doctor With Kroll, there's a similar problem. Norwegian *Rektor* is an academic status, and strikes a more elevated note than our 'Headmaster'. In Scotland too his title would be 'Rector' (and his school would be an 'Academy'); but in England or Ireland the 'Rector' would be Rosmer (see above) – which shows how complex this issue of translating style and title can be. Hence my *School Principal*, with its sterner associations. As to address, Kroll is never styled *Doktor* in the original, but it's a fair presumption that he would have an academic Doctorate: here, *Doctor* is the clearest, most practical and expressive compromise.

Sir When Rebecca addresses Kroll so, it's a device to express in English her use of the Norwegian formal pronoun, comparable to *vous* in French.

John In her dialogue with Rosmer, it's the reverse: Rebecca addresses him often by surname only. In Norwegian, this can sound quite formal – as suits her position in the household; but it can sound intimate too, in their more private dialogues – and here, in English, only 'John' will do. (In speaking of him to Kroll, she makes a point of never referring to Rosmer by his ecclesiastical title.)

Act One

The Signalling Flame The paper's name is literally *The Flashing Fire*, as in e.g. a watchtower, beacon or lighthouse.

Hedgeman How Ibsen has us first mis-hear this character's name (Norwegian *Hekman*) suggests *hekk*, a nest or a hedge. The effect is to strike in us some subliminal glimpse of the man about to appear, as a tramp-like figure walking the roads, rather like the fallen Troll-King in the last Act of *Peer Gynt*. The character's true name *Brendel* carries a Germanic suggestion of a firebrand, but lesser and smaller. A downfallen Light of the World is one of several aspects in which Ibsen will invite us to see him. For all his emptiness, and pathetic pretensions, he is a complex dramatic creature, and never so demonically accurate as when he is mistaken. In the cosmos of the play, he is a refraction of Rosmer reduced to the absurd: and later, his Light will go entirely out.

Whom I most have loved A Biblical echo: traditionally, 'John' was the Beloved Disciple, though in none of the six references to him in the Gospel is he named.

Old man Brendel doesn't address Kroll so in the original; but, amidst all the gibberish of academic titles he lavishes on Kroll, he presumes to use the familiar pronoun too.

Turning of the year *lit.* a 'storm-driven solstice'. Some commentators suggest, because of the 'storm' element, that Ibsen is thinking of an *equinox* here – and committing a common solecism. I think we should trust a Scandinavian of all people to mean 'solstice' when he says it. Others suggest that it's a character-point, a solecism of Brendel's – but that wouldn't 'read' as such on stage. Ibsen's image is perfectly coherent and clear.

A la bonne heure In the original, *A la bonheur* – inaccurate French, but sounding correct – so it won't be heard as a malapropism of Brendel's, therefore it can't be intended as one. Here, the error does seem to be Ibsen's; and most translators quietly emend it.

Deserter Rosmer's offence, in Kroll's eyes, is literally that he is *frafalden*, an 'apostate'. 'Deserter' is not that, but has something of the emotive force that Kroll intends; and, with the notion of 'defection', is more recognizable in the modern theatre, albeit secular. Apostasy, to modern audiences, has lost its immediacy as a concept.

...about Freedom's work Another Biblical echo (conscious, I'm sure, on Rosmer's part), and a famous one (Luke ii.49): '...I must be about my Father's business.' The Christian ethic, libertarianized.

Rebecca my dear... At the end of the Act, at last alone together, Rosmer and Rebecca adopt the intimate pronoun with each other.

Act Two

Morning-coat What Rebecca is wearing is literally a 'morning-skirt', not quite a dressing-gown, but *déshabille.*

Mortensgård Properly pronounced 'Mortensgaur'; but for the Norwegian *-gård* a Germanic pronunciation 'gard' is conventional practice – as can be printing the *å* as *aa*. (As with **Aase** in *Peer Gynt.*) It's one of the few difficult names in Ibsen, who took care to evolve names for his characters that would travel clearly and well. It's dangerous to be pedantic in this matter of pronunciation. 'Miss Vest', for example.

...in the twilight A subtly melodramatic note. Intended or not, it will soon recur, and suggestively: here, 'in the twilight' Mrs Rosmer's unhappy letter is brought to Mortensgård's house; soon, toward the end of the Act, Rebecca will speak nostalgically of how she and Rosmer would sit downstairs 'in the twilight' and plan their future. The two actions are darkly connected; and the simple symbolism is telling – in each case, a sinister hint at 'night' to come.

Act Three

Kroll's paper In the original, Rosmer simply echoes the paper's name. A modern audience, less attentive, might need reminding that this is the paper newly-bought by Kroll and his faction.

Gamvik Rebecca's mother's surname carries a linguistic overtone suggestive of ancient Nordic social landscape.

Act Four

Coachman Because the word 'coach' no longer immediately suggests the horse-drawn vehicle that Ibsen intended, I have reworked references to a coach as references to its driver.

One or other must go under Rebecca's image of her struggle with Beäta is in the original a struggle for survival 'on an upturned keel': just such a struggle as Ibsen had dramatized twenty years ago – in *Peer Gynt* Act Five Scene Two.

Unfathomable mystery Ibsen is plainer: 'insoluble riddle'. Rather as 'in the twilight', this notion recurs suggestively. Here some motivic echo certainly does seem intended. Kroll has spoken (Act Two) of the 'mystery' of the millrace as being for Rosmer to 'fathom'. Toward the end of that Act, Rebecca rebukes Rosmer for precisely that – brooding on 'unfathomable mysteries'. Now at last for Rosmer, the 'unfathomable mystery' proves to be Rebecca herself.

Let your old teacher be a lesson to you This is literally 'Take a *Beispiel* from your old teacher'. Not everybody in an English-language audience will understand the German word, so I translate the whole line – but with a Brendelesque clumsiness and confusion of usage.

Pre-requisite that must be satisfied Brendel's words echo, not verbally but morally, Kroll's (Act Three) 'requirement that must be met'. What both amount to, is that Rosmer must marry. For Kroll, it was a matter of legitimizing a sexual relationship that in fact did not exist. For Brendel, it's a matter of expunging Rebecca's sexuality from the relationship that does exist. The lady's pink little finger, and her ear, are like a 'Freudian' dream-displacement of the female sexual parts. I think a Brendel can play these amazing moments only from within the specific clarity of a visionary state. Thanks largely to this pitiful man, our sense of Rebecca becomes from now increasingly demonic. Her white shawl acquires the presence of a deathly-seductive attribute – Mrs Helseth will later mistake it for the White Horse: Rebecca is indeed a mermaid of a sort, deadened from the waist down, luring the – Kroll's words – 'bewitched, unseeing' Rosmer to his doom below water.

Goes over to the window, opens it... When Rebecca does this, two important advances are achieved in the dramatic process. At the very beginning of the play, the act of closing this window served to introduce Kroll into the process, and initiated the action. Now the window is opened again, and it is as though all that Kroll signified is put behind. The other effect is anachronistic, because it did not technically exist in Ibsen's theatre – but I'm sure he heard it in his head: the sound of the millrace will from now be audible.

Not one word more When, at the last, Rebecca asks Rosmer what could she do that would restore his faith in her, his reaction reciprocates and verbally echoes hers earlier, when he proposed marriage at the end of Act Two. This resonance marks how far the play's inward process has advanced: from the travesty of a *mariage blanc* that Rosmer was broaching there, to the final broaching here of the marriage-in-death that – tragic, or absurd, or both – is all of which these two half-paralyzed souls are capable.

WHEN WE DEAD WAKEN

Here again (and with even more cause, this play's language being so spare), the translator must render with rigour. There is further reason. Spare it might be: on close study this text proves an organism densely alive with motivic growth; and a translation must make this organic activity clear. (Hence, in the notes that follow, an emphasis on this aspect.) Again, as with *Rosmersholm*, I have reproduced Ibsen's punctuation – the character's energy-rhythm – except where unnatural English would result. (Once or twice, for similar reasons, I've inverted the Norwegian clause-order in a sentence.) Again as there I have translated all Ibsen's stage-settings in full; but with this play I have fully translated the character-instructions too. This, because of the problematic status of the text (see *Foreword*).

Nuances in style of address Even more so than in
Rosmersholm, these are a subtle instrument in use here
between one character and another, and are almost always
untranslatable. The entire dramatic process is imaged in
shifts in modes of address:

Maja and Rubek, as husband and wife, address each other
by the intimate pronoun. For the distinction between
Norwegian's intimate and formal pronouns there is no
English equivalent. I touch the lines here and there with
'my dear', 'my love' and so on for the one, and with more
distant third-person phrases where the polite form is used.
– Yet Maja never calls her husband by his first name, he
is always 'Rubek'. This can be sometimes in fact a quite
tender effect (though some distance between them is
always there); but it's not natural in English, and normally
to translate by the Christian name would not be wrong
(cf. Rebecca and Rosmer). In this play, however, Maja's
use of the surname is a story-point, and has to be retained.
(Conversely, the other lady will always speak to him on
first-name terms.)

Rubek has a repertoire of terms for his wife – patronizing,
sardonic, rôle-affected. At the outset, he once or twice
styles her in German – *mein Kind* ('my child'), *Frau Professor*
('Mrs Professor' *i.e.* Professor's Wife) – a mildly mocking
effect. These German expressions might not be so readily
assimilated by an English audience as by a Norwegian, so
I've Englished them. But it's a matter of judgment, and the
German can always be restored.

(At the critical moment, mid-Act Two, where she emancipates herself from him, Maja will repay this in kind: '...I can find myself a new life... Don't you worry about me, *Professor Rubek...*' As she departs at the end of that Act, she'll call to him 'Goodnight' from afar, and he is simply *Professor* now; no name. At their cold re-encounter, mid-Act Three, she will address him as though he were a client or a stranger.)

Squire Wolfheim, even when they first meet, will never acknowledge Maja as 'Mrs Rubek'. Wolfheim too will develop a repertory of 'rôle' terms for her: his echo Rubek's, but reverse their effect; and bring himself and Maja *closer*. Finally, she'll be a 'bear-slayer' just as he is: identification complete. Yet even at his very last exit, carrying Maja in his arms, Wolfheim never uses the familiar pronoun with her.

Act One

A matter of life or death *i.e.* that Maja come north this summer. It is. For Rubek too.

Meaningless Rubek, coming home from abroad, after crossing over into his native Norway, hears at every country station two Norwegian railwaymen talking, 'meaningless' in the night. And it's his own language – which suggests how far gone is his estrangement from his native land and people. In a counter-image, the Spa Supervisor, native Norwegian and living here, has overheard the two ladies 'from abroad' conversing in a language 'lost on him'. Their language could be German perhaps, if the lady's companion is German; or French, even Russian... The Lady herself will prove to be Norwegian, but before she even appears, the Supervisor thus makes a 'stranger' of her too.

Great work Norwegian *mesterverk* is usually here rendered 'masterpiece', but that is strictly the work with which an apprentice offers himself for graduation to 'master'. A pedantry, but one that in practice I respect. In America, 'masterwork' would be acceptable.

Domestic circus This motif has history in Ibsen's own
artistic practice: he privately thought of his characters in
just this way – for instance, the sly and cunning editor
in *Rosmersholm* is given specifically foxy colouring. The
motif's function here is that no-one perceives this coded
bestiary in Rubek's art, and Maja is not interested: the joke
is sterile, for the solipsistic Rubek to enjoy alone – until
in Act Three it's startlingly turned inside-out, when Maja
herself will see a living man's animal aspect in the flesh.

All the glory of the world A Scriptural garble – rather like
some of Peer Gynt's misquotations, though not so absurd
as those. Here the resonance is exact, and central to the
meaning of the play. At Matthew iv. 8–9 (= Luke iv. 5–7),
the Devil, having failed to tempt Jesus either to turn stones
to bread, or to launch himself from the Temple pinnacle
and fly, next

> .. taketh him up into an exceeding high mountain, and
> sheweth him all the kingdoms of the world, and the glory
> of them; and saith unto him, All these things will I give
> thee, if thou wilt fall down and worship me.

Ibsen thus suggests a satanic aspect to Rubek's contract
with Maja. For comfort and well-being, she must 'sell her
soul' – (again like Peer Gynt) gain the whole 'world' and
lose her 'self' – in inauthentic life with him. The 'high
mountain' itself will figure more and more as a motif – and
in its physical presence. Other elements of the Temptation
narrative will feature too.

It's a turn of phrase Later, Rubek will be challenged by the
other lady also, on something he once said. There too he
will appeal to his mode of speech.

Our Professor's Lady Here Rubek uses, not the German
term as before, but the native Norwegian word: one shade
closer, though addressing Maja in rôle-aspect still. A wan
flicker of some empathy in him, as though he realises he
has cut her too deep: but now all between them is too far
gone.

Supervisor No English is quite equivalent to *Inspektør*, nor elegant in spoken dialogue. (In performance, 'Doctor' might be preferable.) His looks, on the surface, a thankless rôle. (Even James Joyce, the play's most zealous early apologist, acknowledged he could give only short shrift to this figure.) But he has his poetic dimension too. In his very first exchange of courtesies with Mr and Mrs Rubek, he brings their marital predicament into the light of morning. Every night the wife sleeps like a 'stone' – Rubek's deathly 'matter': translators who anglicize this stone to a 'log' miss a thematic point here – while the husband cannot sleep at all. Their psychic predicament too: Rubek sleepless, with a sleeping statue by his side. Next, the *Inspektør* articulates Rubek's 'dream' for him – and authenticates it. Then he offers 'to throw light' on the matter. His word here, *forklaring* (here 'illumination') is the very word that Irena and Rubek will later be using in the sense 'transfiguration' – a word that they will have much used long ago in their 'creative days'. This *Inspektør*'s choice of words has a dreamlike accuracy. And line by line he is eliciting Rubek's *perception* too. His first word describing the mysterious lady guest is *fremmed*, which can mean both 'strange' and 'foreign'. Rubek's first reflex is to distance her: 'foreign' he assumes her to be. But this *Inspektør* has already heard her speak 'regional' Norwegian – he assures Rubek that she can not be 'foreign'. He permits Rubek no evasion of the lady's identity. In the day-scheme, the *Inspektør* is a functionary showing courtesy to a distinguished guest. In the cosmos of the drama, he is a psychagogue bringing Rubek gently to the threshold of a convulsive recognition. In all this, mere Mrs Maja Rubek's occupation's gone. But the *Inspektør* is introducing her redeeming figure too…

Wolfheim The Norwegian would originally have been *Ulfhjem* but Ibsen himself has already simplified the *–hjem* to *–heim*. I Germanize the *Ulf–* for clarity: the character's animal-aspect, overtly present. (Rubek's 'portraits' speech should have primed us.) Wolfheim is also immediately associated with another beast of the wild: he'll rapidly acquire four

nicknames – 'slayer', 'hunter', 'shotsman', and 'murderer'
of the Bear. (These names don't translate naturally, but
something of their fable-like quality has to be attempted.)
Wolfheim's own language colours his bear-hunting
exploits with imagery of sexual perturbing and conquest:
he virtually identifies the 'bear' as Maja's sexuality.
But Wolfheim has come not to deliver Maja alone. He
precipitates Rubek's emancipation too. First, he caricatures
Rubek's secret artistic method: his very first gesture is
to characterize someone else onstage in animal terms.
But publicly, and with vitality. Next, he will consciously
identify himself with Rubek: each alike, he says, is a hewer
of obdurate 'matter' – in his own case, though, not lifeless
stone but living sinew. It is as though, to detach Maja from
Rubek, Wolfheim must for a while, in transition, briefly
resemble him. More and more, he appropriates aspects of
Rubek, to make them vital. He too invites Maja up a 'high
mountain', but where Rubek's temptation was satanic,
Wolfheim's diabolism is life-saving. Again, he characterizes
'Rubek's sea' as festering and hellish. In Freudian terms
he is correct: Rubek had promised himself a journey by
sea, distanced from all contact with 'the people and the
life', and ending in the Northern frozenness. Now, thanks
to Wolfheim and the 'strange' lady, this sterile journey is
not to be. And from that same 'far north' comes the lady
herself. Wolfheim has attributes in common with her too:
a knife to hand, for an emergency; and he will introduce
the notion of death as 'the other side', where soon the lady
herself will say her dwelling is. With Wolfheim's entry, the
process of transformation has begun.

The strange lady Ibsen does not name her in his character
list; he denotes her as 'a lady travelling'. In the text itself,
he attributes her first lines to 'the Lady'; only after Rubek
onstage has twice called her 'Irena', does Ibsen himself
begin to denote her so – as though only at her first question
about their 'child' does she take on her identity as 'Irena',
and the process that entails. – Two motivic points. On her
first entrance, she quite theatrically presents herself to the

world and to Rubek as a statue in white stone – which is all she has become to him. And white is her motivic colouring, in one manifestation or other throughout – at her first appearance, even her food and drink are white.

Irena's two husbands These seem real men in Irena's past – though she could possibly be inventing them, or in her visionary insanity have 'created' them. No matter. In the cosmos of the play, they are refractions of Rubek himself. One has death in his head, and a statue holding him in his grave; the other dwells among far mountains (I've presumed to add 'high' here, to point up the Temptation resonance), grubbing for gold. Both are 'foreign'; and Rubek is nowhere so 'foreign' as among his own. 'For whom should she grieve' indeed.

I did you no wrong A nice reversal of melodrama and tradition here. The artist Rubek 'wronged' the naked model Irena by *not* laying hand on her. (And yet she had a 'needle' with which to protect herself… For the implications that arise from this, see *Foreword.*)

Fall at your feet… Satanic elements of the Temptation in Irena's surrender to Rubek too. Which doesn't inhibit Rubek from imbuing himself in a God-like colouring: '…in your image I created her'. Ibsen's intractable morality again: Rubek can be at once a man of artistic greatness, and sanctimonious.

Journey upward… And in a sudden reversal of rôles now it is Irena herself who will call Rubek to come with her up the 'high mountain'. But no promise from Irena of 'all the glory of the world'. She offers him a challenge: 'Have you the courage to encounter me a second time?' In Ibsen's own inner psychic drama, his wounded creativity is offering him a second chance, urging him upward to one last visionary phase of authentic creation. Likewise, Wolfheim 'tempts' Maja up the mountain – and again not with spurious promises of glory: his are revolting 'lies' about the 'life up there'. Ghastly, frightful etc she finds the prospect, yet 'strangely enticing'. Maja confronts this essential ambivalence in what Wolfheim has to offer, and moves toward vitality. In these two challenges, the motif of Temptation is itself transformed.

Act Two

Where ordinary urban people could never enter The covert sexual jibe is clear enough; but informing it is the larger theme, of two sorts of life-inheritance. The one – urban, cultured, and contained – Maja is leaving for the other – more elemental, wilder. This duality is imaged in the presence of the two sorts of children – town clad and country clad. (Before his transformation began, Rubek had 'seen more than enough' of the people and their life; now he will find himself watching.)

Some other real reason for wanting to come Yes; and this is as near as he can come to articulating it: his soul's compulsion to encounter Irena again and pass through death and resurrection with her.

Yes actually I can The very same (albeit common) somewhat testy formula with which Maja had answered him at the play's beginning, when Rubek patronized her as one 'hearing the silent'. He is disparaging her 'clairvoyance' now. Note, however, Maja's more impatient rhythm here.

Suddenly lets the thought drop Why? Maja has said (literally) '…that model you at one time used for – ' For what? Maja does not (will not?) connect the other woman with the work of Rubek's greatness. She must instead invalidate Irena: 'people say she is mad'. When Maja resumes the broken thought, it has passed that dangerous connection by.

Eighteen months or so I'd gone In *Rosmersholm* also, after the loss of a woman, for 'eighteen months' the man is left 'alone and brooding'. This 'dream-doubled' nine-month term suggests a psychic gestation, toward emotional rebirth.

I have lived a whole lifetime through, in these few years This echoes Rubek's acknowledgment, early in Act One, that these years had been a 'long long time' and on occasion 'tedious'. Yet he seems to imply here that they have gone by at speed. It's no contradiction. Then, he had been talking of the tedium of idleness, his essential self unoccupied. Now, since his re-encounter with Irena, he is conscious of so much potentially creative time so swiftly lost.

I am tired now His tiredness is not like Maja's earlier, when she lay in the heather, relaxed and drowsy – after love-making, the implication is. But when Rubek had spoken there of the tiredness that comes on 'after the excitement', perhaps that wry knowing was already informed with the deeper bitterness we're hearing from him now. He has in the past felt some 'excitement' with Maja perhaps, when like a child she sat on her husband-father's knee. Now that is over; and a deeper, existential weariness sets in.

Shading his eyes Maja's gesture, too, when searching for her partner at the beginning of the Act.

The long sleep, deep and dreaming This (and healthily) gives the lie to Rubek. He had originally conceived of his Virgin of the Resurrection as waking from a 'dreamless' sleep: even her unconscious, chaste and empty. It gives the healthy lie also to Irena's earlier posturing as a woman dead: her 'sleep' in fact has been charged with vitality.

Regions of the dead Again, she gives Rubek the lie. From this high mountain where she and he actually are now, the vista is not of 'all the glory of the world'. She points instead to a landscape of the dead.

Cry of deliverance Rebecca, too, utters an exultant shriek: when Rosmer at last offers his stumbling proposal of marriage – that secretly she knows she can never accept. These cries of Ibsen's women are Aeschylean, Klytemnestra-like: and the devil to play, in Ibsen's context of what purports to be naturalistic 'prose'.

In spirit and in truth Again Rubek imbues his creativity with Scriptural colouring (John iv. 23–24). In what proportion his artistic integrity co-exists with pompous humbug, is for actor and director to determine. But, the more one thinks about it, the more one sees 'in spirit and in truth' as chillingly exact.

At best a shape in the mid-ground Hereabout occur certain echoes of Rubek's opening scene with Maja. The house that Rubek 'built' for Maja and himself was 'spacious' too, as was the extended plinth he made to accommodate his degenerating art. He assured Maja that he was 'merry' – 'in a sense'. Here he assures Irena that her image is still 'transfigured' – 'in a sense'. And it's as a mid-ground shape that Irena, some nights past, has made herself manifest to him again – pale amid dark trees, as though emerging from the 'muted' gloom to which he had relegated her among his writhing forms of foreground stone.

Not a term I'm given to using Maja in Act One had challenged Rubek on something he once said; there too he dismissed it as merely a formula of his. Here too he appeals to his mode of speech – but in reverse vein.

Shake ourselves free of what's heartsore and sad A similar escapist urging, Peer Gynt to his dying mother: '...[put out of our minds] what's hurtsome and sore...' (Act Three Scene Four.)

There must be no huntsmen on board though, to trap them The children that were playing onstage have long gone now – sent away by Irena when she came. Now Irena and Rubek are the children before us: and, poignant though it be, we see their child-like play as a regressive thing. The Norwegian means simply '...no trappers on board'; I acknowledge that I render elaborately – it's to point up the motivic process at work here. Irena does not want her bird-selves to be caught; yet, 'free' though they are, they can only drift, and cannot swim, let alone fly. In contrast, Maja goes gladly into the arms of her huntsman, and will 'fly away, free'. The revolting enticing ambivalence that Maja exultantly accepts, Irena and Rubek cannot. The game of petals and leaves is the regressional paradise in which they are locked. Irena later will say as much: their way of life together 'has no resurrection in it'. Only a death can set them free, to rise again.

When our work for the week was done Underlying their picture of their creativity too, a Godlike presumption: the story-pattern of the Genesis creation myth.

Great downy leaf Usually rendered as 'dock' or 'burdock'. Botany is not the issue here; but burdock is spiny and tough and doesn't grow near water. I think water-dock – plentiful in Northern Europe, large-leaved and growing by water's edges – may be the leaf that Ibsen had in mind; but it is not 'downy', and the question remains open, if question of identification properly exists at all.

I've made a rhyme about it Rubek has 'done no poetry' since Irena left him. Now Maja meets Wolfheim, and spontaneously creates a rhyme.

Dark summonings The Norwegian here is a compound word from the *troll* family, as are the 'dark powers' exerted on Irena by the Sister in black. In thinking of the later Ibsen as a 'prose' dramatist, we overlook the poetic process at work in a play such as this; we're missing too how *demonic* a landscape Ibsen's is. Traditionally, the troll lives underground, and if brought out into the light of the Sun, will turn to stone. More than once, Ibsen quickens his portrait of Rubek with a touch of the troll. Irena too has her troll-like attributes. A troll-woman has no 'back' – in Jungian terms, no 'shadow side'. Irena is all virginal white; the black-clad Sister is her 'shadow', split from her and silent. And Irena has been in more than one sense turned to stone, and (her 'padded grave' in Act One) buried alive. It's a healthy instinct of Wolfheim's, to abhor this troll-like couple's good wishes as 'dark'.

High wild land Norwegian *vidde*, mountain plateau, way above the tree-line (and in fact bitterly cold, even at midsummer). It has no equivalent in our English landscape, so the translator must offer the audience some mental picture.

The filthiest luck on earth This moment is truly demonic. The couples have re-matched. The 'dark' potency, first sensed by us as something incoming, in the alien person of the Sister, is now shown as informing the very character, Rubek, who has been governing our perspective all along. The tables are turned on Rubek and on us. With a joking adaptation of reverse values – light for dark, and dark for light – Rubek uncovers a capacity for laughter, and 'jovially' hands Maja over to the other man.

When we dead waken The Norwegian line is quite plain, and I hear in Irena's words here almost a factual tone. The traditional English '*a*waken' is rhetorical, rather descriptive in effect – it lacks the urgency and the injunctive note it needs. (The even plainer *wake* would almost do it, but its waking sounds passive and arbitrary.) These sensings commit me to an untraditional rendering of the title too, for of course the title must be the line.

Act Three

Here at last we are high on the 'promised' mountain. No spa nor sanatorium here; the healing process entirely elemental. The two couples here will cross, Rubek with Irena passing upward, Maja with Wolfheim passing below. Maja and Wolfheim cannot *thematically* be coming 'from above', but obviously the couples' journeys must be felt to cross onstage: it is neat how Ibsen contrives an effect of Maja and Wolfheim entering physically downward onto the scene. Rubek's element, stone, here lies everywhere about him, cleft and fallen. The half-collapsed hut, that Act One's 'overgrown pavilion' has 'become', is also what Rubek's 'splendid lakeside villa' now truly is. It acquires further meanings as the Act proceeds.

So help me: never Wolfheim's oaths are no longer hellish; from now they imply, and ultimately name, a Power above. In Wolfheim too some transformation is happening.

Living image of a faun Rubek's secretly animal aspect to his art (and, as such, invisible to Maja), here reversed: Wolfheim, assuming another of Rubek's sterile attributes, and charging it with life. A revelation to Maja in her own right.

Was it there, you were telling me...? Rubek's spurious
promises of a vision from the mountain are transformed to
Wolfheim's mythscape of sexual fable. (Rubek's 'glory of
the world' will soon prove, with Wolfheim, a horrendous
and potentially lethal chasm into which Maja must
descend, to live at all.)

Good mistress comrade of the chase Rubek's sardonic
and distancing 'Frau Professor' et cetera are in process of
transformation too, and drawing Maja closer.

A whole summer, come to that Rubek and Irena had
whiled away 'a whole summer' by Lake Taunitz: the 'little
farmhouse' is suddenly visible before us – a half-collapsed
bothy, and its promise of escapist idyll which Maja now
rejects.

Kid gloves Not in the original: but the Norwegian 'with the
hands' implies in this context a special tender care. 'Kid
gloves' seem suitable for a faun. The solution comes from
Fjelde's translation, and I acknowledge.

Dash her foot against a stone Another echo (and accurate
now) of the Temptation narrative. Urging Jesus to launch
himself from the Temple pinnacle, the devil assures him
(Matthew iv. 6 = Luke iv. 11) that the angels

> shall bear thee up lest at any time thou dash thy foot
> against a stone.

Again, a satanic element of Rubek's contract, that
Wolfheim takes over and transforms. But the stroke
is complex. In the story he's telling here, his knightly
courtesy diabolizes him: the girl abhors his 'soiling', and
Wolfheim grows horns. These have stigmatized him, made
him exile as much in his solitary physical restlessness, fiend
ever hunting, as Rubek has been, slave ever toiling at his
stone. Now, with Maja, the Satan that Rubek the Tempter
was is transformed to the Pan that Wolfheim *is*, and the
regeneration of Wolfheim too begins.

Serve her damn well right Wolfheim's last, isolated diabolic oath goes with the extinct Rubek-Maja pairing into the dead past.

Castle...with splendid hunting land for miles around On the scree of his shattered stone, here stands the ruin to which Rubek's splendid villa and park have been essentially reduced.

We shall shoot him a bullet in his wing! This is the moment of Maja's and Wolfheim's 'marriage'. Maja sheds Rubek, distancing him to a guardian icon, much as is Irene's black-clad Sister; and in the same stroke, makes Rubek himself the trophy she had promised him she'd bring. Here, at last, Wolfheim first calls Maja by name. (He had not once so much as acknowledged her as 'Mrs Rubek' before.) And it is 'we' – Maja and Wolfheim – who shall wing the oppressive father-husband and bring him down.

His strange lady With the very adjective *fremmed* with which the Inspektør had described her on her first entrance, Wolfheim now describes Irena on her last.

One born to slay the bear No longer now merely a 'bear-sticker's wife', Maja is herself a 'bear-slayer' in her own right. Confronting Rubek, and facing him out as she will, she is ready now to 'slay' her own 'bear'. But the Norwegian word (= 'bear-slayer') is given in masculine form. A 'pre-Lawrentian' touch again (and by that token, to us one hundred years later, politically 'incorrect'): Maja's transfer to Wolfheim's 'masculine' domain is complete, and by that act her womanhood is brought to life.

Hood of swansdown Irene's white is now all that of creature (albeit dead), not of stone.

The two of us meet yet again? The coin of Irena's earlier (Act One) 'Dare you encounter me a second time?' is here paid in reverse. (Staging note: As did Maja at her crucial re-entrance at the end of Act One, so does Rubek here begin to speak while still half-seen.) Maja in reply satirizes her earlier aspect as servant to Rubek. She honours Rubek with no name nor style nor mode of address, but speaks to him with objective courtesy, as to a client, or stranger – or visitor to her own home.

Climb-locked In Norwegian the beautiful *bergfast* that defeats us all. One traditional rendering, 'treed', is alien to the play's image-system.

God forbid Having put paid to the devil and Rubek in his previous oath, now at last Wolfheim invokes 'God' in his swearing. This completes the 'exchange of values' between Wolfheim and Rubek.

A matter of life or death [up here] Just as Maja had made it, in insisting (Act One) on coming 'up North' to Norway at all.

You know now Again, a common formula, but exactly the wording that had underlined (Act Two) Rubek's ultimate confession that he could no longer continue his 'life' with Maja.

You wait…in the bothy there The bridal lodging – hunting-lodge and castle before – is now offered to Rubek and Irena, naked of all mythic aspect. But it would be relevant to Rubek and Irena only if they were returning to earth, to the life that has failed. As Maja had, on her way downward, so Irena and Rubek reject it on their way above.

No one shall be let lay hand upon you Absolutely.

That love, that was of our earthly being… From here, the text lifts more and more into the beat and flight of song, a love-duet to the music of the rising storm. It's a late-nineteenth century apotheosis, with affinities with the sentiments of the closing chorus of *Faust* (which Peer Gynt had once ludicrously garbled), and bearing kinship too to the finales of *Tristan* and *Siegfried.* (Ibsen wasn't interested in Wagner; all in his own right, he deploys 'Wagnerian' motivic process – particularly in this play. It has only come home: Wagner learned it from Aeschylus…) The issue with song is that the words must be plain, the music does the work. Here we have no outer music. So the translator's words, while remaining strict perforce, must do by choice and placing all the singing they can.

Topmost towering pinnacle above At the very moment of climax, Ibsen sets a culminating word that's strangely chosen: Irena says literally 'all the way up to the peak of the *tower...*' A mountain feature might well be referred to as a 'tower', but in this climactic elemental context the echo of a human construct does strike a surprising note. Does Ibsen intend resonances here? One, private to himself, might be the Master Builder's spire, here attempted by equal man and woman – and with presumably no falling. Another, thematic to the play, could well be the 'pinnacle' of the Temple, scene of the Temptation to fly – and here, once and for all, the satanic would fail.

Masses of snow, and buried in them Return of the repressed elemental water, the avalanche is what Irena's white at last becomes. The ending itself is life-giving ambivalence. In its negative aspect, it's an elemental murk of death, in which both are justly engulfed because they made death of their lives. It has its triumphal aspect too: Rubek and Irena are at the last vouchsafed a glimpse of the glory.

Pax vobiscum! The Sister's benediction, in Latin in the original – but one can no longer presume that an audience will understand. Again, a matter of judgment, but *Peace be with you* can possibly be preferred.